RECLAIMING AMERICA

DISCARD

DATE DUE

RECLAIMING AMERICA

Nike, Clean Air,
and the
New National Activism

RANDY SHAW

UNIVERSITY OF CALIFORNIA PRESS
Berkeley   Los Angeles   London

University of California Press
Berkeley and Los Angeles, California

University of California Press, Ltd.
London, England

© 1999 by the Regents of the University of California

Library of Congress Cataloging-in-Publication Data
Shaw, Randy, 1956–
    Reclaiming America : Nike, clean air, and the new
national activism / Randy Shaw.
        p.   cm.
    Includes bibliographical references and index.
    ISBN 0-520-21359-9 (alk. paper).—
    ISBN 0-520-21779-9 (pbk. : alk paper)
    1. Social action—United States.   2. Community
organization—United States.   3. Political participation—
United States.   I. Title.
HN65.S484   1999
361.2—dc21   98-28700
                                                         CIP

Manufactured in the United States of America
10   9   8   7   6   5   4   3   2   1

For Anita and Ariel

Contents

Acknowledgments

This book greatly benefited from the insights and analyses of the activists whose struggles are described here. Their work to reclaim America inspired me to write this book. I am grateful to all who agreed to share their ideas with me, and I have tried my best to include their comments in the text.

I am particularly indebted to those who reviewed portions of the manuscript and provided valuable feedback. Thanks to Aileen Alfandary, Marjorie Alt, John Byrne Barry, Lora Jo Foo, Tim Lee, and Larry Shapiro for their candor, insights, and attention to detail. David Lubell's research on chapter 4 proved invaluable. I owe special gratitude to my longtime friend Chris Tiedemann for reviewing first drafts of most chapters, and to Jeffrey Ballinger for his careful scrutiny of my discussion of the campaign he launched against Nike. Diane Mechling kindly provided me with ample news clippings about Nike as I was beginning the book, and Mary Beth Pudup generously provided ongoing feedback on the framing of my analysis.

As always, Naomi Schneider, my editor at the University of California Press, was helpful and supportive.

I could not have written this book without the support and editorial assistance of my wife, Lainey Feingold.

Introduction

Once upon a time in America it was rare to see people sleeping in doorways. Sweatshops were read about only in history books and images of mothers and children begging for food were associated with photographs of the Great Depression. Much of America's manufacturing work force earned a union or living wage and enjoyed a living standard that was the envy of the world. Barriers that had denied economic opportunities to racial minorities and women were eroding. The New Deal's social safety net programs, such as Social Security and aid to poor families, appeared sacrosanct, while funding for the myriad programs of Lyndon Johnson's Great Society—including public broadcasting, Head Start, college tuition assistance, and subsidized housing—rose steadily. President Richard Nixon signed into law the National Environmental Policy Act, signaling the wide bipartisan political support for federal laws protecting America's air, water, and natural resources.

This picture of America is no fairy tale. Rather, it is America in the 1970s, when social and economic injustices were still widespread but the nation was moving toward the equitable society envisioned in the ideals of its founders. This progress was achieved by citizen activists and their organizations working on national struggles that significantly shaped the country's future. At the time, few would have imagined that the 1970s would represent a high point for America's commitment to progressive ideals and that national progressive activism would steadily decline following a period of such great success. Even fewer would have suspected that their hard-won gains would actually be reversed.

Following the 1970s progressive activist participation in national struggles steadily gave way to a nearly exclusive focus on local issues. Many local-oriented activists and organizations continued to recognize that their work often represented the "same struggle, same fight" as national campaigns, but their direct participation in such broader struggles declined. It is almost as if progressive activists took too literally the bumper sticker adage "Think globally, act locally." As progressive grassroots activists increasingly focused on local issues, they watched with shock and bitterness as one after another of their national victories were overturned.

For many years it was easy to attribute these reversals to the Reagan and Bush presidencies. After all, these Republican presidents repeatedly vetoed increased funding for human needs and largely opposed expanded civil rights for racial minorities, women, and gays and lesbians. As Democratic Party control of Congress grew during the Reagan-Bush years, many progressive observers thought that it would only take the election of a Democratic Party president to return America to its correct path. The election and reelection of the Clinton-Gore ticket in 1992 and 1996 roundly disproved this analysis. The Clinton years did not stem the nation's growing social and economic inequality. On the contrary, the Clinton administration built a bridge to the twenty-first century with policies that brought America closer to conditions prevailing at the end of the nineteenth. Today more than a quarter of the nation's children live in poverty, more than thirty million Americans are ill-housed and ill-fed, and millions of children and young women toil in sweatshops at home and abroad. Even as America's overall economy improved during the 1990s, the bottom 80 percent of its population received a smaller share of the nation's total income than it did in the 1970s. Clinton's early years dashed hopes that citizen activists and their organizations would again provide the mobilizing base necessary for implementing a progressive national agenda. Worse, the first Democratic president to hold office in more than a decade actually aligned his party with policies, such as the North American Free Trade Agreement, that had been advanced by his Republican predecessors. The party was over before it had ever begun.

America's corporate and political elite has succeeded in controlling the national agenda because citizen activists and organizations are not fully participating in the struggles shaping national political life. As the constituencies central to reclaiming America's progressive ideals bypass national fights to pursue local issues, their adversaries have faced surprisingly little opposition in dismantling federal programs achieved by six decades of national grassroots struggle. Citizen activists and organizations have steadfastly maintained their local focus even as national policy making drastically cut the resources flowing to communities. From 1979 to 1997, for example, federal aid to local communities for job training, housing, mass transit, environmental protection, and economic development fell by almost one trillion real dollars.

As federal funding to address local needs diminishes and federal policies undermine local decision making, citizen activists and organizations often resemble Sisyphus, condemned by the gods to forever pushing a boulder up a hill only to have it fall back down as the pinnacle nears. Local antipoverty efforts have been restricted by the 1996 repeal of federal welfare entitlements. Activists can fight over state and county implementation plans, but the new federal time limits and eligibility requirements circumscribe what can be achieved. Community strategies to reduce homelessness have been devastated by the lack of sufficient federal housing subsidies, the declining number of public housing units for the very poor, and the termination of federal disability benefits for mentally disabled drug users and alcoholics most at risk of becoming homeless. Dwindling federal allocations to local bus and regional mass transit systems have forced fares steadily upward, worsened daily commutes, reduced alternatives to the automobile, and caused pitched battles among public transit supporters over how to divide what little funding remains. Meanwhile 50 percent of America's discretionary tax dollars continues to bankroll the military with little public outcry.

National politicians recognize that they face weak or nonexistent opposition from progressive citizen activists and their organizations, and have become emboldened in their destruction of the nation's safety net. The early Reagan years brought nationwide protests against proposed cutbacks in federal programs, and this national activism forced that conservative icon to sign an emergency federal jobs bill in 1983. By contrast, there were no massive public protests in the 1990s when federal funding for the arts, humanities, legal services, and housing was savaged. Protesters hit the streets when the Reagan administration sought to reduce the number of new families receiving housing assistance, but the Clinton administration's total elimination of new certificates in the 1996 housing bill occurred without noticeable dissent. The thousands of local nonprofit housing development corporations and tenants' organizations advocating for low-income families lacked a vehicle for successfully mobilizing against the subsidized housing program's demise.

The proposed repeal in 1996 of New Deal–era federal welfare entitlements was expected to cause progressive activists and organizations serving human needs to launch an all-out war to prevent the reversal of one of national activism's greatest gains. Instead welfare's repeal represents perhaps the decade's most striking example of the decline of progressive national activism. Other than a rally organized by the Children's Defense Fund in Washington, D.C., several weeks before the congressional vote, there was precious little evidence of mass grassroots mobilizing to defeat the repeal of welfare. Various organizations and elected officials made public pronouncements against the measure, but the sense of crisis or urgency in urban America did not even rise to levels commonly seen in local development controversies. Local-oriented antipoverty advocates lacked a vehicle for influencing the national welfare reform debate, and even elected federal officials dependent on urban voters, hearing little public protest, did not hesitate to cast their votes to end welfare during an election year.

Significantly, two major constituencies whose local-oriented activists maintained their connection to national struggles—environmentalists and abortion-rights activists—successfully mobilized to repel nearly all of the challenges to their prior gains. Legislation seeking to weaken federal environmental protections in 1995 and 1996 was almost entirely defeated. Politicians emboldened by their success in cutting domestic programs moved against existing environmental legislation, only to be overwhelmed by a massive opposition campaign from national and local environmental groups. By the time the dust cleared even House Speaker Newt Gingrich declared himself to be an environmentalist, and concerted attacks on existing environmental protections have since diminished. Similarly although abortion rights have been curtailed in several states, activists and organizations have repeatedly mobilized to defeat new federal restrictions. Bill Clinton remained steadfast in support of abortion rights even as he was waffling or buckling on other controversial issues. Unlike other progressive constituencies, prochoice activists working at the local or state level continued to actively participate in the national arena.

Recent national policy reversals demonstrate that "people power" is undermined when it is only exerted locally and does not also challenge the political and corporate insiders who seek control over America's future. From AIDS activists fighting locally to save lives while federal funding for essential treatment remains inadequate to environmentalists fighting to preserve national forests while the federal government subsidizes private logging roads, activists have seen local agendas sabotaged again and again in the national arena.

This book seeks to inspire activists and organizations working at the local level to play central roles in national struggles. Through what I describe as the "new national activism," I suggest how citizen activists and organizations can work in their own backyards on national campaigns seeking to reclaim America's progressive ideals. This book challenges the prevailing view that influencing the national agenda requires hiring expensive Washington lobbyists or making large campaign contributions. Instead I argue that the nation's priorities can often be shaped most effectively by national campaigns operating outside the electoral process. When federal action is required and dealing with national politicians is unavoidable, I show how building grassroots power in local communities, rather than depending on political allies in Washington, is the key to success.

The new national activism recognizes that national struggles should enhance the political influence, resources, constituency base, and organizing skills of activists and their organizations. In this new activism citizen activists and local-oriented organizations are not mere cogs in a big machine. Rather these campaigns provide the vehicles necessary for enabling community and campus groups to become partners in national struggles. This occurs through such methods as organizer outreach, national synchronized protests, and the creative use of e-mail as an outreach and coordinating vehicle. Most critically, the new national activism forges agendas that link local problems to national solutions.

Creating vehicles for citizen activists and their organizations to solve local problems through national activism enlarges grassroots participation in the struggles shaping America's future. For example, grassroots environmental organizations are more likely to join national struggles that address problems—such as local air and water pollution caused by facilities several states away—clearly requiring federal action. Activists seeking to improve the lives of immigrant garment workers can often best respond by launching national anti-sweatshop campaigns. Community-based antipoverty and social service groups will only obtain the resources they need to meet increased demands for affordable housing, job training, and education assistance by joining the national struggle for new federal budget priorities; in these and countless other cases local advocacy must work hand in hand with national activism.

I focus on three issues to demonstrate how the new national activism can overcome the corporate and political elite's stranglehold on national political life. In part 1 I discuss how activists and organizations working in their own backyards and outside the political process have mobilized in national anti-sweatshop campaigns to rewrite the allegedly "ironclad" rules of the global economy. My chief focus is the David versus Goliath struggle waged by activists and organizations against Nike's overseas labor abuses. The anti-Nike campaign, along with national anti-sweatshop struggles against Jessica McClintock, Inc. and Guess, also profiled, have fundamentally altered the American public's perception of unrestricted free trade. Anti-sweatshop activism has forged links between national and local-oriented economic fairness campaigns that provide the best opportunity yet for a national movement for a living wage.

Unlike anti-sweatshop campaigns the issues of environmental protection and national budget priorities require a new national activism that can succeed inside the Beltway. Part 2 of the book discusses how the Sierra Club and the network of state-based Public Interest Research Groups (PIRGs) used national grassroots mobilizing in 1997 to win tough new standards for the federal Clean Air Act. The national mobilization of local-oriented environmentalists overcame industry opposition, including a $20 million advertising blitz. The Clean Air Act victory was not only environmentalists' biggest success in more than a decade, but it was won while congressional hearings into campaign financing appeared to send the message that big money always wins. Rather than surrender to this prevailing wisdom the Sierra Club and the PIRGs demonstrated that a new national activism can achieve victories when it reconnects local-oriented individuals and groups to national struggles.

Part 2 also seeks to mobilize citizen activists and their organizations to devote resources toward redirecting Pentagon spending to human needs. As post–Cold War military spending continues to devour 50 percent of America's discretionary tax dollars, resources are desperately needed to rebuild the civic life of the nation. Community-based nonprofit organizations are left to divide a declining share of federal funds while military budgets equal to the Cold War average are approved—and then increased above the Pentagon's own requests—with little dissent. I discuss how a new national activism is the best strategy for making progressive budget priorities for the twenty-first century.

In the final section I discuss the role of community-based nonprofit organizations (CBOs), the media, and the Internet in building grassroots participation in national campaigns. CBOs receiving federal funds have a particular financial and philosophical interest in creating new national budget priorities. A CBO's staff, membership, board, constituency base, newsletter, and unrestricted funds can all play critical roles in the national effort to reclaim America's progressive ideals. Community-based organizations must go beyond their typically local focus to join the national struggles that increasingly shape community life.

Linking all of the chapters is a call for national struggles to actively recruit and engage campus activists. Student participation in national campaigns has proved critical to, if not determinative of, their success. Curiously, this point has been lost on a generation of adults whose greatest activist successes came during their student years. Student interest in combating sweatshops, fighting for the environment, and making a better world in general has perhaps never been greater. This tremendous reservoir of talent will be squandered unless national campaigns find ways to fully integrate student activists.

In offering a road map for reviving a national grassroots activism I recognize the practical impediments. Faced with seemingly omnipotent corporate power, multimillion-dollar election campaigns, and a national media largely supportive of the status quo, many citizen activists are more convinced than ever that local struggles are the last, best hope for winning progressive change. Neighborhood issues often have more immediate and visible impacts and their smaller scale provides a sense of democratic participation that is harder to replicate in national campaigns. Residents come to know town officials on a first-name basis and see them at Little League games and the supermarket, whereas federal officials spend most of their time in Washington, D.C., and even when at home are rarely seen outside their official capacity. Local struggles evoke the favored image of a New England town meeting. National activism calls to mind backroom deal making by an elite.

Some activists have abandoned national struggles because of misleading rhetoric about transferring or "devolving" federal programs to states and localities. Such shifts, as in welfare "reform," are simply political cover for even more drastically slashing resources for the poor. The idea of state government as an incubator of progressive policies and a bastion of social reform should no more captivate activists than did earlier calls for "states' rights" to justify Jim Crow laws. On virtually every issue, including abortion rights, crime, welfare, and environmental protection, most states maintain policies far more regressive than the federal government. State governments are often even more captive to special interests, and statehouses' typical distance from major population centers and the comparative absence of ongoing media coverage of state governments give free reign to secret deals and lobbyist control. During the 1990s most states increased the tax burdens on low- and moderate-income people while cutting taxes for the affluent. Activists should not be fooled into believing that their agenda can be more easily achieved in the state arena. So-called devolution typically increases environmental destruction and social and economic unfairness.

I have worked on local issues for two decades and would be the last person to denigrate local struggles or to suggest that citizen activists abandon local campaigns. The continuing necessity and genuine benefits of working on local issues are beyond dispute. As a result of the dramatic rise in community activism since the 1970s millions of Americans have revitalized neighborhoods and rekindled democratic ideals. Grassroots activists and organizations have mobilized to defeat the entry of large chain stores and the siting of toxic incinerators that threaten community life. Struggles for rent controls, open space, curbside recycling, and equitable city budget decisions are but a few of the issues on which working locally is essential. In struggles such as those to enact city laws authorizing needle exchange, local action is necessary until a sufficiently large and powerful constituency approves national action. The virtues of working on local issues—from the capacity to set policy through city ballot initiatives to greater access to local officials— are not minimized in this book.

Still I believe citizen activists and organizations cannot reclaim America's progressive ideals by pouring all their efforts into local issues. Harry Boyte, the leading chronicler in the 1970s of citizen activism's "backyard revolution," recognized that grassroots citizens' movements also had to transform the "macrostructures" of the national arena. Robert Fisher in his analysis of neighborhood organizing in America similarly cautioned that local activism disconnected from a national movement "will win limited reforms but not address the continued incidence of powerlessness, prejudice and poverty in the United States." Both Fisher and Boyte hoped for the emergence of a federated national organization that could unify grassroots activity in local communities. But this entity never developed. In its stead citizen activists and organizations became extraordinarily proficient at winning local battles, but their very success may have created a false sense of security—particularly after the election of Bill Clinton—about the durability of their gains. It has become clear that, like it or not, community-based organizations and grassroots activists must fully engage in national struggles not only to further a progressive national agenda but to protect local victories.

While activists have followed the bumper sticker prescription of thinking globally and acting locally, their conservative and corporate opponents have used their control of the national arena to win concrete successes on global and local issues. Turned off by the big-money, sleazy politics associated with Washington, D.C., citizen activists have unwittingly given free rein to those largely responsible for their repugnance: the corporate lobbyists, national politicians, and their media allies, who together increasingly monopolize national political debate.

The lack of citizen activist participation in national struggles means that the chief force for challenging corporate and political insiders at any level, the mobilizing capacity of "people power," is only rarely exerted in the national arena. Social and economic inequality, child poverty, racial prejudice, and powerlessness are either ignored or worsened by the federal government.

Activists and organizations primarily working on local issues must recommit themselves to greater participation in national campaigns. The progressive rallying cry identifying local and national battles as the "same struggle, same fight" must translate into action. Without reenergized national activism, the agenda of the corporate and political elite will continue to undermine local efforts to improve community institutions and the quality of neighborhood life. Citizen activists and organizations have achieved success by being flexible, resourceful, and tireless. These same traits must now motivate them to act nationally as well as locally to reclaim America's progressive ideals. It is not an either/or choice.

Part One

Reclaiming America outside the Electoral Process

National Anti-Sweatshop Campaigns and the Movement for a Living Wage

Chapter 1

Just Don't Buy It

Challenging Nike and the Rules
of the Global Economy

When Jeff Ballinger was in Indonesia to monitor wages and working conditions from 1988 to 1992, he played on a softball team with employees of the Beaverton, Oregon–based Nike corporation. Nike had contracted with Korean and Taiwanese factory owners to operate production facilities for Nike shoes in Indonesia. Ballinger was not very familiar with the emerging structure of labor practices in the developing world and assumed that his teammates were directly managing Nike-owned factories in the country. The players were talking one day and Ballinger mentioned that he was in Indonesia to help protect the rights of workers producing goods for American corporations. One of the Nike employees laughed and told Ballinger, "I am your worst nightmare." The exchange was part of ongoing banter, and Ballinger did not ask the Nike employee what he meant by his comment.[1]

Soon after this conversation Ballinger was monitoring wage data on Indonesia's sneaker industry. He discovered that Nike's Indonesian workers were being paid only fourteen cents per hour. Ballinger began to investigate the wages and working conditions of the mostly female Indonesian workers making Nike shoes. He learned that Nike's subcontractors were not even paying the below-subsistence wage required by Indonesian law. Ballinger also found abusive and often physically coercive working conditions. Based on his observations Ballinger examined the factors that appeared to lead Nike to shift its production facilities to Indonesia. He found that Nike had closed its last U.S. plants in Saco, Maine, in the 1980s, and during the 1970s had shifted most of its shoe production to South Korea, whose workers earned

nowhere near the U.S. rubber-shoe industry average of $6.94 per hour.
When South Korea's prodemocracy movement of the late 1980s gave
workers the right to form independent unions and strike, Nike's work
force won higher pay. The new salaries remained far below American
standards, but Nike wanted a better deal. Indonesia, with its cheap labor costs and dictatorship whose military ensured labor peace, seemed
the perfect choice.

As a result of his findings Ballinger wrote an article for the August
1992 *Harper's*, "Nike, the New Free-Trade Heel: Nike's Profits Jump
on the Backs of Asian Workers." The piece consisted of Ballinger's
commentary on a copy of a pay stub of an Indonesian worker named
Sadisah. The stub indicated that the employer was not Nike but Sung
Hwa Corp., a Korean-based company now serving as Nike's subcontractor in Indonesia. Nike was the first athletic footwear operation to
fully subcontract its production facilities. Because the workers were
not employed by Nike, the corporation could avoid legal responsibility for their wages and working conditions.

Ballinger described how Nike's shifting of factories to increasingly
cheaper labor pools had meant solid growth for the company. In 1991
Nike had its best year yet, with a record net profit of $287 million. As
Sadisah's April 1992 wage stub showed, however, those making Nike's
shoes had not reaped the benefits of the company's success. Sadisah
was earning only fourteen cents per hour, less than the Indonesian government's standard for "minimum physical need." The International
Labor Organization found that 88 percent of Indonesian women working at such wages were malnourished. Sadisah's wages allowed her to
rent only a shack without electricity or running water.

Her wage stub showed Sadisah to be a very hard worker. She had
worked sixty-three hours of overtime during the pay period and received an additional two cents per hour. She assembled 13.9 pairs of
Nike shoes every day; the labor cost for a pair of Nike shoes selling
for eighty dollars in the United States was about twelve cents. Ballinger concluded by observing that in order for Sadisah to earn as much
as the $20 million annual endorsement fee paid by Nike to basketball
superstar Michael Jordan, she would have to continue working six
days a week, ten and a half hours per day, for 44,492 years.[2]

Ballinger's description of Nike's labor practices was graphic and compelling. His *Harper's* article is the type of original historical document that should be included in the Smithsonian Institution, where many of America's archival materials reside. Like other social change visionaries, however, Ballinger had produced a critique of Nike and of global free trade that was ahead of its time. Nike had already achieved a nearly mythic status in America, and its advertising had connected its brand name to too many positive images for a critical two-page article by an unknown human rights activist, even published in an elite liberal magazine, to be noticed. Like activists who opposed the Vietnam war before 1965 and those attacked as "premature anti-Fascists" for going to Spain to save the republic from Franco and Hitler in 1936, Ballinger's viewpoint lacked sufficient public support to be espoused or endorsed by the mainstream media. Thus his groundbreaking analysis of Nike was not soon followed by broader media coverage of the company's Indonesian labor practices; Ballinger may have been alone in foreseeing that his article would lay the groundwork for a national campaign challenging Nike's labor practices and the prevailing rules for corporate responsibility in the global economy.

Ballinger's critique of Nike's labor practices emerged during a decade in which the leadership of both of America's national political parties strongly embraced unfettered free trade and escalating economic globalization. At an eight-nation economic summit meeting in June 1997 President Clinton declared globalization to be "irreversible" and thought it "difficult to imagine that this is even a serious debate right now." Clinton's view was promptly echoed by his purported chief ideological adversary, Republican House majority leader Dick Armey, who urged recognition of unrestricted free trade as a "basic human right." Armey also asserted that free trade was "liberating" for Chinese workers forced to work as either slaves or for meager wages making goods for American import. This bipartisan support led many to conclude that the national political arena was not a hospitable venue for activists seeking to rewrite the allegedly "ironclad" rules of free trade and the global economy.[3]

Jeff Ballinger, however, believed that a successful challenge to the global labor practices of one of the world's most successful and popular corporations could establish a precedent for similar national grassroots campaigns. As impossible as a national campaign against Nike appeared at the time, the ensuing years brought results that have revised and may ultimately rewrite the rules for the global economy and change the substantive meaning of free trade. The anti-Nike campaign's success against overwhelming odds shows the continued power of national activism to reclaim America's progressive ideals.

Activists versus Nike: The Obstacles to Success

Jeff Ballinger's goal of inspiring Americans to force Nike to reform its global economic practices faced at least five formidable obstacles. These included Nike's positive corporate image; the difficulty of interesting Americans in Indonesian affairs; Nike's contracts with major college and university athletic teams; its adoption of a Code of Conduct that conveyed the message, albeit erroneous, that it carefully monitored its subcontractors' wages and working conditions; and the public perception that it was unfair to target Nike when other footwear companies allegedly engaged in similar practices. The impediments were so great that embarking on an anti-Nike campaign in 1992 seemed to violate the standard organizing rule of picking only potentially winnable fights; the growth of the anti-Nike campaign in the face of such obstacles demonstrates not only the power of activists acting nationally to rewrite the rules of the global economy, but the triumph of the activists' vision of what is possible over prevailing mainstream assumptions that have too often deterred social change efforts in all fields.

Nike's Image: Just Do It

Ballinger's exposé appeared during a period of dramatic growth for Nike. Nike's profits tripled from 1988 to 1993, and unlike Microsoft or other hugely successful corporations of the 1990s Nike was identified with hipness and style as well as dependability. The popular image of the Nike sneaker as a vehicle for personal transformation was imprinted on the public's consciousness through advertising campaigns whose budgets rose from $250 million in 1993 to $975 million worldwide in 1997. Nike's television advertisements have consistently proven as persuasive and evocative as any of their surrounding programming.

In the 1980s Nike's ads featured a series of vignettes between basketball superstar Michael Jordan and film director Spike Lee; the idea was spawned when a member of Nike's ad agency saw that Lee's Mars Blackmon character in his film *She's Gotta Have It* refused to take off his red and black Nike Air Jordans even while making love. Nike's "Bo Knows . . . " ads featured multisport superstar Bo Jackson to emphasize the sneaker's versatility. In the most famous of the "Bo knows" series, Nike displayed its clout and hipness at once by including in one commercial tennis star John McEnroe, hockey star Wayne Gretzky, Jordan, and a renowned blues original whose identity was revealed by his tag line: "Bo, you don't know Diddley."

Nike's reliance on African-American sports stars in its commercials was a dramatic break from the past. Before Nike's advertising campaign, even the greatest African-American superstars such as Hank Aaron, Willie Mays, Bill Russell, and Jim Brown failed to receive the national endorsements of their less successful but Caucasian peers. Nike's willingness to break the marketing stereotypes that had denied endorsements to African Americans both helped sell Nike shoes in inner cities and contributed to the company's progressive image.

Also contributing to Nike's progressive identity was its choice of subjects for its "Just Do It" campaigns. For example, in 1988 Nike's "Just Do It" ads featured a wheelchair racer competing at racquetball and basketball, a forty-two-year-old female New York City Marathon champ, and an eighty-year-old who ran seventeen miles through the streets of San Francisco each day. The ads conveyed the idea that Nike sneakers were worn by people of all ages, genders, and disabilities, and that the buyers of Nike shoes had the grit and determination to take on the type of challenges included in the advertisements. A widely distributed Nike poster reflected the company's apparent recognition of the country's social, economic, and racial injustices. The text, "There are clubs you can't belong to. Neighborhoods you can't live in. Schools you can't get into," appeared above a photo of a lone runner on a country road. The text then concluded, "But the roads are always open. Just Do It." Wearing Nikes offered a route to spiritual if not political salvation in an unjust world.[4]

By 1992 Nike's advertising strategies had convinced millions of Americans that paying up to $150.00 for a pair of sneakers costing $5.00 to

make was a small price for certified acceptance into the world of the
socially hip and adept. Nike even defined such a purchase as a revolutionary act, using the Beatles' song "Revolution" to pound this point
home in a 1980s advertising campaign. Wearing Nike shoes brought
status and security to young people, while trying other brands risked
peer group criticism. The Nike swoosh had become a seal of approval;
if it was good enough for Michael Jordan to wear, no kid could challenge its preeminence.

As a result of its creative advertising campaigns, in 1993 Nike was
one of the first three companies to be inducted into the American
Marketing Association Hall of Fame (the others were Coca Cola and
Absolut Vodka). This honor was bestowed only upon brands that "represent innovative and trailblazing marketing and have had a dramatic
impact on our lifestyle, becoming enshrined as American icons." In
light of the icon status of Nike sneakers and of the company's progressive and racially groundbreaking image, is it any wonder that Ballinger's *Harper's* article was widely ignored? The larger question seemed
to be how Ballinger and other activists could successfully challenge
the labor practices of a company that had achieved a cultural status
that seemingly rendered it impervious to activists' campaigns.

Indonesia: The Lost World

The second obstacle to the growth of a national anti-Nike campaign
was that Nike's wrongdoing through 1992 was occurring in distant and
little-known Indonesia. By moving its production facilities to Indonesia, Nike had chosen one of the most brutal regimes of modern times
as its guarantor of labor peace. Indonesia must have seemed the country least likely to permit worker unrest over wages and working conditions. Traditional assumptions about American attitudes toward social and economic injustice in other nations also made Indonesia a
seemingly safe harbor for Nike's production facilities. The fourth most
populous country in the world, Indonesia is a nation of thirteen thousand
islands and several hundred ethnic groups located south of Malaysia
and northeast of Australia. Relatively few Americans have visited Indonesia, there is no sizable or politically potent Indonesian immigrant
community in the United States, and therefore Americans do not have
strong religious, ethnic, or racial ties with Indonesia like those that

have mobilized them to focus attention on other foreign countries. Indonesia's longtime dictator, President Suharto, was barely known in America in 1992, and as a strong ally of the United States, Suharto did not engage in the confrontational posturing that raised public awareness of Libya or other distant lands. Although Indonesia aroused controversy among human rights groups for its 1975 invasion of neighboring East Timor and its subsequent murder of more than a quarter million East Timorese, this genocide brought little American media attention, and Suharto retained bipartisan political support. The dictator had provided a safe and stable profit-making environment for multinational corporations since coming to power in a CIA-backed coup in 1965; if the American public and media had not been aroused by Suharto's genocide and reign of terror, there was no reason to expect them to be outraged by stories of poor wages and working conditions of Indonesian workers making Nike shoes.

The University of Nike

A third obstacle to a national anti-Nike campaign was the company's nearly total control of the sneakers worn by the country's top college basketball teams. Having conducted a survey that found strong links between the shoes preferred by local college sports teams and the sneaker preferences of the kids in the stands, Nike began seizing control of the college basketball team market as early as 1978. The company accomplished this by paying six-figure annual salaries to coaches of elite basketball programs such as Jerry Tarkanian of University of Nevada at Las Vegas, John Thompson of Georgetown University (who subsequently joined Nike's board), and Dean Smith of the perennial powerhouse University of North Carolina. Duke's coach, Mike Krzyzewski, was given a million-dollar signing bonus in addition to his annual Nike compensation. In exchange for such lavish deals, these coaches gave a few clinics and, far more important, they outfitted their teams with Nike sneakers. In 1985 Nike had all of the Final Four basketball teams under contract and twenty-three of the sixty-four teams in the tournament. The rules governing intercollegiate sports stated that no player could be forced to wear an endorsement shoe, but rejecting a shoe endorsed by the coach who awarded the player's athletic scholarship and determined his or her playing time was unlikely.

Such rejection could even be construed as criticism of the coach's ethics. When Jim Calhoun, the University of Connecticut's basketball coach, was asked about Nike's abuse of Indonesian workers and his fifteen-year "relationship" with the company, he replied, "I don't think that it's something that, when we get the various sneakers that we think of who made them. Maybe that's ignorance on our part, but it's a very honest ignorance." Nike's role as supplier and underwriter of male and female college athletic programs would grow throughout the 1990s. By 1992 Nike sneakers were already linked with college basketball success. Convincing kids in the stands that they should wear a different and, by implication, inferior product seemed an insurmountable task.[5]

Nike's Code of Conduct

The fourth obstacle to the growth of an anti-Nike campaign was the company's formal adoption of policies that conveyed the message that Nike zealously protected the interests of those workers making its shoes. Nike adopted its Memorandum of Understanding and Code of Conduct for its Indonesian "business partners" following Ballinger's article in 1992. Nike's Memorandum required its subcontractors to comply with local laws regulating wages and working conditions and mandated that documentation of compliance with the Memorandum be maintained for Nike's inspection. The Memorandum also required subcontractors to adhere to environmentally safe practices and to certify that they did not discriminate on the basis of gender, race, religion, age, ethnic origin, or sexual orientation. Incorporated into the Memorandum was the Nike Code of Conduct. The Code stated that Nike seeks "always to be a leader in our quest to enhance people's lives," which means that at every opportunity, including in the areas of human rights and equal opportunity, "we seek to do not only what is required, but, whenever possible, what is expected of a leader."

It would be nice to think that a journalist reading of Nike's extraordinary commitment to human rights, worker rights, and an equal opportunity provision so progressive that it specifically protected Indonesian gays and lesbians from discrimination in the workplace would investigate whether such rules were actually being implemented under the Suharto dictatorship. But the American media in 1992 was uninterested in putting resources toward verifying whether Nike's subcontractors adhered to the Memorandum or Code; the very existence of such formalized policies enabled Nike to deter media inquiries and to readily defend itself against charges of labor mistreatment. The anti-Nike campaign would have to develop its own credible information sources establishing Nike's failure to monitor compliance with its Code in order to overcome Nike's repeated refrain that it was a leader in protecting workers' rights in the global economy.

Why Single Out Nike?

Finally, an anti-Nike campaign had to overcome the notion that it is unfair to attack Nike for labor practices endemic in the developing world. Jeff Ballinger's strategy was to focus on a particular company and its abuses to demonstrate the need for broader reform. However, if Americans felt that Nike could not compete in the global economy without relying on workers earning below-subsistence wages, they might feel that Nike could not be blamed for the workers' plight or be held responsible for initiating reforms. Further, if the entire system of corporate exploitation of workers in the global economy was the problem, it could be argued that focusing on any one company was pointless. As frustrating and irrational as it is, the stance that "all corporations are evil so there's nothing to be done" has been a remarkably effective rationalization for inaction in the face of injustice. For an anti-Nike campaign to develop, activists had to demonstrate that Nike was not merely a symptom but a leader and perpetrator of global economic injustice and that it could readily institute reforms without sacrificing market share or plunging into insolvency. Activists' challenge to Nike's labor practices and global economic impact therefore had to surmount obstacles beyond those typically associated with national corporate campaigns. Unlike such past targets as the J. P. Stevens company, corporations doing business in apartheid South Africa, and the agribusiness interests that fought Cesar Chavez's creation of the United Farm Workers, Nike was a powerful adversary that also had a positive public image. Nike's founder and CEO, Phillip Knight, has often described Nike as a marketing rather than footwear enterprise, and Nike had a massive advertising budget to counter whatever negative publicity activists could generate about its labor practices. Nike's control of the college sports team market ensured that the brand would remain identified with athletic success, and there was no reason to believe that Americans would suddenly become interested in addressing Nike's labor abuses in a nation few could even locate on a map. Despite these obstacles, Ballinger's fundamental strategic analysis was correct: a successful anti-Nike campaign that forced the company to ensure a living wage for those producing its goods would set a precedent for other American companies seeking to take advantage of free trade by operating in nations that sanction exploitative wages and working conditions. If activists were to overcome the inauguration crowd's allegedly ironclad rules for the global economy, Nike, the model for these rules, had to be fought regardless of the barriers.

1993–1995: The Campaign Slowly Begins

Soon after his *Harper's* story appeared, Ballinger left Indonesia for Istanbul, Turkey. He continued to monitor Nike's Indonesian labor practices and every two months sent packages of information on Nike to thirty media outlets worldwide. In the year following his exposé of Nike's labor abuses, however, there was little evidence that Ballinger's charges had made any impact. Although the basic themes of the national anti-Nike campaign emerged in 1992, it would take more than three years for activists' critique of Nike's labor practices to reach the American public's consciousness. The pace of national social change struggles often is slower than activists would like and frustration can build as years pass without any guarantee that small victories and flurries of momentum will ever become a larger, more coherent movement. It is helpful to recall that nine years passed between the Rosa Parks–triggered Montgomery bus boycott and the passage of the first meaningful federal civil rights legislation in 1964. The escalation of the Vietnam war in 1965 brought few public or campus protests; the largest such events did not occur until 1969 and 1970. The year following Ballinger's exposé was thus not atypical of a nascent movement's formative years. In 1993 Nike posted a record profit of $298 million and its U.S. gross revenue reached nearly $2 billion. Nike's most prominent advertising spokesperson, basketball star Michael Jordan, was paid $20 million to tout the company's sneakers; this amount was four times the total earnings of the twelve thousand Indonesian women who made Nike's shoes. While the U.S. State Department worldwide report on human rights for 1993 acknowledged that Indonesia's government sanctioned attacks on workers' rights, the document did not connect Nike to any abuses.

Nineteen ninety-three did bring a breakthrough in public understanding of the full meaning of free trade. In a bitter campaign that continued for much of the year, President Clinton and his corporate allies ultimately won passage of the North American Free Trade Agreement (NAFTA). NAFTA's enactment was justifiably seen as a defeat for labor and human rights groups, which had argued that "free trade" would restrict America from preventing the import of goods made under labor, environmental, and social conditions unacceptable, if not illegal, in this country. The fight preceding passage, however, was an all too rare moment when everyday Americans focused on the impact of trade policies on workers' living standards at home and abroad. When NAFTA opponents discussed the shift of American jobs to low-wage workers abroad and linked free trade to corporate exploitation of overseas workers, Nike's labor practices in Indonesia could be understood as part of a broader global economic agenda. The NAFTA debate put the perils of free trade in terms understandable to the millions of Americans who lacked advanced economic degrees and who had never heard of the World Bank, and left those opposed to the treaty eager to find examples of the policy's abuses. Further, NAFTA's passage did not end the broader public discussion over trade policy. The Clinton administration was negotiating the proposed General Agreement on Tariffs and Trade (GATT) during the NAFTA debate. Although GATT did not attract as much media coverage, the American public received heightened exposure to trade issues through GATT's passage in late 1994. The debates over NAFTA and GATT enabled the American public and mainstream media to perceive a context to Nike's labor practices that may not previously have been evident.

As Americans' interest in corporate practices in the global economy was increasing, author Donald Katz presented Phil Knight with an idea for a book. Katz had written a cover story on Nike for *Sports*

Illustrated in August 1993.[6] Now he urged Knight to cooperate in a book portraying Nike as "the company of the future seeking to define culture through the power of sports." Katz told Knight that the book "could describe the trick of creating the kind of jobs people really want in an advanced economy. Nike was becoming something of a model for the global, post-industrial enterprise."[7]

Having identified Nike as a positive model for the future of work in the global economy, Katz was forced to explain how Nike's global search for low-wage workers and its Indonesian labor practices were consistent with this theme. He asked the leadership of the self-proclaimed "company with a soul" to explain the situation. Knight, whose $6 billion net worth made him one of the ten richest Americans, denied charges that Nike exploited Indonesian workers: "There's no question in my mind that we're giving these people hope. This happens to be the way countries move ahead. I don't think we are doing anything wrong." Dave Taylor, Nike's vice president for production, was equally emphatic that Nike had nothing to do with alleged abusive labor practices: "We don't set policy within the factories; it is their business to run."[8]

Mirroring the response many readers would have to such comments, Katz observed that although Nike's "moral neutrality" toward the plight of workers making its shoes was "well within historic tradition, bucking tradition has been a larger part of Nike's history than falling in line. It was hard to imagine that shareholders would mind some kind of required minimum wage safety net—which competitors were sure to be forced to copy." Realizing that he had just made the case for Nike's critics, Katz quickly backtracked, reminding readers that Nike had given employment opportunities to people who were so poor that their grandparents were "forced to eat bark off trees." Nevertheless, many readers of *Just Do It: The Nike Spirit in the Corporate World* would likely join its author in questioning how a "company with a soul" would allow its shoes to be made by sweatshop labor.[9]

Katz's best-selling book provided the broadest publicity yet of Nike's labor practices in the global economy. Its primary value to the development of a national anti-Nike campaign, however, was not the few doubts it expressed in the course of its overwhelmingly admiring account. Rather it was the book's depiction of Nike as the chief exporter of a free trade revolution that would reduce workers' wages and living standards, a revolution that would be culturally sanctioned through the power of sports. Nike was not simply surfing the wave of the global economy; it was creating a model other companies would follow of a corporation seeking repressive governments and below-subsistence-wage workers to host its operations. Because Nike was the trendsetter for the unprecedented exploitation of workers in the sneaker industry, activists could readily explain to the public why Nike was their target. Further, Katz showed that Nike took pride in its Indonesian operations and insisted—against all evidence—that its Code of Conduct was ensuring decent wages and working conditions for those making Nike shoes. To counter the feeling of many Americans that all big corporations are morally corrupt so it is unfair to target any one, activists could show how Nike's relentless self-promotion and self-congratulatory stance toward its exploitation of workers set it apart. Nike's attitude toward its labor practices was akin to the apartheid South African government repeatedly praising its leadership on the issue of race relations. Nike's willingness to brag about its Indonesian operations opened itself up to charges of hypocrisy that could not be made against corporations that simply espoused a commitment to the bottom line. Activists could begin to turn public sentiment against Nike by showing that the company's claims about its Indonesian operations were false and that Nike's vaunted leadership was most pronounced in the field of hypocrisy. Nike's affirmative misrepresentations about its labor record repeatedly fueled the anti-Nike campaign. As Jeff Ballinger later acknowledged, "we could not have eventually built such a broad campaign without Nike's help."

Ballinger demonstrated how activists could transform Nike's rhetoric into assertions of corporate hypocrisy in a series of full-page advertisements he produced in November 1994. The ads were designed to produce subscribers to the *Nike in Indonesia* newsletter produced by Press for Change, a group formed by Ballinger that year to gather and distribute information about the abusive production practices of Nike's contractors in Indonesia. Each of the advertisements was titled with the Nike slogan "Just Do It!" Underneath the title was a quotation from either a Nike advertisement or Phil Knight, and below the quotation was a corresponding photograph. For example, the Nike advertisement stating, "There's really no time to be afraid. So stop. Try something you've never tried. Risk it. Demand a raise," appeared above a photo of an Indonesian woman described in the caption as having been "murdered for asking for a raise." The remainder of the ad detailed the woman's case and noted that Nike gave away $7 million in sports equipment to colleges in 1993, while the total wages paid to its twelve thousand Indonesian workers that year was only $5 million. A second ad coupled the Nike slogan, "You know when you need a break. And you know when it's time to take care of yourself, for yourself. Because you know it's never too late to have a life," with a photograph of a young Nike sweatshop worker. The next paragraph discussed how Indonesian women had no time to "take care of themselves" because they are forced to work sixty hours a week, often for even less than the government's minimum wage of $1.80 per day. It also notes that when Nike's female workers tried to organize in order to "have a life," their efforts were defeated by government security forces.

In the ad quoting Phil Knight's explanation of Nike's corporate philosophy—"Everyone up to speed. Everyone on the same squad"—a director of a U.S.-funded wage monitoring campaign is quoted as having been told by a Nike Indonesian manager, "I'm your worst nightmare." The ad then asks, "Same squad?," as a photograph of Nike workers showing proof of illegally low wages is juxtaposed with Knight's photo, carrying the caption, "Phil Knight. Billionaire."

The clever inversion of Nike advertisements would become a consistent hallmark of anti-Nike activism. The ads, which ran in alternative weeklies in Boston, Portland, and Los Angeles, appeared prior to sufficient public consciousness of Nike's labor practices and did not result in a massive outpouring of subscriptions to Ballinger's *Nike in Indonesia* newsletter. The strongest reaction to the advertisements came from Nike's attorneys, who contacted Ballinger claiming that his statements in the ads were erroneous. No lawsuit against Ballinger was filed, however; Nike's attorneys cannily denied the activist the opportunity to prove the accuracy of the advertisements in a high-profile trial. Although the *Boston Globe* and the *New Republic* ran articles in 1994 on Nike's labor practices, the mainstream media's lack of consciousness of the issue became clear during President Clinton's visit to Indonesia in November of that year. Clinton used the trip to laud

Indonesia's commitment of free trade, and neither he nor the accompanying media discussed Nike's labor practices or addressed what free trade actually meant for Indonesian workers.

The media's lack of interest in Nike's Indonesian affairs persisted throughout 1995. The chief media advancement that year came from a major article by Cynthia Enloe in the March/April *Ms.* magazine. Enloe's article ("The Globetrotting Sneaker") exposed Nike's exploitation of women workers to an audience that would be particularly interested in the issue and emphasized the contrast between Nike's advertising campaign stressing women's empowerment with its reliance on female sweatshop labor. Enloe described how in the 1980s women workers in South Korea had overcome their society's traditional notions of feminine duty and had organized independent of male-dominated unions to win significant pay increases. The women also made sure that management addressed such issues as sexual harassment and health care. But she noted that Nike's "Just Do It" advertising slogan then took precedence over its women's empowerment campaign: "In response to South Korean women workers' newfound activist self-confidence, the sneaker company and its subcontractors began shutting down a number of their South Korean factories in the late 1980s and early 1990s." Nike then shifted its facilities to China and Indonesia, both of which "are governed by authoritarian regimes who share the belief that if women can be kept hard at work, low paid, and unorganized, they can serve as a magnet for foreign investors."[10] Enloe's piece was the longest description of Nike's overseas labor practices yet to appear. It was also the first to highlight Nike's women's disempowerment strategy, providing an analysis that has helped draw women activists to anti-sweatshop campaigns. Nike's spokesperson did not dispute any of Enloe's facts but disparaged the article by claiming that, unlike the *New York Times* or the *Wall Street Journal*, *Ms.* "has an agenda—to improve women's rights worldwide." Was this not also the agenda Nike claimed to espouse in its ads?[11]

No major media followed up on Enloe's piece or on Nike's provocative response. Activists continued to have difficulty through the end of 1995 getting mainstream media coverage of Nike's practices. Max White, whose Portland, Oregon, Amnesty International chapter focused on Indonesia and led him to help found the organization Justice! Do It Nike, was particularly frustrated by his inability to get material on Nike published in the media market that included Nike's headquarters. White recalls that as late as 1995 "it was a major coup for me to even get a letter to the editor printed in the *Oregonian*."[12]

In case the mainstream media's lack of interest in Nike was not sufficiently discouraging, 1995 was a banner year for the company. Nike's revenues rose 26 percent to more than $5 billion. Nike's spectacular profits no doubt led some to conclude that the activists' efforts to reform Nike had failed. A truer picture, however, could be seen from Phil Knight's introduction to Nike's 1995 annual report. Knight wrote that, as successful as Nike had been in 1995, he remained "angry and frustrated" at attacks on Nike's labor practices. As the company's founder, Knight had clearly been wounded by activist criticism. His sensitivity to attacks that had not yet appeared in major mainstream media outlets and of which most Americans remained unaware showed that a strategic opening for pressuring Nike existed regardless of the company's economic success. In 1996 activists were finally able to seize this opening and mobilize nationally against both Nike and the corporate approach to the global economy of which Nike was the most prominent proponent.[13]

The Movement Emerges

Several factors led to the transformation of activists' opposition to Nike into a broad, publicly recognized movement in 1996. In addition to Ballinger and others having laid the factual and thematic groundwork for a national campaign, the seemingly sudden emergence of widespread public criticism of Nike's labor practices was attributable to the exposure of Nike's wrongdoing in the *New York Times* and other mainstream national media, the public and political fallout over talk-show host Kathie Lee Gifford's connection to Honduran sweatshops, the entry into the anti-Nike campaign of key groups such as the faith-based investment community and Medea Benjamin and the labor and human rights group Global Exchange, and public exposure of Nike's misdeeds in Vietnam. Associated with all of these factors was the anti-Nike campaign's ability both to capitalize on media opportunities and to create events that enabled a now-interested media to continually cover the issue.

The first crack in the national mainstream media protective covering of Nike came from a source held up by Nike as the model for
journalistic objectivity: the *New York Times*. Reporter Edward Gargan's March 16, 1996, article told the story of twenty-two-year-old
Tongris Situmorang, who worked at a Nike factory until he was fired
for organizing workers to demand an increase in their $2.10 daily
wage. After his dismissal Situmorang was locked in the Nike plant
and interrogated for seven days by the Indonesian military, eager to
learn of his labor activities. Gargan noted that government crack-
downs on worker organizing had grown increasingly common in Indonesia, a development that led the blue jeans giant Levi Strauss to
leave the country in 1994. Gargan stated that by contrast, "Nike, whose
shoes are made in thirty-five plants across Asia, has expanded in the
region to take advantage of cheap labor." Nike spokesperson Donna
Gibbs is quoted by the *Times* as saying that she was unaware of Situmorang's case, but then saying that "our information is that workers
were not held for a week." Gibbs subsequently claimed Gargan's article was "highly distorted or an outright lie," saying that the factory
was instituting a new bonus program and only "seven out of 15,000
workers had a problem. Those workers taunted and harassed the others." Gibbs did not dispute the claim that workers had been fired and
the military brought in, but argued that there was no "coercion" by
the military.[14]

Gargan also confirmed a key argument of Nike's critics regarding
the requirement in Nike's Code of Conduct that its subcontractors
pay the local minimum wage. "The problem is that the minimum
wage does not provide for minimum subsistence," an Asian diplomat
told Gargan. "And beyond that, the companies don't always pay what
is required by law." The head of the Indonesian finance ministry
stated that "the philosophy of the minimum wage is to make sure
the minimum calorie need per day is fulfilled. That is the formula."
Nike's vaunted Code of Conduct, even when followed, assured workers of wages sufficient to feed themselves but not family members,
and left nothing to cover housing, clothes, transportation, or anything
beyond the minimum caloric intake necessary to survive.

The *New York Times* article, the subtitle of which—"Low Wages
Woo Foreign Business, but the Price is Worker Poverty"—succinctly

captured the perils of global free trade, provided mainstream media confirmation of Jeff Ballinger's repeated charges about Nike's labor practices. Moreover, the *Times* story paved the way for further mainstream national news coverage of the issue. The *Times* is widely recognized as the "gatekeeper" for news stories. As media critics Martin Lee and Norman Solomon have observed, both the *Times* and the *Washington Post* "are integral to the prevailing political power structure. They publish exclusive news stories and eminent punditry that greatly influence the direction and tone of other media." Articles from both papers appear in newspapers across the country, and the *Times's* daily national edition has even further broadened the paper's influence. Jeff Cohen, founder of the media watchdog group Fairness and Accuracy in Reporting (FAIR), sees the *Times* and the *Post* as "sanctifying what is an issue, what isn't an issue, and who the experts are who should address each issue." Once *Times* editors concluded that a story about Nike's abusive Indonesian labor practices was "fit to print," editors at other publications could proceed to cover activist criticism of Nike without fear that their news judgment would be criticized. The protection offered by the *Times* was particularly necessary for controversial stories such as a critical article on the world's largest shoe advertiser. Newspapers like the *Oregonian*, whose August 1992 article on Nike by reporter Nena Baker brought it criticism from the hometown sneaker giant, provided scant coverage of activists' criticism of Nike through 1995. After the *Times* story appeared, the paper provided ongoing coverage of the activist campaign against Nike.[15]

Second, the *Times* story gave unprecedented credibility to activists' charges against Nike. Those who have worked on national campaigns recognize the often disturbing reality that many Americans do not believe a story until it has appeared in the *New York Times*. In *The Activist's Handbook* I discuss how the AIDS Coalition to Unleash Power (ACT UP) used a variety of tactics—including a mass protest outside the home of the *Times's* publisher—to improve *Times* coverage of AIDS issues. The strategically savvy group devoted so much energy to the *Times* because it recognized the paper's influence in framing public opinion. For the anti-Nike forces to have their cause bolstered in the *Times*—and in the Business Day section, no less—was a tremendous coup.

The *Times* story also directly led to the public emergence of critical mainstream institutional opposition to Nike's labor practices. On March 21, 1996, less than a week after the *Times* article appeared, David Schilling, director of global corporate accountability for the Interfaith Center on Corporate Responsibility (ICCR), sent a letter to Phillip Knight. ICCR is a coalition of 275 Protestant, Roman Catholic, and Jewish institutional investors whose combined portfolios were then worth approximately $50 billion. Schilling's letter carefully recounted facts raised in the *Times* article and repeatedly asked how Nike's Code of Conduct and Memorandum of Understanding could have allowed such violations of human rights to occur. Schilling stated, "It is a basic human right to receive a sustainable wage. The problem in Indonesia is that the minimum wage does not provide for minimum subsistence." Schilling urged Nike to adopt an independent monitoring mechanism to strengthen the detection and resolution of violations of the company's Memorandum and concluded the letter by graciously enclosing "a copy of wage definitions for your reference."[16]

It was clear from the timing of Schilling's letter that ICCR was already familiar with the controversy surrounding Nike's labor practices and was ready with solutions. The *Times* story gave the mainstream investment organization the media support necessary in order to make its concerns about Nike public. In addition to contacting Nike about its concerns, the ICCR was assisting the General Board of Pension and Health Benefits of the United Methodist Church in filing a shareholder resolution with Nike seeking independent monitoring of Nike factories. Two weeks after Schilling's letter, the board sent its own letter to Nike. The letter began by praising the company for adopting a Code of Conduct for its global operations. But the letter went on to express the board's "concern and interest in learning about the Code monitoring process" and encouraged Nike to report to shareholders about "initiatives taken to ensure compliance with the Code." The board ended the letter by informing Nike that it was filing the enclosed resolution for consideration at the September 1996 annual meeting of the company. As of April 4, 1996, the date of its letter, the board's investment portfolio exceeded $7 billion, including 75,200 shares of Nike stock. Nike had never received such a polite but potent challenge to its global labor practices.[17]

The entry of ICCR and the United Methodist Church into the Nike campaign immediately enhanced the campaign's credibility. The trustees of even the most socially conscious investment funds must act prudently to serve their beneficiaries' financial interests, and they conduct their own investigation into a corporation's practices before concluding that a problem exists. As a leader in the corporate social responsibility movement, ICCR's credibility was recognized throughout the corporate world; when it celebrated its twenty-fifth anniversary in 1996, the benefit committee included representatives of Coca Cola, Pfizer, General Motors, and Capital Cities/ABC. The criticism of Nike's labor practices by ICCR and the United Methodist Church's General Board confirmed the allegations of Ballinger and other activists and created pressure on Nike from a source—its shareholders—that it could not simply ignore. Shareholder resolutions have been frequently used by religious institutions, public employee unions, and other socially responsible investors seeking reforms in corporate practices. This tactic is most effective when combined with a broader campaign that can use the resolution to attract media attention and to launch other public education efforts.

The board's proposed shareholder resolution ultimately became a public relations nightmare for Nike. Rather than trying to reach an accommodation with the church representatives, Knight allowed his anger to prevail. He rejected discussion of the resolution's call for Nike to commence independent monitoring, and when a church representative stated that his group would like to continue a dialogue with Nike about the issue, Knight told him to speak with longtime Nike spokesperson Donna Gibbs. When the representative called Gibbs the following Monday, he was told she was no longer with the company. Knight's performance at the September 16, 1996, meeting and the ruckus created by the board's resolution were seen in October by eleven million viewers of CBS's weekly show *48 Hours*. Nike avoided similar negative publicity at its 1997 annual meeting by persuading the pension board to withdraw a shareholder resolution calling for independent monitoring of Nike factories. Nike publicized the pension board's decision at its annual meeting and in press releases as evidence of the organization's satisfaction with Nike's labor practices. But pension board representative Vidette Bullock-Mixon accused Nike of deliberately exaggerating the board's action, claiming that Nike, like the rest of the industry, "have a long way to go." Bullock-Mixon noted that "Nike is a savvy PR organization. They put their spin on everything."[18]

In addition to the ongoing challenge to Nike's labor practices by ICCR and the United Methodist Church, many other religious groups have joined anti-sweatshop campaigns. On October 23, 1996, Labor Secretary Robert Reich held a press conference with representatives of thirty-six religious groups committed to using their power and resources to oppose sweatshops. Reich's claim that "the power of the pulpit will have a dramatic and sustained effect" was no exaggeration; one cannot imagine activists' successfully challenging the harm to workers caused by free trade and the escalating global economy without faith-based support. The anti-Nike campaign's initial difficulty attracting such support may have been due to the lack of unifying religious affiliation between Nike's predominantly Muslim Indonesian workers and most Americans. As other anti-sweatshop campaigns, particularly the Guess struggle discussed in chapter 2, brought more religious institutions into the cause, the campaign against Nike's labor abuses also benefited. By 1997 groups like the Union of American Hebrew Congregations, whose Reform Judaism was probably not shared by any of Nike's Asian work force, had adopted strong anti-sweatshop resolutions. Such resolutions did not single out Nike nor any other company, but they did underscore the association of Nike—one of the most high-profile targets of anti-sweatshop campaigns—with child labor and other worker abuses.[19]

Before April 1996 ended the anti-Nike forces gained tremendous publicity from an unlikely source: Kathie Lee Gifford. Gifford, host of the national talk show *Live with Regis and Kathie Lee*, had followed the lead of many other celebrities by establishing her own clothing line. The Gifford line was sold at Walmart with little fanfare until Charles Kernaghan of the New York–based National Labor Committee told a congressional committee on April 29, 1996, that Gifford's clothes were made by Honduran girls earning thirty-one cents per hour laboring in sweatshops. Kernaghan's statement led to the type of media feeding frenzy that increasingly surrounds revelations about celebrities. Gifford initially denied the charges, but when confronted with the evidence, quickly broke down in tears on her morning show and vowed to use all of her power and media access to end sweatshop labor. As Gifford's story brought the modern-day reality of sweatshops to such unlikely places as *People* magazine and *Entertainment Tonight*, reporters and media outlets were eagerly searching for other examples of celebrity-backed sweatshop apparel. The search quickly led to Nike, whose $20 million endorser, Michael Jordan, was in the midst of displaying his skills during the NBA playoffs. When asked by *Time* magazine whether Nike exploited its workers, Jordan replied, "I'm not really aware of that. My job with Nike is to endorse the product. Their job is to be up on that." Jordan's comments became a staple of stories about Nike's labor practices and even led sportswriters to unfavorably compare Jordan's attitude with that of Jackie Robinson and other socially conscious African-American sports stars.[20]

The Kathie Lee Gifford controversy created a critical but brief opening for expanding media attention to Nike's global labor practices. If anti-Nike activists could not seize this opportunity, the issue would soon be forgotten and the best chance for winning sympathetic coverage of their campaign lost. There was also a risk, as evidenced by *Time*'s June 17, 1996, coverage, of the pro–free trade media actually using the celebrity sweatshop issue to hurt the growing anti-Nike cause. The *Time* story argued that "if child-labor and safety laws were truly enforced, whole industries in many countries would collapse, at great cost to both developing and developed economies." Although *Time* quoted Labor Secretary Reich on the subminimum wages and appalling working conditions prevalent in the garment industry, it distinguished Nike from the pack. "We've taken a leadership role in trying to promote trade and act in an ethical way," Nike spokesperson Donna Gibbs told *Time*, whereas "human rights groups have their own agendas." *Time* noted that although the fifty-cent-per-hour wage of Nike's Indonesian work force "seems little more than slavery, it's roughly twice the country's minimum wage. . . . [O]verall, the lot of Indonesian workers is improving." *Time* acknowledged that Nike's claim that it met Indonesia's labor standards actually meant little, but then, acting as if it had never read any material from Nike's critics, the national newsweekly claimed that in response to criticism, "Nike declared last week that its contractors have agreed since 1991 to a Memorandum that binds them to rules on child labor, worker, and environmental safeguards." Rather than ask activists or cite the *New York Times*'s March 16 analysis of Nike's lack of compliance with its Memorandum, *Time* concluded by quoting Nike's Gibbs: "We feel that over time, our consciences, our way of doing business, has influenced the families that own these factories."[21]

The dominant theme of the *Time* sweatshop story was that the primary beneficiaries of free trade and the escalating global economy are people "making pennies an hour" who must sacrifice child labor and safety laws to improve their lot. Nike's claim to have taken a leadership role in acting ethically was used as a pull quotation, and a reader who only knew of Nike's Indonesian practices through *Time* would likely view activists' criticism of the company as bizarre. The *Time* article is a good reminder that activists should not expect the same mainstream media that opposes progressive social change campaigns to suddenly convert to the cause because of heightened public interest in the issue. Fortunately the anti-Nike activists understood the need to cultivate the support of sympathetic reporters and to create media events that accurately and powerfully conveyed their message. The campaign accomplished this by placing stories through columnists and by engaging in creative actions that helped overcome their adversary's multimillion-dollar advertising campaign.

The anti-Nike campaign's emphasis on columnists rather than news stories made perfect sense for a struggle whose agenda was strongly opposed by the mainstream media. The national mainstream media's universal support for free trade and an expanding global economy was often a direct expression of its own economic self-interest and meant that the campaign against Nike's labor practices would not receive even the scattering of sympathetic news stories that had benefited earlier national movements for civil rights, against the Vietnam war, for South African divestment, and against aid to the Nicaraguan contras. Jeff Ballinger had long recognized the need to achieve positive mainstream coverage through other vehicles and had been sending material on Nike to columnists for years with little result. With the media looking for sweatshop stories in the wake of the Kathie Lee Gifford affair, Ballinger's hard work paid off when he was contacted by *New York Times* columnist Bob Herbert. From June 1996 to June 1997 Herbert devoted eight entire columns to Nike's labor practices, thus

ensuring continued coverage of Nike's travails in the nation's most
influential newspaper. Herbert's columns combined colorful titles—
"From Sweatshops to Aerobics," "Nike's Pyramid Scheme," "Trampled
Dreams"—with extremely persuasive text. Herbert's columns fostered
growing opposition to Nike in three key ways. First, his initial column
identified Ballinger and Press for Change as working to reform Nike's
Indonesian labor practices. This enabled interested activists and organizations to contact Ballinger, share information, and coordinate
efforts. Second, Herbert's columns consistently pointed out the con-
tradictions in and outright hypocrisy of Nike's multimillion-dollar advertising campaigns. He noted that Nike's advertising campaign to
corner the women's shoe market had won industry awards without
anyone finding it "peculiar" that "a company could ride a so-called
women's empowerment campaign to new heights of wealth while at
the same time insisting that most of its products be made by grossly
underpaid women stuck in utterly powerless and often abusive circumstances." Herbert was also among the first to publicly criticize
Michael Jordan as an "uncaring multimillionaire celebrity" making $20
million a year from a company that worked young Asian women "like
slaves." Herbert's attacks on Nike's advertising and its celebrity en-
dorsers helped undermine the power of such messages or at least led
some to view Nike commercials in a new light.[22]

Herbert's columns, and those of Steve Duin in the *Oregonian* (part
of the Newhouse media conglomerate), Mitch Albom in the *Detroit
Free Press* (owned by the Knight-Ridder chain), Stephanie Salter in
the *San Francisco Examiner* (owned by the Hearst empire), and many
others made a far more powerful and convincing argument against
Nike than anything that would potentially appear in their papers' news
sections. Further, because columnists are paid to give opinions, they
had the editorial freedom to harshly criticize Nike without being attacked for bias, as reporters frequently are. Whereas reporters have
lost their jobs for accurately exposing negative corporate or government behavior, columnists are seldom dismissed for such reasons. Herbert's predecessor at the *Times*, the Pulitzer prize–winning Sydney
Schanberg, was the exception, having been terminated for criticizing
New York City land use policies strongly backed by his editors. Schanberg's article "Six Cents an Hour," which appeared in the June 1996

issue of *Life* magazine, described Nike's reliance on Pakistani child labor to sew together its soccer balls. Whether the Schanberg article spurred Phil Knight to approach the *Times* editorial board about Herbert is unknown, but Knight met with the *Times* after Herbert's fourth column. Recognizing the power of Herbert's columns, Knight requested that the *Times* stop Herbert from writing future pieces about Nike. The *Times* told Knight that it could not tell its columnists to stop writing about a particular subject, and denied his request.[23]

National social change efforts have increasingly had to purchase full-page advertisements in major newspapers in order to get their messages out. By cultivating relationships with columnists Ballinger and his fellow activists achieved effective publicity that was cost-free. The anti-Nike campaign was particularly media-dependent because its adversary was spending nearly one billion dollars annually to cultivate a positive image. Activists could never come close to matching Nike's advertising budget, but through the media prowess of Medea Benjamin and Global Exchange the anti-Nike campaign created publicity events that expanded its base and put its powerful multinational adversary on the defensive.

Global Exchange Joins the Struggle

When it comes to generating media coverage of labor and human rights abuses, few organizations have been more successful than Global Exchange. Founded in San Francisco in 1988, Global Exchange practices an activist approach to human rights. The organization has sent human rights/fact-finding delegations to nearly every political hot spot around the globe, including often inaccessible places such as Iraq, Cambodia, and Mozambique. The delegations are made up of writers, policy makers, professors, human rights advocates, and others who meet with all sides in the conflict. Upon their return many delegates become part of the organization's critical base of support by speaking out on human rights issues at universities, doing media interviews, and meeting with their congressional representatives. Global Exchange also gives people a firsthand look at countries around the globe through its "Reality Tours." The tours combine socially responsible visits to places like Guatemala, Cuba, and Mexico with the unique opportunity to meet with government and opposition political figures, local human rights activists, labor representatives, and others who can give an insight into their country that would not be available to tourists staying at Club Med. A longtime critic of unfettered economic globalization, Global Exchange has developed its own Fair Trade program to create markets for artisans in more than thirty-seven countries. The organization pays a fair price for the goods they buy and then sells the goods through its three Global Exchange Fair Trade Craft Centers. The organization's goal of developing community-based economic alternatives for third-world people has helped support more than three hundred Mayan women operating a cooperative in Guatemala and sixty people selling goods through the Grahamstown Crafts Co-op in South Africa. As a living model for socially responsible economic globalization, Global Exchange brought its credibility and nationwide activist support network into the anti-Nike campaign. The group also committed its full-time in-house public relations expert, Tony Newman, to work exclusively on building media support for the struggle.[24]

Global Exchange became involved in the anti-Nike campaign after a visit to its offices by East Timorese human rights activist Jose Ramos Horta in May 1996. Horta, who was awarded the Nobel peace prize later that year, discussed Nike's labor practices in Indonesia and suggested the organization address the issue. Medea Benjamin, codirector of Global Exchange, immediately seized upon the idea as an excellent opportunity to both assist the struggle for human rights in Indonesia and educate and mobilize Americans about Nike's and other corporations' exploitation of workers in the global economy. The organization's first action was to bring Cicih (pronounced chee-chee) Sukaesih (Su-KAY-zee) to the United States for a tour. In 1992 Sukaesih was fired by a Nike subcontractor for organizing workers to demand payment of the Indonesian minimum wage, then $1.30 a day. Ballinger recognized the potential galvanizing impact of her presence but he lacked the resources to bring her to the United States. Global Exchange had the $7,500 needed for the tour and, more important, the nationwide institutional support network necessary to carry out a series of high-profile media events surrounding Cicih's visit.

Sponsored by Global Exchange and Ballinger's Press for Change,

Sukaesih's American tour was a brilliant and successful media strategy on several levels. The tour was scheduled from July 15 to 27, 1996, and to build interest in Cicih's arrival she was interviewed by *Times* columnist Herbert shortly before leaving Indonesia. Herbert's July 12, 1996, column, "Trampled Dreams," told the story of the dismissal of Cicih and twenty-three of her coworkers for "daring to demand that their employers pay the minimum wage." Although the abusive Nike subcontractor who fired the workers had been replaced, Cicih and her coworkers were not rehired and "she has no money of her own and her prospects are dim." Herbert noted that many of Nike's women workers have "come to the cities to work but do not earn enough to have their children with them. . . . [T]hose who live with their children face a struggle each day just to feed them. And then it's back to work in the shadow of the Nike 'Swoosh.'" After speaking to Cicih, Herbert spoke with Phil Knight. Knight stated that Indonesians were lining up to work in factories making Nikes, and said that "it would wreck the country's economy if wages were allowed to get too high." Herbert made Cicih a celebrity even before her arrival and his column no doubt contributed to Nike's sudden openness to its need for reform.[25]

Cicih's visit began in Washington, D.C., during a "Fashion Industry Forum" called by Labor Secretary Reich. The Forum was part of a series of high-profile media events triggered by the Kathie Lee Gifford upheaval; since Gifford committed herself to being on the front lines fighting sweatshops, the Clinton administration had little choice but to at least appear to be doing something about the problem. On the eve of both the forum and Sukaesih's visit Knight told reporters that "there is no question that Nike can do a better job" monitoring labor practices at its Asian facilities.[26] While Knight claimed that the press had inaccurately portrayed Nike, he committed the company to "get more independent monitoring so that the public is reassured." Prior to the prospect of Sukaesih's imminent arrival Knight had consistently maintained that Nike's accounting firm, Ernst & Young, already monitored its subcontractors. He had never even allowed the words "independent monitoring" to pass his lips. Nike's public change of position showed how the decision to schedule the tour was paying dividends even before Sukaesih's arrival.

Sukaesih's first stop in Washington, D.C., was at a Nike Foot Locker shoe outlet. After checking the shoes to see if they were made in her factory, she noticed the ninety-dollar price tag. It would have cost her two months' salary at Nike's Indonesian plant to afford the shoes, which she tried on for the first time. Although she and other anti-Nike activists were refused entry to the Fashion Industry Forum, Sukaesih met Kathie Lee Gifford and the two joined in a smiling photograph that was distributed nationwide. Sukaesih's appearance with Gifford and with the legislators and apparel makers who attended the forum represented the first opportunity ever for Nike's Indonesian work force to be publicly recognized as having a voice in decisions affecting their labor conditions. Sukaesih's presence automatically raised questions why she, or another Indonesian labor representative, was not formally participating in the process of developing new initiatives to combat sweatshops. After leaving Washington, Cicih went to New York, where she met with UNITE and human rights groups and participated in a demonstration at the Manhattan Niketown. She then went to Chicago to meet with the General Board of Pensions of the United Methodist Church, whose shareholder resolution would be considered at Nike's September annual meeting. While in Chicago Cicih sought to meet with Chicago Bulls basketball star Michael Jordan; he was unavailable.[27]

Cicih's next stop was in Portland, Oregon, adjacent to Nike's head-quarters and the home of Justice! Do It Nike, a strong grassroots organization that had long been involved in the labor issue. Global Exchange had sent a letter to Phil Knight on July 18 requesting that he meet with Cicih anytime on July 23 so that she could tell him her story. Knight, who did not become a billionaire by falling into obvious traps, responded the following day. Knight stated that the company was "well aware" of Cicih's situation and noted that the factory in which she worked was under new management that had addressed worker grievances and paid the minimum wage. Knight described this development as "an example of the benefit Nike brings in upgrading labor practices in emerging market societies." While noting Nike's participation in the Fashion Industry Forum and other coalition efforts designed to improve and expand its monitoring system, Knight stated that Nike preferred to work with groups that "are interested in constructive, proactive solutions, not those who announce their intentions through news conferences and mean-spirited media campaigns."[28]

Like all great activists Benjamin and Sukaesih were not dissuaded by their adversary's intransigence. They began their day in Portland by visiting Niketown so that Cicih could inspect and try on shoes. This seemingly innocent conduct led to their immediate removal from the store by Nike security. The two then proceeded to Nike headquarters in an effort to discuss Cicih's story with Phil Knight. The resulting episode further proved Portland activist Max White's point that "Nike is a genius at advertising, not public relations." Nike treated the activists like alien space invaders trying to break into the earth's stratosphere. Nike security staff with radio transmitters verbally monitored the two women's progress as they approached the grand lobby at the center of the Nike compound. Upon their reaching the lobby a guard picked up his phone and said, "They're here." It was a hot July morning in Portland and Cicih and Benjamin were thirsty after their long walk. When they reached for water glasses that Nike maintained in the lobby for its visitors and began pouring water, a guard grabbed the glasses away, claiming they were private property.[29]

One would think that Nike would have known what to do next. A low-level functionary should have greeted the activists and apologized for the guard's behavior. The official should have poured water into the women's glasses and then offered to spend the remainder of the day hearing Cicih's story. Nike could then have argued that it had nothing to hide and was pleased to have had the opportunity to discuss its labor practices with Cicih. Nike could even have offered Cicih a high-paying job on the spot. But Nike took none of these preemptive actions either because of its arrogance or, more likely, because of Phil Knight's strong dislike for what he had already described as the "terrorist tactics" of Benjamin and Global Exchange. Instead, here is what Nike did: After the women were told that Knight was not available they said that they were happy to meet with the company president instead. When told that he was in a meeting Benjamin stated that they had plenty of time and would wait for the meeting to end. Nike staff found this response unacceptable and told Benjamin that they were calling the police to have her and Sukaesih removed. Benjamin immediately recognized the publicity value of Nike's arresting two activists who had simply come to their headquarters seeking to discuss the company's Indonesian labor practices. It suddenly dawned on her, however, that an arrest might cause special problems for Cicih, including the possibility that her visa to enter the United States could be revoked. Benjamin asked Cicih if she had any problem with the police coming. With a big smile Cicih replied, "For the first time since I have been in the United States, I feel right at home." The women were ultimately forced to the edge of Nike's facilities, where they were surrounded by television cameras and other media eager to learn of their treatment by Nike officials.

Cicih's tour brought the anti-Nike campaign its broadest media coverage to date. Local media stories accompanied her visits to each city and her appearances at Niketowns and Foot Locker stores educated consumers as to the disparity between the $2.00 daily wage of Nike's workers and the $70.00–150.00 retail price of its shoes. Her visit energized anti-Nike activists in each city and won new converts to her cause. Phil Knight was so concerned about the impact of her trip that he not only expressed a willingness to implement independent monitoring but on August 2, 1996, he appeared with President Clinton and the ever-present Gifford for the announcement of the formation of an anti-sweatshop task force. The *Oregonian* published a story titled "Nike Joins Ranks of Sweatshop Opponents" and reporter Jeff Manning referred to "the new, conciliatory Nike company line." While insisting that "Nike is in the third world to stay," Knight stated that "consumers want assurances that the products they buy are not made in abusive situations, and we look forward to working with this coalition to develop solutions." The Portland-based *Business Journal* quoted Knight's commitment to "more independent monitoring" and his remarkable admission that the focus "on the international nature of business and how consumer products are made is healthy."[30]

Neither Clinton nor Knight offered any specifics on eliminating industry abuses, and the six months that industry leaders were given to report back to Clinton were clearly designed to allow public interest in sweatshops to dissolve. Nevertheless, Nike had agreed to serve on a task force with such critics of its practices as the ICCR and UNITE, a stance that only a few months earlier would have been unthinkable. As Medea Benjamin told Manning, "we have a healthy skepticism, but it's very positive that Nike is engaging. For so long they just ignored the issue."

While Kathie Lee Gifford put the spotlight on sweatshops, Benjamin and Ballinger forced Nike to stop ignoring the issue by using Sukaesih to personalize its abusive labor practices. Cicih was the first victim of Nike's global free trade agenda that most of the American public and media had ever met and her engaging personality and courageous story touched people's hearts and minds as even the most persuasive articles and columns could not. National social change movements are often propelled by people's sense of moral or emotional anger and it was difficult to arouse such feelings among an American public generally indifferent to events in Indonesia. Cicih provided the human face of Nike's victims that had long been absent and it is to the enormous credit of Global Exchange and Press for Change that they recognized the star quality of the leader of a four-year-old dispute. It is not easy to find female sweatshop workers who are willing to jeopardize their lives by becoming leaders in a labor struggle. Cicih Sukaesih carried with her a moral power that even Nike feared to directly contest; her American tour was a powerful blow to the political and corporate elites' sugar-coated vision of the benefits of a burgeoning global economy.

The Momentum Builds

July 1996 marked a turning point for the anti-Nike campaign. The combination of Cicih's tour, continued publicity about sweatshops generated by Kathie Lee Gifford, and the identification of independent monitoring as a critical compliance strategy by Labor Secretary Reich at the Fashion Industry Forum forced Nike to publicly pledge to reform its labor practices and to reposition itself as a leader in the fight against sweatshops. But a danger emerges when the target of social change campaigns publicly expresses a willingness to revise its conduct and become part of the solution. As the media reported Nike's newfound commitment to anti-sweatshop activism many consumers likely believed what they read and felt that the anti-Nike campaign could declare victory and disband. Phil Knight stood next to President Clinton and Kathie Lee Gifford at an August 2 press conference announcing the formation of a coalition that would meet for six months and then report back to the president with recommendations for combating sweatshops; what better evidence was there of Nike's new commitment to resolve its labor problems?

In order to prevent Nike from winning public acclaim through words rather than deeds and to forestall an at least six-month delay in Nike's implementation of overdue reforms, the anti-Nike campaign had to show the public that Nike's promises were a sham. The first action the campaign took toward these ends was to coordinate its members' activities by creating the Working Group on Nike. The working group described itself in its initial July 23, 1996, letter to Phil Knight as "representing shareholders, financial services firms, human rights organizations, and religious groups concerned about the treatment of workers at the overseas factories where Nike contracts." Its letter to Knight focused on Nike's need to adopt independent monitoring and enforcement of its Memorandum and Code of Conduct and pointed out that The Gap had agreed to such a system for its El Salvador operations. The group reminded Knight that three Indonesian nongovernmental organizations had written to him on July 3 offering to set up independent monitoring processes for Nike's facilities but had received no response. The letter urged Nike to open a dialogue on the issue "before the controversy becomes a threat to Nike's image or before one of your competitors becomes the first to adopt independent monitoring."

The working group's letter essentially said: We have read your press statements; now put up, or else. It was followed by an August 5, 1996, letter to Secretary Reich asking him to encourage the dialogue that the group's July 23 letter had failed to produce. Noting that Nike had rejected independent monitoring in a letter to a Group member while publicly claiming to support the practice, the letter emphasized the concern that "Nike could use its position on the Clinton administration's advisory committee to evade issues relating to its contractors in Indonesia." This letter, written by group representative Trim Bissell of the national Campaign for Labor Rights, essentially said: We all know the game Nike is playing with your administration and we expect you not to let Nike get away with it.

The working group took the immediate action necessary to let Nike and the Clinton administration know that the anti-Nike campaign expected prompt and concrete changes from Knight's Rose Garden appearance with the president. Absent such action the group would "continue to mobilize public opinion" against Nike. The creation of the working group also served two other important purposes. First, it set forth a set of unified demands so that Nike could not marginalize particular groups or partially address a problem and then claim that it had done everything its critics had asked. The demands for independent monitoring, an end to child labor, respect for the right to organize, and payment of a living wage were certainly nothing new, but having all of the groups agree to a unified agenda prevented Nike from successfully defining its opposition as anticapitalist radicals. Nike repeatedly described Global Exchange in such negative terms, but such charges could not tinge a coalition that also included major investors like the ICCR. The working group's formation and unified demands forced Nike to deal with all of its opponents, denied it the ability to cut a separate deal with the investor opposition with which it felt most comfortable, and provided a specific focus helpful in movement building.

The creation of the working group also enhanced communication and trust among the diverse anti-Nike organizations. As I discuss in *The Activist's Handbook*, without careful understanding of the nature of coalition politics, coalition activism can lead to division and recrimination when groups of divergent styles unify for a specific goal. Unifying groups willing to engage in militant, confrontational tactics like Global Exchange and the Campaign for Labor Rights with stylistically moderate investment groups like the ICCR and General Board of Pensions of the United Methodist Church meant that each coalition participant had to understand the basis for the others' actions. This did not mean that the ICCR would try to prevent Global Exchange from engaging in a particular tactic; rather the working group fostered the dialogue necessary between the various organizations so that all would understand why and how a particular entity saw its action as advancing the cause.

All of the organizations comprising the anti-Nike campaign played important roles in focusing public attention on Nike's annual shareholders meeting in September 1996. The meeting would include the United Methodist General Board's shareholder resolution on Nike's labor practices, and represented an important opportunity to attract media attention to Nike's actual labor practices following its claim to have joined the fight against sweatshops. Global Exchange prepared for the shareholders meeting by leading a delegation of professors, religious leaders, labor organizers, and human rights observers from eight countries on a ten-day fact-finding trip to Indonesia in early September. Global Exchange had written to Phil Knight asking permission to visit the Nike factories but was denied on the grounds that they were not objective observers. The delegation then tried to simply visit the factories informally but were turned away by security guards at every facility. The delegation was also prevented from meeting with the accounting firm Ernst & Young, employed by Nike to monitor its subcontractors' compliance with its Code of Conduct.[31]

Even without formal factory tours the delegation spoke to many Nike workers about wages and working conditions. The workers' descriptions contradicted Nike's claims that worker rights were being protected in its plants. Overtime was mandatory at nearly all of the plants surveyed and workers reported they were not always paid for all overtime hours worked. Ernst & Young was not trusted by the workers, who feared reprisals if they told the truth to the firm. Workers reported that Ernst & Young monitoring teams were interested primarily in product quality and whether production quotas were being met; workers in three separate factories were unanimous in stating that the monitors "never ask questions about the workers or conditions in the factories." Delegation member Clayola Brown, a vice president of UNITE and a member of the national board of the AFL-CIO, met with a group of thirty to forty Nike workers and asked them what change they wanted most. Unused to being asked such a question, the workers hesitated until one said, "We want the same minimum wage you have in your country." The rest of the group quickly joined in agreement.[32]

Global Exchange incorporated its findings in a September 16, 1996, "Report on Nike." The Report juxtaposed "Nike Claims" versus "Reality" regarding its abuse of workers, its failure to pay a living wage, and the ineffective oversight by Ernst & Young. Timed for release on the day of the Nike shareholders meeting, publicity about the report was enhanced by a demonstration/press conference that day organized at Nike headquarters by the Portland Green Party and the Justice! Do It Nike coalition. Phil Knight's anger at Global Exchange's effort to undermine Nike's new image as a leader in the fight against sweatshops led him to single out Global Exchange at the shareholders meeting as a suspicious organization with "ulterior motives." The group's report may have led to Knight's tactically foolish decision to have Nike's board vote down the General Board's shareholder resolution regarding independent monitoring without discussion and before many shareholders had even had the opportunity to vote. Rather than try to split the anti-Nike movement by contrasting the "terrorist tactics" of Global Exchange with the working through the system approach of the corporate socially responsible investment community, Knight alienated both. Knight's treatment of the church representatives confirmed that, despite his joining with President Clinton to denounce sweatshops two months earlier, Nike was not serious about eliminating sweatshop conditions for the workers making its shoes.

Nike's Vietnam Syndrome

Knight's contemptuous attitude toward even his most mainstream and polite critics was witnessed by millions of Americans when an episode on Nike was shown on the October 17, 1996, CBS News show *48 Hours*. Correspondent Roberta Baskin had been following Nike's labor practices for years and had been given ample material by Jeff Ballinger. As far back as 1993 Baskin had prepared an exposé on Nike's labor practices for the short-lived CBS weekly documentary *Street Stories*. The network ran Baskin's piece that year on the night of July 3, which may well have been the night on which such a story would attract the smallest possible audience. Ballinger and his friends may have been the only viewers and at the time he was greatly disappointed at the missed opportunity to direct public attention to Nike's labor abuses.

Baskin's October 17, 1996, story, however, was a revelation. With nearly all of the activist and media attention on Nike's labor practices in Indonesia, few were aware that Nike also maintained plants in Vietnam. The *Portland Business Journal* had reported on May 5, 1995, that Nike was planning to open five sneaker factories south of Ho Chi Minh City by August of that year. The *Journal* article cited Vietnam's high unemployment rate and monthly minimum wage of only thirty-five dollars, two factors that led a Nike executive to describe the former Saigon as a place with "a lot of opportunity." The piece suggested that Nike was launching its Vietnam operations quietly so as to avoid the type of press criticism it had received for its Indonesian practices.[33]

Until Baskin's television report Nike had indeed succeeded in avoiding scrutiny of its Vietnamese operations. Her story described workers paid less than minimum wage in miserable conditions while making shoes for a company headed by the sixth richest man in America. Abuse of workers was so widespread that the phrase "to Nike" someone meant taking out one's frustration on a fellow worker, a common occurrence in the factories. But even worse for Knight than the exposure of Nike's Vietnam labor practices was Baskin's depiction of Knight's attitude toward reports of abuse. The CBS crew was covering the shareholders meeting when Knight reported that in a Vietnamese plant a woman was hit with a shoe. According to an eyewitness interviewed on camera by Baskin, however, Knight's portrayal of the incident was slightly askew. The supervisor "hit all fifteen team leaders on the side of the neck and the head two or three times each," said a Nike worker at the facility. The supervisor was ultimately convicted for assaulting the fifteen women workers, further confirming that Nike's CEO was either misinformed or intentionally deceitful about the company's Vietnam operations.[34] Baskin's attempts to do a follow-up story were rebuffed by CBS, and the network vetoed a summer rebroadcast of the episode. Baskin eventually sent a highly publicized memo to the network charging that Nike's sponsorship of the 1998 Winter Olympics, to be televised on CBS, led the network to muzzle critical stories about Nike's labor practices.[35]

Baskin's investigation of Nike's Vietnam practices would have far-reaching and unforeseen implications for the anti-Nike campaign. In contrast to its lack of ties with Indonesia, America has a significant, educated Vietnamese population that maintains personal as well as business ties to Vietnam. Among this group was Thuyen Nguyen who came to America from Vietnam in 1975 when he was eleven years old. Nguyen was employed as a technology consultant for a New Jersey financial services company when he viewed the *48 Hours* show. Outraged and shocked by what he saw was happening in his native country, Nguyen decided to form his own organization, Vietnam Labor Watch. Nguyen had never engaged in anything that could be described as activism. Like many of the great citizen activists, however, Nguyen was not deterred by his lack of experience. He began contacting other Vietnamese Americans as well as his friends in Vietnam. He also contacted Nike, whose labor practices manager, Dusty Kidd, invited Nguyen to tour the company's Vietnam plants to prove to himself that all was well. Nike was presumably still relying on the same information source for its Vietnam operations that led to Phil Knight's false account of the shoe incident; its decision to invite Nguyen to Vietnam would prove even more damaging to the company.[36]

Nguyen visited three of Nike's Vietnam factories and interviewed thirty-five factory workers. As a nonactivist technology consultant unaffiliated with any of the Working Group on Nike, Nguyen must have appeared to Nike as the perfect counterweight to its adversaries. Nike hoped that once the independent Nguyen, a person to whom nobody could ascribe a hidden agenda or motive, verified that Nike's Vietnam factories were in compliance, all the controversy caused by Baskin's story would be put to rest. Nike seemed to have everything figured out this time and it is not hard to imagine the expectant glee felt by Nike's besieged public relations department while awaiting Nguyen's report. There was only one problem with Nike's strategy: the reality of its Vietnam operations.

Nguyen's March 1997 report on his three-week trip to Vietnam that month included the most shocking revelations ever produced about Nike's overseas labor practices. Unfortunately, Nguyen's press release about his findings was completely ignored by the media. Lacking any personal media contacts and affiliated with an organization whose name had never appeared in the press, Nguyen's release was probably not even read before being tossed into the recycling bin. Frustrated by the lack of media response, the relentless Nguyen contacted Global Exchange, whose San Francisco headquarters was three thousand miles from Nguyen's New York home. Global Exchange's crack media team, led by Tony Newman, immediately disseminated Nguyen's report to a now very interested national and local media. Following the best activist strategy of always giving reporters who have helped your cause in the past the opportunity to break a new story, Newman first contacted *Times* columnist Bob Herbert.

Herbert's March 28, 1997, column, "Brutality in Vietnam," powerfully and persuasively revealed Nguyen's findings to a public that was largely unaware that Nike even operated production facilities in Vietnam. Herbert's main revelation from Nguyen's report was the events on March 8, International Women's Day, witnessed by the independent observer at a factory making Nike shoes:

On March 8, International Women's Day, 56 women employed at a factory making Nike shoes in Dong Nai, Vietnam, were punished because they hadn't worn regulation shoes to work. Factory officials ordered the women outside and made them run around the factory in the hot sun. The women ran and ran and ran. One fainted, and then another. Still they ran. They would be taught a lesson. They had worn the wrong shoes to work. More women fainted. The ordeal didn't end until a dozen workers had collapsed.

Herbert, quoting from Nguyen's report, noted that "Vietnamese all over the country were outraged that on International Women's Day, when most companies in Vietnam give women flowers and other gifts, twelve Vietnamese women were so abused they had to spend the day in the emergency room." Nguyen's report "found the same kind of demoralizing and debilitating abuses that a wide array of Nike critics have been spotlighting for a long time. Nike set up shop in Vietnam because labor there is even cheaper than in Indonesia. But apparently not cheap enough."[37]

As set forth by Herbert and by subsequent widespread national and local media coverage of Nguyen's report, what the independent observer stumbled upon during his three-week visit at Nike's invitation was business at usual in Nike's Vietnam factories. Nguyen concluded that "it was common" for workers to faint from exhaustion, heat, or poor nutrition during their shifts and that Nike's business partners regularly physically beat the workers to enhance their productivity. McClain Ramsey, Nike's newest in what was becoming a series of chief spokespersons, expressed outrage upon learning of Nguyen's recitation of the March 8 incident. She told Herbert that "Nike is completely horrified" that that was allowed to occur in a factory, and "has called for a full investigation." Whereas "cynics might say that Nike is horrified that the story got out," Herbert reminded readers of the central point of the growing anti-Nike campaign:

Rather than crack down on the abusive conditions in the factories, Nike has resorted to an elaborate international public relations campaign to give the appearance that it cares about the workers. But no amount of public relations will change the fact that a full-time worker who makes $1.60 a day is likely to spend a fair amount of time hungry if three very simple meals cost $2.10.

Prior to Nguyen's trip to Vietnam Nike's then chief spokesperson Dusty Kidd had sent him a copy of Nike's Code of Conduct and Memorandum of Understanding so that his report presumably could intersperse Nike's stated commitment to "trust, honesty, teamwork and mutual respect" with what they expected Nguyen to witness in Vietnam. Instead, Nguyen's report had concluded that Nike treated its workers "like animals." The reverberations of Nguyen's report would prove significant. First, Nguyen's report came as Vietnamese-American response to the October 1996 *48 Hours* story on Nike's Vietnam practices was starting to build. In late February the student council of the University of California at Irvine voted twenty-five to one for a resolution condemning labor abuses by Nike and other corporations. The motion was sponsored by the Asian Pacific Student Union with support from the campus's Vietnamese American Coalition. The Irvine resolution was the first anti-Nike measure passed by a major American university, but as important as this action was, further impetus for greater student involvement in the anti-Nike campaign was required. Nguyen's report, coming from a Vietnamese native and detailing terrible abuses against the Vietnamese people, provided the necessary spark. Demonstrating the speciousness of claims that students' "identity politics" have subverted and replaced national economic justice struggles, Asian-American and Vietnamese student groups intensified their anti-Nike activism following Nguyen's report. There may be few Indonesians on American campuses but there are thousands of Vietnamese Americans; their organizations' entry into the anti-Nike effort provided the key on-campus links for Global Exchange and its allies to mobilize national student opposition to Nike.[38]

Second, the publicity generated by Global Exchange about Nguyen's report was astounding. Nguyen's report made front-page news throughout the United States, including in *USA Today*. The Associated Press sent out a major story about Nguyen's March 28 press conference and continued to pursue the story in the following days. Bob Herbert wrote a second column on the report on March 31, 1997 ("Nike's Boot Camps"), and Mitch Albom of the *Detroit Free Press*, Steve

Duin of the *Oregonian*, Stephanie Salter of the *San Francisco Examiner*, and perhaps most significantly cartoonist Garry Trudeau in the nationally syndicated *Doonesbury* all wrote powerful pieces about Nike's latest outrage.

Albom's April 5 piece began by describing a recent commercial featuring African-American baseball stars thanking Jackie Robinson for breaking the color line. A surprising number of sportswriters and other journalists used the occasion of the fiftieth anniversary of Robinson's 1947 breakthrough to contrast Robinson's social consciousness with Michael Jordan's lack of concern about Nike's workers. Albom's column went deeper, exposing the sinister agenda of Nike's commercials featuring Robinson and others:

It is a touching tribute, grainy film footage mixed with heart-felt messages. But when the moment peaks, and your heart is open, what's the last thing you see? A Nike Swoosh. Same way you see a Nike Swoosh after those Tiger Woods commercials, in which the children of the world—all races, mind you—dream of being Tiger. . . . By its founder's admission, Nike is no longer in the shoe business; it's in the image business. It wants you to feel a certain way. It wants you and your kids to desire the swoosh subliminally, under the skin, without even knowing why.

Call it planned addiction. First, Nike wants your mind. Then it takes your wallet.

In fact, when it comes to exploiting poor people, Nike seems to have a motto. . . . Let's do it.

After describing Nguyen's report as showing that Nike's Vietnam factories "are treating women like slaves," Albom returned to Nike's hypocrisy: "Ask Michael Jordan the last time he got slapped for talking. Ask Phil Knight why none of the cute kids in his commercial is seen hunkered over a machine stitching shoes." Noting that Nike is the only athletic shoe company that "tries to paint itself as such an angel, while doing so much of the devil's business," Albom concluded:

I have purchased my last pair of Nike anything. They may own every famous athlete, every pro and college team. They may spend billions on brain washing disguised as advertising, sticking their swoosh on every noble thing that ever happened in America and claiming it as their own. But they're not getting my mind. It's the only thing I have left to detect evil. I plan to protect it.

Albom's attack was published in a chain-owned newspaper whose attempt to break up the *Detroit Free Press* union showed that it could hardly be described as having a "proworker" agenda. It is doubtful that any major newspaper in America would have printed as part of a news story any of Albom's harsh attack on one of the country's largest advertisers. Had Global Exchange and its allies tried to pay for an ad making such charges against Nike, they might well have been refused. Albom's column redefined the campaign against Nike as an Orwellian struggle by free-thinking humanity against the mind-controlling, freedom-depriving tactics of "Big Brother" Nike. The Orwellian 1984 had passed and the Cold War was over, but Nike's advertising images remained to threaten us.[39]

Albom's theme of Nike as an Orwellian threat was also expressed in Stephanie Salter's *San Francisco Examiner* column following Nguyen's report. Ironically, Salter's assertion that Nike's "power and influence has reached grotesque proportions" was immediately confirmed when for only the second time in the award-winning columnist's long tenure her column was rejected by her editor. Salter described her conversation with her editor about the piece:

He said the piece was unfair to Nike, that I did not support my allegations after calling Nike obscene and offensive, and that it was a polemic that included no news. Then he said that there had also been discussions as to how the piece would affect the paper's "integrity" in working with Nike on the Bay to Breakers [a race that is the paper's top annual promotion].

But prior to the editors' intervention Salter's column ran on the *Examiner*'s website, the Gate, where it was picked up by the *Miami Herald*. This enabled several alternative weeklies across the country to expand the impact of Salter's piece by either printing it or reporting stories about the paper's censorship.[40]

Salter's column referred to the company as N——e, "since journalists use dashes when they print obscene or offensive words." Salter saw something bigger than the exploitation of "16-year-old garment workers in Vietnam who make $2 a day," asking "what about sublimating your own individuality to be a walking billboard for a company that's already richer than God?" Echoing Albom and the concerns of an increasing number of critics about Nike's larger societal message, Salter explained that she was picking on the company not simply because of its greed and lack of conscience:

I'm picking on N—e because it is the biggest, the coolest. Because it pays the best athletes the most millions to endorse its products. Because you can't walk a block without seeing its logo. Because it is scary to see something as big and influential as N—e with no sense of moral responsibility for counterbalance. I'm picking on it because I have been to N—eTown, where twisted values are showcased every day for children and the parents who want to make them happy.[41]

Bob Herbert's March 31 follow-up column also emphasized the emerging theme of Nike as a threat to rather than enhancer of individual freedom. In a profound insight regarding the company's ability to "buy and sell people at will," Herbert observed, "Nike is paying Tiger Woods a fortune, but it has also slapped its swoosh on his head, and Tiger dare not take off that cap. Nike is important because it epitomizes the triumph of monetary values over all others, and the corresponding devaluation of those peculiar interests and values we once thought of as human."[42]

The media fallout from Nguyen's report went beyond the new perception of Nike as posing a threat to cherished American values of freedom and individuality. Nike's hometown paper, the *Oregonian*, announced in its April 1, 1997, editorial that "Nike and its sports-apparel competitors need to create, pay for and cooperate with an independent organization to audit and report on human-rights conditions in their factories in developing nations. Until independent monitors are the rule, the industry's foreign laborers will not be free of human-rights abuses." The critical tone of the editorial sharply contrasted with the paper's editorial of July 7, 1996, which supported outside monitoring but whose dominant theme was that "Nike appears to be more part of the solution—to the extent there is one—than part of the problem." The *Oregonian*'s editorial staff had clearly grown tired of Nike's claims coming in conflict with Thuyen Nguyen's documented realities; now its editorial read like the General Board of Pensions of the United Methodist Church shareholder resolution flatly rejected by Nike the previous September.[43]

Nguyen's report also brought *Doonesbury* cartoonist Garry Trudeau into the anti-Nike campaign. It is rare for social or economic justice campaigns to enter the popular culture, an absence that some blame for the frequent isolation of such causes from the consciousness of most Americans. Political causes that do enter the world of television or major studio films are often caricatured or watered down and the public exposure is of little utility to activist campaigns. Garry Trudeau's comic strip, *Doonesbury*, has long been that rare example of including progressive political content in a popular medium. Many conservative newspapers obligated to run the strip due to its popularity place it on the editorial page in order to dilute its often powerful message.

Trudeau's main character, Michael Doonesbury, had entered into a romantic relationship with Kim, a Vietnamese-American woman, well prior to the issuance of Nguyen's report. After reading of Nike's labor practices in Vietnam, Trudeau arranged for his fictional Kim to visit a cousin working for a Nike subcontractor in Vietnam while in the country for her honeymoon. In the strip's first week of columns about Nike, Kim sees the difficult working conditions her cousin and the other women are forced to endure and grows suspicious of the factory manager's responses to her inquiries. During her tour of the Nike plant, Kim is told that "despite what you might have heard . . . there is a . . . feeling that employees get when they know they're working for something bigger than just themselves." To prove this point Kim is shown a shrine where all workers are allowed five minutes a day to worship, not Buddha, but Nike icon Michael Jordan. The week of strips ended on May 31, 1997, with Kim telling Mike on their flight home: "I just don't get it, Mike—Nike could easily pay its work force living wages and still make humongous profits." Kim then vows to take the issue to stockholders and the media, while in the last panel the plant manager asks a subordinate to confirm his golf plans.

Trudeau's second week of strips, June 23–29, 1997, was even more explicit about Nike's wrongdoing. Kim begins the week by taking Michael's running shoes, "the ones made by the company whose name has become synonymous with chronic violations of minimum wage laws." She then decides that the couple's new business will be to maintain a website documenting Nike's misrepresentations "one lie per page." Directly lifting from Nguyen's report, Kim tells Michael and the strip's more than fifty million readers that Nike boasts "they pay twice the $200 per capita annual income in rural Vietnam. But

Doonesbury   BY GARRY TRUDEAU

Doonesbury   BY GARRY TRUDEAU

the factories are in suburban Saigon, where annual income approaches $1000! They also claim they offer free medical care, English lessons and training—none of it true! Nike's image is held aloft by a web of deceit!"

Nike was understandably angry that the seemingly innocent vehicle of a comic strip was sending an anti-Nike message to millions of readers each day. The company asked Trudeau's Universal Press Syndicate to prevent future anti-Nike columns, but to no avail.[44] Trudeau stayed on the Nike story and used a week of strips to publicize the International Day of Protest against Nike on October 18, 1997. The strips showed Kim using e-mail to convince the two hundred Nike-sponsored college athletic teams to observe the day by refusing to wear their swoosh-enhanced uniforms. In the October 18 strip a player removes his uniform and scores a touchdown as the announcer praises him for "doing well by doing good." Trudeau ended the series with a Sunday, October 19, 1997, strip that echoed the idea of Nike as a threat to individual freedom. The football coach asks his college president about all the grief they are catching about their Nike gear (Trudeau has the uniforms and helmets covered entirely with swooshes). The president says the free apparel makes it possible for the school to field a team and "promotes a brand loyalty that helps transition kids to a world filled with confusing consumer choices." But most important: "One day we'll all be living on Planet Nike, and it would be irresponsible for us not to prepare our kids to function in a hyperswoosh environment." When the coach asks if "we developed that load in-house," the president demurs: "No, no, they sent us a kit."

My inquiries have led to the conclusion that more people learned about Nike's Vietnam practices through *Doonesbury* than through the original media coverage of Nguyen's report. In addition, *Doonesbury* was clearly the leading media source for the October 18 protests. This is not surprising when you consider that most people do not read every article in the newspaper each day but they do make sure to check out their favorite comic strip. In addition to exposing millions of loyal readers to Nike's Vietnam abuses and emphasizing that "the amount of misinformation Nike puts out is amazing," Trudeau also helped the anti-Nike campaign in two potentially significant ways. First, *Doonesbury* readers include millions of liberal college graduates and baby boomers who are the population group most likely to turn against Nike if exposed to facts about its exploitation of those who make its shoes. Nike's tremendous emphasis on winning the inner-city basketball shoe market may have obscured the fact that it rose to predominance through striking a chord with the baby-boomer-turned-jogger of the 1980s. The company's focus on this group is reflected in its sponsorship of the Nike World Masters Games, an Olympic-style competition for men and women over the age of forty most recently held in Portland on August 19–22, 1998. When *Time* magazine did a cover story on the baby boom generation it quoted a social historian saying that the generation's ethos could be summed up in the phrase "Just Do It." Garry Trudeau's generation spent its formative years engaged in challenging America's conduct in Vietnam and is likely to be particularly attentive to addressing Nike's misconduct in that country. In addition, Nike's focus on the women's sneaker market has particularly targeted precisely the group of liberal, college-educated women most likely to share Kim's anger at the company's mistreatment of female workers making its shoes in Vietnam.

Trudeau's strips also made the important point that individuals are not powerless to redress the injustices of an unfettered global economy. Like Thuyen Nguyen, Kim had never considered becoming an activist and was employed in the high-technology sector. She met Michael Doonesbury in the spring of 1996 at a meeting for Republican presidential candidate Steve Forbes, a leading advocate of unrestricted free markets. Kim's exposure to her cousin's abusive treatment by a Nike contractor in Vietnam transformed her attitude toward Nike; she even wants to shift her plans from using the Internet for making money to using it to expand the anti-Nike campaign. Few *Doonesbury* readers will likely follow Kim's lead and abandon their work plans to focus on anti-Nike activism, but many may choose to support Trudeau's idealistic vision by refusing to purchase Nike shoes.

Nike recognized well before the avalanche of media criticism that its invitation to Nguyen had backfired and began operating in full damage control mode. First, Nike's business partners in Vietnam flatly denied Nguyen's charges. A senior executive of Pou Chen Vietnam Enterprise, a Taiwanese factory whose Vietnam facility employed eight thousand workers making Nike shoes, insisted that "we obey the labour laws and pay the minimum salary." He confirmed the salary for a six-day work week was forty dollars per month. He also confirmed Nguyen's account of the International Women's Day incident at the plant but emphasized that the supervisor was dismissed (and was eventually convicted) for mistreating the employees. Second, Nike announced to the media that it had suspended the manager of the plant where the incident occurred. Third, Nike dispatched a Nike spokesperson from Hong Kong to inspect its Vietnam plants. In Nike's third damage control measure within ten days of the release of Nguyen's report a representative told the *Vietnam Investment Review*, in a story distributed internationally, that the company was prepared to take "tough measures if suppliers did not toe the line."[45]

Nguyen's report had hit Nike at a particularly bad time. On February 25, 1997, Nike had won widespread media attention for hiring former civil rights leader, Atlanta mayor, and U.N. ambassador Andrew Young to evaluate its subcontractors' compliance with its Code of Conduct. Nike's press release described Young's firm, GoodWorks International, "as dedicated to promoting positive business involvement and investment in developing countries and America's inner cities." Max White, coordinator of the Portland-based Justice! Do It Nike, spoke for many in the anti-Nike campaign when he observed that although he admired Young, he "was not very familiar with [Young's] organization." White urged Young to make an independent review rather than simply conclude what Nike wanted him to conclude.[46]

White's response cleverly expressed support for Young while raising doubts about the virtually unknown organization's capacity to fairly investigate the company that was paying its bills and controlling its work product. Nevertheless, Nike's appointment of the well-respected Young could have provided great public relations for the company had Nguyen's report a month later not set a much more damaging image in the public's mind. As it was, *Times* columnist Herbert's March 28 column had used Nguyen's report to slyly mock the Young appointment. After detailing all of Nike's "Brutality in Vietnam" Herbert noted Young's appointment and concluded by quoting Nguyen that, in light of the massive human rights abuses he uncovered, "Mr. Young has a lot of work to do."[47]

An important impact of Nguyen's report that was not discussed in the media was that it very likely embarrassed the Vietnam government. In its zeal to take advantage of Vietnam's low-wage work force, Nike, like America in the 1960s, may have too quickly entered unfamiliar political terrain. As Cynthia Enloe, whose work on international women's labor issues led her to write about Nike for *Ms.* in 1995, points out, Vietnam remains an avowedly socialist society despite its desire to attract multinational corporate investment. This seeming contradiction is easily reconciled when companies like Coca Cola become major investors in the country but also pay a living wage. Vietnam is not China, whose socialist rhetoric confuses nobody, and it is certainly not Indonesia, where even speaking about socialism brings imprisonment. The Vietnamese political leadership is not yet prepared to follow China's model of ignoring the substance but keeping the outward trappings of a socialist state. As noted by Phan Duc Binh, a lawyer in the country's labor ministry, "this is not only a country that needs foreign investment. We need to build a system of law that protects the worker." This means that the Vietnamese government is still figuring out how far down the capitalist path it can go without popular dissent. When such dissent emerges, as it did when, as Nguyen's report was being released, 250 workers walked off the job of a Nike subcontractor to protest substandard wages and working conditions, the government's proworker patina is put at risk.[48]

The Vietnamese government could not have been happy to read coverage of Nguyen's report in international dispatches throughout Asia, Europe, Australia, and Canada. The state news media itself reported that the six thousand workers at a factory at Cu Chi that supplies Nike routinely are subjected to sweltering heat, corporal punishment, and degrading remarks from supervisors; Vietnam's labor ministry has repeatedly warned the factory's Korean managers to stop such practices, but to no avail. According to Nike's regional spokesperson Martha Benson, "it's important for Nike to be seen as the best employer in Vietnam." Nike apparently feels it can achieve this status despite paying those who make its goods less than workers at Reebok, Pepsi, or Coca Cola. Vietnam experienced twenty-four major strikes in the first three months of 1997 and the government is tired of rising worker unrest fueled by factories controlled by foreign investors. The state media's willingness to publicize labor abuses in Nike factories, reflecting Vietnam's still-ambivalent relationship toward the company, would be less likely in China or Indonesia. There is no way of knowing whether Nike and the Vietnam government discussed Nguyen's report, but it is likely that the government has joined activists in pressuring Nike to resolve its labor problems.[49]

The Empire Strikes Back :
Nike Attacks Global Exchange

Nike responded to growing criticism of its labor practices in 1997 by attacking its fiercest public critic, Global Exchange. In less than a year Global Exchange had engaged in a series of actions that Nike found objectionable. Phil Knight had criticized the group for inviting Cicih on her American tour and for issuing its report on Nike's Indonesian abuses on the eve of the company's annual shareholders meeting. Nike would certainly have learned from its own press contacts that Nguyen's damaging report would never have received media attention had Global Exchange not picked up the report and implemented a media strategy that brought Nike its worst publicity since the campaign against the company began. It had come to seem that Nike could not stage a media event without Global Exchange showing up and undermining the company's intended message. For example, Nike scheduled a major press conference and media tour for Thursday, February 20, in connection with the Saturday opening of its Union Square Niketown in San Francisco. Global Exchange had scheduled its own media event for Saturday but then learned of the Nike event and held its own press conference an hour before the start of the tour. As a result coverage of the competing media events in both the *San Francisco Chronicle* and the *San Francisco Examiner* focused almost exclusively on activist criticism of Nike's labor practices. Even worse from Nike's perspective was that the company had attracted the media to an event that resulted in negative headlines and huge newspaper photographs of Nike protesters. The *Chronicle* story was titled "Not Sold on Nike" and the *Examiner* piece, which pictured Global Exchange's Medea Benjamin standing in front of a giant papier-mâché puppet whose eyes had dollar signs and whose forehead read "Nike Exploitation," was titled "Protesters Lace Nike Labor Practices."[50]

If Nike was not sufficiently embarrassed at having spent thousands of dollars on a media tour hijacked by Global Exchange, the company had to be humiliated at its inability to deliver its own message or to counter that of Global Exchange. Nike had brought to the tour one of its star endorsers, Jerry Rice of the locally beloved San Francisco 49ers football team, as well as San Francisco mayor Willie Brown. But neither was prepared to answer questions from reporters about Nike's labor practices. Meanwhile, Global Exchange had brought the head of the San Francisco Labor Council and a representative of UNITE, both of whose criticism of Nike was extensively quoted by the media. The *San Francisco Chronicle* story observed that twenty high school students were on a field trip to witness the Nike media tour. Asked about the prospect of a boycott to support the plight of Nike's Indonesian workers, Courtney Engel, age sixteen, replied, "It's totally justified. I think they need a boycott," to the approving nods of her classmates. "We're here for our marketing class. This is very bad marketing."[51]

Global Exchange's intervention in Nike's event not only became a publicity bonanza for the anti-Nike campaign but it showed high school students looking down upon the prowess of a company that has almost redefined the entire concept of marketing when shoes, rather than human rights, are involved. To top it off, Global Exchange proceeded with its planned Saturday protest, which again brought media coverage of its message.

Faced with the ever-present irritant of Global Exchange, Nike sought to destroy the group's credibility. The best means to accomplish this would be to show the media that Benjamin and Global Exchange were liars who should not be granted mainstream media access. Nike sought to accomplish this on April 23, 1997, in a press release titled "Nike Critic Again Ignores the Truth in Latest Attack." The release focused on a media alert by Global Exchange on April 2, 1997, claiming that three Nike subcontractors in Indonesia had sought exemptions from the twenty-cents-per-day increase in the minimum wage that took effect on April 1. The Indonesian government has the power to grant exemptions to the minimum wage for companies that can prove economic hardship, which led Benjamin to be quoted in the April 3, 1997, edition of the *Oregonian* emphasizing that "Nike raked in record profits of over $670 million and now the subcontractors say it would be a hardship to pay their workers 20 additional cents a day."

Nike, which was still responding to the fallout from Nguyen's report of the previous week, immediately contacted the *Oregonian* to dispute Benjamin's claim. As a result the paper's April 3 story, "Nike Plants Balk at $2.36 a Day," was followed the next day with "Nike Factories in Indonesia Will Pay $2.36 Minimum Wage." The second article quoted Nike spokesperson Jim Small as saying, "We've told all our subcontractors they're expected to pay the minimum wage, no exceptions." The article stated, however, that the March 20 edition of *Bisnes Indonesia* had reported that the three Nike subcontractors had requested the wage exemption, thus confirming Benjamin's account.[52]

The entire matter of Nike's compliance with the new minimum wage would likely have been forgotten had the subcontractors complied with Small's alleged directive. Instead, a few weeks later more than ten thousand workers at a factory making Nike shoes in Indonesia burned cars and ransacked the factory's offices over the company's refusal to pay the new minimum wage. According to the April 28, 1997, *Wall Street Journal* Nike was monitoring talks between the two sides but its spokesperson, Jim Small, disputed the workers' claims that the minimum wage was not being paid. Small told the *Journal* that the workers were in fact "making more than the minimum wage" and expressed concern that such rising wages could mean that "Indonesia could be reaching a point where it's pricing itself out of the market."[53]

One would think that it would be in Nike's interest to shift media attention away from the fact that Global Exchange had proved better informed about wages in Indonesia than a company claiming to closely monitor its Indonesian subcontractors. But Nike somehow saw an opportunity in the dispute to discredit its adversary and issued an April 23, 1997, press release denouncing the group's "third misleading attack in the last month." Jim Small argued that Global Exchange's claim that the subcontractors would not be paying the new minimum wage was "reckless and inflammatory. If this were baseball, or the court system, Global Exchange would be 'out' on a third strike." Small then gave an extremely convoluted account of how workers were confused because Nike's subcontractors had eliminated their attendance bonus to "remain competitive" after the new minimum wage law took effect. His explanation only confirmed the position of the workers and Global Exchange. Nevertheless, Small vowed that Nike "will not be deterred by those that choose to use exaggerations and mistruths in an attempt to serve their own purposes." Nike thought that its effort to delegitimize Global Exchange was a good idea but such a strategy required a factual basis the absence of which in this dispute only undermined the company's charges.

As Global Exchange continued to take the offensive, Nike began to see a far more sinister agenda at work. On the eve of Nike's September 22, 1997, shareholders meeting Global Exchange released a report by two Hong Kong human rights groups detailing child labor and brutal working conditions in Nike's China factories. The report by the Asia Monitor Resource Center and the Hong Kong Christian Industrial Committee was based on interviewing workers at four sports-shoe subcontractors. The findings parallel those found by the Vietnam Labor Watch: Nike's Code of Conduct was "flagrantly violated," workers routinely were beaten and inhaled toxic fumes, and generally were treated "as though they were in a prison labor camp." The report also found children as young as thirteen working at the plants.[54]

This report, which publicly linked Nike to a country widely known in America for brutal repression, apparently sent Phil Knight over the edge. Although Global Exchange did not produce the report, it released it to the media and held a press conference across the street from Nike's annual meeting to highlight the findings. During the meeting Knight focused on rebutting the report and according to media reports "took particular pains to trash Global Exchange." Charging the group with continuing to go public with "half-truths, misinterpretations and lies" about Nike, Knight expressed frustration over the media's failure to examine the group's background. Knight claimed that Global Exchange's three chief causes were "supporting the Chiapas rebels in Southern Mexico, supporting Fidel Castro's regime in Cuba and criticizing Nike." He added that "it's the first time that Nike and Castro have been in the same boat." This last remark "drew hoots" from the audience and led a shareholder to urge Nike to spend more time addressing its labor problem than in dismissing critics. The shareholder told Knight, "You can't write people off as extremists. You sounded like [Richard] Nixon." Knight responded that he "doesn't classify all critics as extremists, just Global Exchange."[55]

Knight's attacks on Global Exchange were indeed coming to resemble Nixon's paranoid identification of his political opponents as enemies. Knight had even argued at the annual meeting that Global Exchange had a financial motive to lie about Nike, claiming that the resulting publicity had increased the group's donations by 50 percent. Since Global Exchange's accounts of Nike's labor practices had consistently proved more accurate than the company's, Knight's criticism was a transparent effort to deny the group's credibility through redbaiting. Ironically, Knight had announced earlier in the annual meeting that four subcontractor factories in Indonesia were being fired for failing to pay the minimum wage or for violating other provisions of Nike's Code. Knight therefore attacked the veracity of a group while confirming its charges of continued Indonesian labor abuses by Nike subcontractors. Nike's combative strategy continued despite the media's lack of interest in shifting its focus from Nike's labor practices to "looking into the background" of Global Exchange.

The Andrew Young Seal of Approval

On February 24, 1997, Nike appointed Andrew Young and his firm GoodWorks International to review Nike's operations in Asia. The action sought to forestall escalating anti-Nike activism and negative media coverage. Young's background as a civil rights activist and as an outspoken advocate for human rights while serving as U.N. ambassador during the Carter administration ensured that Nike's announcement would be positively received by an increasingly skeptical media. Young declared that he chose to become involved because "Nike has expressed its determination to be a leader for positive corporate change. Their commitment can result in growth and opportunity for the communities around the world where they operate." Young's specific task was to review Nike's Code of Conduct for its overseas factories, providing, in Phil Knight's words, "yet another level of input and oversight." Nike's use of Young to rebuild its image won the company short-term plaudits but the strategy also required Young to eventually produce a report that would be closely scrutinized by Nike critics. In the wake of the media frenzy following the release of Thuyen Nguyen's report the following month, Young, as Nguyen told Bob Herbert, indeed had his work cut out for him. If Nike had allowed its marketing rather than public relations department to handle Young's final product, the review could have caused a major blow to the anti-Nike campaign. Young's report could have best helped Nike by verifying Nguyen's account of brutality in Vietnam and Ballinger's and Global Exchange's own fact-finding into labor abuses in Nike's Indonesian plants. Young could then have urged Nike to create an entirely new subcontractor oversight department so that the terrible abuses that have disturbed so many Americans would never recur. Young would graciously donate his services to the oversight department because of Nike's commitment to improve living standards around the globe. Knight would then enthusiastically concur with all of Young's recommendations and vow to create a new era for Nike in the global economy. The media would take a "wait and see" stance for at least six months, thus stopping the escalating publicity about Nike's labor practices in its tracks. The anti-Nike campaign's momentum would also have been slowed if not halted, as the general public followed the media's lead in holding off judgment about the company until Young's reforms had time to work.[56]

Nike did not use Young's report in the manner that its marketing department could have predicted would best derail anti-Nike activism and forestall consumer unease about purchasing Nike sneakers, because this approach would have required Phil Knight to acknowledge for the first time that Jeff Ballinger and Global Exchange had been correct in their critiques of Nike's Asian labor practices. Knight may have become a six billion dollar man by bucking tradition, but no financial motive or strategic imperative would allow him to concede the truth to his adversaries. As a result of Nike's putting its public relations and founder's self-image ahead of its need to stifle growing public opposition to its practices, Young's June 24, 1997, report accomplished little. On the second page of its business section on June 25, 1997, the *New York Times* ran a short story titled "Nike's Asian Factories Pass Young's Muster" emphasizing the subjectivity of Young's findings. Although the story led with Young's conclusion that he found "no evidence of widespread or systematic mistreatment of workers," Medea Benjamin of Global Exchange was quoted describing the report as "extremely shallow." The article's concluding paragraph noted that although Young maintained that he was working independently, "Nike officials accompanied him on all his factory tours, and he presented his findings to the company's board and senior management a week before making them public." This conclusion could readily be seen as undermining the report's validity.[57]

Perhaps anticipating that the national media would not sufficiently boost Young's report, the company took out full-page advertisements in the *Times* and other newspapers on June 25, 1997, when the news stories appeared. The ads highlighted Young's claim that it was his "sincere belief that Nike is doing a good job . . . but Nike can and should do better." Claiming that "after six months of investigation . . . this was how Andrew Young concluded his independent seventy-five-page report," the ad emphasized that "Nike agrees. Good isn't good enough in anything we do. We can and will do better." The advertisement's brief text surrounded by a largely empty white page mimicked Nike's distinctive use of its motto or swoosh on a black background in television commercials. But the newspaper ad substituted heavy-handedness for Nike's customary subtlety in emphasizing Young's "independence," and inexplicably asserted that Young's investigation lasted six months when he had not even been hired until less than four months prior to completing his report.[58]

The anti-Nike campaign had obtained a leaked copy of Young's report prior to its release and Global Exchange faxed a detailed critique of the study's shortcomings to the media on the morning of Young's press conference. This strategy probably reduced media coverage of the report and affected media attitudes toward its credibility. Global Exchange's key criticism was Young's admission that "GoodWorks was not asked by Nike to address compensation and 'cost of living' issues, and had no desire to do so." Such a glaring omission was emphasized by the media since it meant, as a *Business Week* editorial observed, that "the report all but ignores what may be the most important concern of Nike's foreign workers—wages." Quoting Medea Benjamin's contention that excluding the wage issue rendered the report "meaningless," the editorial stated that Young's recommendations "seem inconsequential unaccompanied by a discussion of wages." This support of Benjamin's critique by a publication strongly supportive of free trade and economic globalization showed that even the corporate sector distrusted Nike's defense of its labor practices and also demonstrated that Nike's attempt to undermine Global Exchange's mainstream media credibility had failed.[59]

Thuyen Nguyen, whose findings differed markedly from Young's, had joined Benjamin in the day-long media counterattack against the GoodWorks report. Nguyen's critique found its way into the familiar hands of *New York Times* columnist Bob Herbert. Herbert's column included wonderful tidbits from Young's report omitted from other accounts, such as the author's admission that he did not bring his own translators to the Vietnam plants but relied on those provided by Nike. This acknowledgment was amazing, since the first week of Garry Trudeau's *Doonesbury* strips had already shown plant translators lying about what workers were saying and one would think that Nike would make sure that Young's report could not be discredited over this issue. Whereas Young found no evidence of "widespread or systematic worker abuse," Nguyen told Herbert that in Nike's less than two years in Vietnam one factory manager was convicted of physically abusing workers, another was under indictment, and a third had fled the country to avoid prosecution. Herbert cited Young's claim that the notorious International Women's Day incident in which female workers were forced to run around their factory until they fainted was attributable simply to a "culture clash." Young said, "This was the way they do things in Taiwan. You run around to get your blood pressure up, race your motor." Herbert's columns further demonstrated that the primary effect of Young's report was further media coverage of the anti-Nike campaign's charges against Nike.[60]

The clearest evidence that Nike's use of Young had backfired did not emerge until nearly two months after his report was released. In the *New Republic* on September 8 and 15, 1997, writer Stephen Glass used a periodical hardly identified with progressive interests to lambaste Young's report. The story's reference to the "GoodWorks game" and the "reputation racket" accompanied a sordid tale of a report that was "a classic sham, marred not just by shoddy methodology but by frequent misrepresentations." Unlike the newspaper reporters and columnists who reacted to the report upon its release, Glass had had time to contact those on the report's list of thirty-four "nongovernmental organizations with whom GoodWorks met or spoke." Although these sources were designed to give Young's report credibility, Glass found that many on the list had never spoken to Young or anyone from GoodWorks; one name appeared because it was on a GoodWorks memo "to be called," and a child labor expert's name appeared because she had asked for a copy of the final report. Glass even investigated the report's photographs of smiling Vietnamese workers who were identified as union representatives. The Vietnamese Confederation of Labor had never heard of the workers and Nike publicist Veda Manager confirmed that they were actually Nike employees with no connection to the union.[61]

The significance of Glass's reduction of Young's hefty seventy-five-page report to its actual thirteen pages of text and to its function as a "highly unprofessional public relations ploy" is that it appeared in the *New Republic*. If the views of its publisher, Martin Peretz, are any guide, the *New Republic*'s readership likely consists of many influential people who would not be swayed against Nike by Bob Herbert, Garry Trudeau, or any of the groups primarily involved in the anti-Nike campaign. Peretz fired his editor after this issue for being too critical of the Clinton administration, and he is notorious for carefully monitoring the viewpoints expressed in his periodical. The *New Republic* article gave a neoliberal, New Democrat stamp of approval to the anti-Nike campaign.

Although Andrew Young's report was widely challenged, Nike's public relations staff continued to rely on its findings to fend off activist criticism. This all changed, however, when readers of the *New York Times* on November 8, 1997, woke up to find a front-page story reporting that Nike's own accountants, Ernst & Young, had submitted an inspection report to the company the preceding January that found Nike's Vietnam workers subjected to the dangerous working conditions denied in Young's review. Ernst & Young had found that workers at a factory near Ho Chi Minh City were exposed to carcinogens that exceeded local legal standards by 177 times. Seventy-seven percent of the employees suffered from respiratory problems and the full workforce was required to work sixty-five hours a week, in gross violation of Vietnamese law. In exchange for working long hours in unsafe conditions, the workers were paid ten dollars per week.

As reporter Steven Greenhouse noted in his opening sentence, the Ernst & Young report's main impact was in "undermining Nike's boast that it maintains model working conditions at its factories." Greenhouse observed that it had only been five months earlier that the company had taken out full-page ads excerpting Young's conclusion that Nike was doing a "good job" in its treatment of its workers. The message was clear: Nike had either deceived Young by withholding the Ernst & Young report from his review or Nike had knowingly encouraged Young's intentional misrepresentation of Nike's Vietnam labor conditions. Either way, Nike's credibility was severely damaged in what the *Times* described as "yet another embarrassing episode in a continuing saga."[62]

Having appeared on the front page of the nation's most influential newspaper, the Ernst & Young report subsequently received widespread national media coverage. Despite its importance, the report would likely not have received such attention had Thuyen Nguyen of

Vietnam Labor Watch not intervened to give Greenhouse an early exclusive. The Transactional Resource and Action Center (TRAC), a San Francisco–based group, had obtained the report from a disgruntled Nike employee and had scheduled a press conference for Monday, November 10. When TRAC distributed its press release to the media on November 7, the media embargoed the story until the Monday event. When reporters contacted Nike about the release, the company sent out its own press release on Friday, November 7, to preempt the story. Since any press coverage of the report on Saturday would only have Nike's "spin," it was essential that the anti-Nike campaign get its own viewpoint to reporters so that it would supplant Nike's version. Nguyen had also received calls from reporters about TRAC's press release and recognized that the story could not wait until Monday as planned. Nguyen had developed a good working relationship with Steven Greenhouse of the *New York Times* and, in coordination with TRAC, the *Times* was given an exclusive that would run on Saturday, November 8. As a result Ernst & Young's report on Nike's unsafe working conditions, rather than the company's spin, framed the debate.[63]

Nike: Building Girls' Self-Esteem

While Nike's efforts to destroy Global Exchange's credibility and its use of Andrew Young to deter future criticism failed, Nike was simultaneously working on a far more powerful response to its adversaries: a campaign to build American girls' self-esteem. As discussed above, Cynthia Enloe's 1995 *Ms.* article ("The Globetrotting Sneaker") and Bob Herbert's June 24, 1996, *New York Times* column ("From Sweatshop to Aerobics") briefly addressed the contradiction of Nike's commercials stressing women's empowerment while the company was doing everything in its power to destroy the hopes and dreams of the overwhelmingly female makers of its shoes. Nike's overseas work force is more than 80 percent female, predominantly from poor, rural backgrounds, and typically aged eighteen to twenty-one. Nike had long sought to capture the woman's sports and fitness market, but with girls' participation in athletics steadily rising while the boys' sneaker market remains stable, Nike's ability to build strong bonds of brand loyalty among girl athletes may pose the greatest challenge to the anti-Nike campaign.

Nike began focusing on the women's market in 1987 but had no success until two years later when it launched an advertising campaign created by women advertising staff. The campaign emphasized non-athletic themes and linked women's participation in sports to personal growth rather than to competition and the joys of winning. The ads included a *Women's Source Book* that could be obtained by calling an 800 number; more than a quarter million calls were received during the campaign's first two years. Nike's advertising strategy led to 20 percent increases in its sale of women's sneakers in each of the campaign's first three years. But as girls' and women's participation continued to grow Nike became even more sophisticated in attracting this market. The company has become a sponsor of a wide variety of girls' sports activities designed to build upon the well-established link between girls' participation in sports and improved body image, academic performance, and self-esteem. For example, Nike was a sponsor of a Girls First conference in Los Angeles in 1997, in which athletic officials worked on strategies for increasing girls' participation in sports. During 1997 Nike provided a matching fifty-thousand-dollar grant to Smith College for staff to coordinate one-day sports clinics for girls in the fifth to eighth grades in the eighty schools surrounding the prestigious women's college. The clinics are run by Smith's coaching staff and athletes and Nike provides each girl with a T-shirt and a free lunch.[64]

Nike's girls' self-esteem campaign is, not surprisingly, linked to a television advertising campaign. The company's "If You Let Me Play" ads feature several young girls praising the benefits of participation in sports. As the refrain "if you let me play" repeats, sports involvement is linked to avoiding domestic abuse ("I will be more likely to leave a man who beats me"), preventive health care ("I will be 60 percent less likely to get breast cancer"), and self-esteem ("If you let me play, I will like myself more"). The young girls portrayed are not focused on winning trophies; they simply want a chance to participate on equal terms in America's sporting life.

Is there anything wrong with Nike providing girls' sports with the resources that schools have often failed to provide despite the enactment in 1972 of Title IX, which requires equal opportunity for females in schools that receive federal funds? Of course not. Should we be happy that Nike is using its power to help girls develop skills that will reduce the chances of teen or unwanted pregnancies and improves their odds of graduating from high school and college? Absolutely. The anti-Nike campaign has not attacked or challenged Nike's commitment to girls' sports, since such an approach would only further align girl athletes with Nike. Instead the campaign had to develop strategies for countering Nike's use of clinics and free T-shirts to build girls' loyalty and for responding to girls asking why they should not buy the sneaker that top male athletes are wearing.

The campaign responded to Nike's girls' self-esteem strategy through a broad educational campaign regarding Nike's exploitation of female workers. Jeff Ballinger's organization, Press for Change, has offered free subscriptions to his *Nike in Indonesia* newsletter to six thousand high school social studies teachers. The nonprofit *Scholastic Update* newspaper, perhaps the most widely circulated current events source in American public schools, devoted its entire March 7, 1997, issue to "World Trade: The Growing Global Economy." The front page displayed a pair of Nike shoes and asked, "Do you know where your sneakers come from?" The story on sneakers began by asking students to consider, when they lace up their Nike Air Force basketball shoes and think about the hundred-dollar price tag, that the shoes may have been made by a "teenager in Indonesia making about 15 cents an hour in a broiling hot factory with no air-conditioning, little lighting, and no breaks during a 14-hour day." Although the article gives Nike's representatives an opportunity to present their case, it concludes with Jeff Ballinger's prediction that many apparel companies "will squeeze every last penny out of every last sweatshop they can."[65]

Although *Scholastic Update* is not part of social change campaigns, the publication seeks stories that interest students who tend to groan when the subject turns to current events. Anti-Nike activists got their message into the schools in the same way they entered newspaper columns: by providing well-documented and thought-provoking stories that attracted the interests of writers for broadly circulated publications. A slightly different approach is being planned by the progressive and reform-minded *Rethinking Schools* magazine. Bill Bigelow wrote an article on sweatshops, "The Human Lives behind the Labels," for the magazine's summer 1997 issue and he and his colleagues are producing a publication focused on sweatshops modeled upon the magazine's extremely successful "Rethinking Columbus" primer. The publication will be geared toward teachers, parents, and students and is specifically oriented toward classroom use. The magazine on Columbus sold more than 225,000 copies and likely reached more than one million students; the anti-sweatshop publication should prove a critical educational antidote to Nike's girl- and youth-focused advertising campaigns. The Campaign for Labor Rights's sixty-page "Global Sweatshop Curriculum Packet" includes classroom exercises, practical suggestions for student action, and a report on teaching sweatshop issues in the classroom.[66]

I know from my own children's school experiences that some teachers will integrate available materials about sweatshops into their curriculums, others will not. Those teachers who ignore or refuse to use the materials, or who are barred from so doing by administrators, may also help the anti-Nike cause; activists can garner publicity by urging local school boards whose districts use corporate materials in the classroom (as well as the commercial Channel One, where applicable) to allow or require teachers to use information about sweatshops and Nike also. For example, a tremendous amount of local publicity was generated in Portland, Oregon, when local activists from Justice! Do It Nike, the Committee for Labor Rights, and other groups joined with Portland school board member Joseph Tam to challenge Nike's contribution in April 1996 of a half million dollars to the Portland school system. The school board voted four to one on August 22, 1996, to accept the donation but the four-month battle likely exposed more schoolchildren to Nike's labor abuses than any comparable strategy activists could have developed on their own during this period. Similarly Maria Sweeny, a fourth-grade teacher at the Hawes School in Ridgewood, New Jersey, won national media attention when her principal stopped her class from presenting a school play depicting the conditions under which Nike and Disney goods and McDonald's "happy meals" toys were made. The children chose the play after reading about Nike in *Time for Kids* and spent a month writing to corporations and worker advocacy groups to get the full story. The principal canceled the play because it did not show "all the good things these corporations do." All the anti-Nike talk generated by the play was also causing "hurt feelings" among students wearing the company's shoes. The principal's action created a news story about kids' exposure to sweatshops, and further publicity was generated when the class performed the play on Broadway on October 27, 1997.[67]

In the spring of 1996, when widespread national publicity about Nike's labor practices was still emerging, the company commissioned a poll of young people thirteen to twenty-five years old, in which respondents listed what Nike meant to them. The results were: (1) Athletics; (2) Cool; (3) Bad labor practices. The survey confirms that students and young consumers are very receptive to learning about the conditions under which their clothes are made. Students exposed to the facts about Nike may not support the company simply because they attended a company-sponsored clinic, received free Nike products, or viewed ads about self-esteem. For example, youths from eleven community centers in the Bronx organized a "shoe-in" at the Manhattan Niketown on September 27, 1997. The decision by the primarily African-American youths to discard their old Nike sneakers through a media event rankled Nike enough that the company sent a spokesperson to meet with the young activists. Although Nike's representative stressed the company's self-proclaimed "leadership," the kids were not convinced. Protester Dulani Blake maintained that "Nike goes to different countries so people can work for cheap." Social worker Michael Gitelson, of the Edenwald Gun Hill Neighborhood Center of the Bronx, helped the kids organize a second sneaker "give back" on January 19, 1998, Martin Luther King Day. Gitelson has countered Nike through his own empowerment strategy, stressing that "real empowerment" means being able to do without Nikes and choosing another brand. By reaching the targets of Nike's self-esteem ads in their schools, community centers, and religious institutions, the anti-Nike campaign, both through its own efforts and those of other anti-sweatshop educational campaigns, can counter Nike's attempt to link the swoosh with enhanced female self-esteem.[68]

The second component of the broad educational campaign necessary to counter Nike's persuasive girls' self-esteem campaign is to focus on the children's parents, particularly mothers. While parents have been exposed to the anti-Nike campaign along with the rest of the public, a particular focus on girls' and women's organizations and publications is essential. Magazines such as *New Moon, blue jean,* and *Teen Voices* that are targeted to progressive/activist-oriented young girls and their mothers represent an excellent vehicle for enabling fifth through ninth graders to resist the siren sounds of Nike's self-esteem advertising. These girls can show how self-esteem can be far more effectively developed through educating and organizing one's classmates around sweatshop issues than by wearing Nike sneakers. Even mainstream magazines geared to the teenage girl makeup and dating scene should be pushed to report on abuses in the shoe and garment industry. The People for the Ethical Treatment of Animals (PETA) has fought the fashion world on its own terms by using glamorous female stars to redefine fashion. PETA succeeded in making wearing fur unfashionable through the personal testimony of supermodels and actresses; the anti-Nike campaign can recruit female celebrities whose assertion that wearing Nikes and other sweatshop goods is unhip and a fashion disaster will reverberate with image-conscious consumers.

On October 28, 1997, fifteen national women's organizations, including the Feminist Majority, the Ms. Foundation, and the National Organization for Women, held a press conference denouncing Nike for its hypocrisy in advertising women's empowerment while exploiting the female makers of its shoes. Tony Newman of Global Exchange had offered the *New York Times* an exclusive on the story, and reporter Steven Greenhouse's October 26, 1997, story—"Nike Supports Women in Its Ads but Not Its Factories, Groups Say"—was featured in the paper's widely read Sunday edition. Greenhouse reported that the women's groups and individuals, including author Alice Walker and Congressional Black Caucus chair Maxine Waters, had written a letter to Phil Knight urging Nike to pay its female workers a living wage and to use independent monitoring to ensure respect for workers' rights. The letter struck at the heart of Nike's female self-esteem strategy:

The women depicted in NIKE advertisements are strong, resilient and empowered by their athletic accomplishments. NIKE's slogan is catchy, "There is no finish line." Unfortunately, this motto also applies to some of their factories overseas where women, according to payslips from Nike factories in Indonesia, work from 100–200 overtime hours a month to make ends meet.

While the women who wear NIKE shoes in the United States are encouraged to perform their personal best, the Indonesian, Vietnamese and Chinese women making the shoes often times suffer from inadequate wages, corporal punishment, forced overtime and/or sexual harassment.

According to some of the country's most influential women's groups Nike's women's empowerment and female self-esteem advertising campaigns sought profits by exploiting female workers. In case anyone missed the point that women should oppose rather than buy Nike, Greenhouse quoted Eleanor Smeal's claim that the return of sweatshops meant that "just like the feminists at the turn of the century fought them, it's incumbent on us to do the same." Nike spokesperson Vera Manager denied the women's allegations and told Greenhouse that Nike's factories had passed Andrew Young's inspections.[69]

As *USA Today* observed in its October 27 story on the charges, 40–45 percent of Nike's annual sales are made to women. Women and girls also constitute more than half of the total athletic footwear market. During 1997 alone some of the world's largest magazine publishers, including Conde Nast, Time Inc., and Weider Publications, sought to capitalize on the women's sports market by launching new female-oriented sports magazines. With girls and women likely to remain the most rapidly expanding demographic sneaker market for years to come, Nike will continue to go all out to win their loyalty. This is why it was so pivotal for the anti-Nike campaign both to counter the company's female-oriented advertising and to argue, as Eleanor Smeal did, that American women have a historic obligation to oppose sweatshops.[70]

In addition to its specific focus on programs linking girls' self-esteem to wearing Nikes (though the company would argue that they simply want girls to play sports), Nike's Participating in the Lives of America's Youth project donates basketball courts, playground facilities, and athletic equipment to inner-city neighborhoods throughout the country. As low-income, predominantly African-American or Latino urban communities have witnessed their parks and recreational centers fall into decay, Nike donations have filled the void created by government neglect. Kids benefiting from these donations may well decide to purchase Nike shoes and it would not likely prove fruitful for activists from outside the community to try to convince them otherwise. However, prior to Nike's move to Indonesia and the controversy created over its sweatshops it faced criticism from Jesse Jackson and other leaders over its marketing campaign to low-income African-American children. Jackson and other critics, who now include prominent African-American athletes like basketball star Chris Webber, raised concern that Nike was connecting the self-esteem of poor children to the purchase of a pair of $150.00 Nike shoes. Reports abounded of kids committing crimes to obtain the money for the shoes or stealing the shoes outright. It may well be the case that factors other than Nike's labor practices will damper consumer demand in the low-income communities that are the recipients of Nike's beneficence.

Nike Calls In the Commander in Chief

The last and most high-profile strategy Nike used in the spring of 1997 to counter its unprecedented level of negative publicity was President Clinton's April 14, 1997, announcement that an agreement had been reached to end sweatshops. The purported agreement was produced by the anti-sweatshop task force created by Clinton with Knight at his side the preceding August. Since that time Nike had routinely touted its participation on the task force as evidence of its leadership as a model for corporate behavior in the global economy. Because the task force included UNITE, the National Consumers Federation, and the Lawyers Committee for Human Rights in addition to Nike and major apparel industry representatives, the accord reached had the appearance of having unified divergent interests behind a common plan. The agreement included a proposal for a "No Sweat" label, a sixty-hour work week with one day off, and some form of independent monitoring. Nike and other task force members agreed to follow the new rules, thereby laying the groundwork for worldwide labor standards for the apparel industry. To confirm the importance of the agreement, the media quoted public interest representatives such as Michael Posner of the Lawyers Committee, who described the plan as a "breakthrough" that "stands to benefit workers around the world." Linda Golodner of the National Consumer Federation was even more effusive, claiming that "the benefit for everyone is what the whole task force was about: that's to make sure consumers can purchase goods that have not been made in a sweat-shop and make sure there's a process in place to check that factories are not sweatshops." Even Charles Kernaghan of the National Labor Committee, whose exposé of Kathie Lee Gifford helped lead to the task force, strongly praised the accord. Kernaghan claimed the agreement would mark a new era for Haitian workers' economic well-being and was as enthusiastic as the industry representatives about the task force's achievement.[71] My own reaction to the agreement was to recall my advice in *The Activist's Handbook*: just say no to task forces. Such bodies inevitably pressure activists to compromise their interests for the benefit of their ostensible political allies and the latter's business supporters. Once the public interest and labor groups agreed to serve, the path was open for Bill Clinton to reach a public accord that could severely damage the growing anti-Nike campaign and other struggles against sweatshops.

This damage did not occur because of the incredible effort of Medea Benjamin, Global Exchange's publicity genius Tony Newman, and their public relations allies at Communication Works. The accord to end sweatshops had barely been announced when Benjamin released a detailed critique of its shortcomings. Benjamin's main point was that the agreement simply required companies to pay the "prevailing minimum wage," which meant that Nike could continue to pay twenty cents an hour in its Vietnam plants. The agreement continued to allow companies to use their own accountants rather than human rights groups as independent monitors, provided no higher pay rate for overtime work, and accepted a sixty-hour work week as the norm. Simply put, Nike could continue to rely on sweatshop labor under the proposal and obtain a "No Sweat" label to boot! Benjamin's critique was featured in the *New York Times*, the *Wall Street Journal*, the *Los Angeles Times*, and many local newspapers. To achieve even wider exposure for her critique Benjamin wrote an op-ed piece for the *Los Angeles Times* that also circulated through various weeklies. When the labor- and public interest–oriented representatives who had initially praised the agreement began hearing Benjamin's analysis, they realized that they had spoken too soon. This was particularly evident on the *News Hour with Jim Lehrer*, in which Benjamin appeared with task force member Jay Mazur of UNITE and a representative of the apparel industry. Mazur had initially termed the agreement "an historic first step" and the "beginning of a long journey." On the nationally televised *News Hour*, however, Mazur was clearly uncomfortable aligning UNITE with the apparel industry rather than Benjamin. As Benjamin raised her criticisms of the agreement Mazur invariably seconded her concerns, giving the impression that UNITE was far more skeptical than it originally seemed. Kernaghan's attitude toward the agreement also changed from unconditional exuberance on the day of the agreement to raising questions about its weak wage and monitoring prescriptions three days later.[72]

Benjamin's role in influencing public comments about the agreement from groups and individuals identified with anti-sweatshop work was not a triumph of sectarianism over sound policy. The eagerness of some activists to stake out an extreme position and then denounce anyone taking a more moderate stance has proved divisive in a range of movements and must not be encouraged. Rather, Benjamin and Global Exchange had taken the time to actually read the proposed new code of conduct for sweatshops and then publicly exposed its obvious shortcomings. As a result an agreement that sought to realize Phil Knight's dream of maintaining Nike's overseas wages and working conditions with a newly minted "No Sweat" label was described in a *New York Times* editorial of April 16, 1997, as merely "a modest start on sweatshops." Describing the proposed code as "littered with loopholes" and emphasizing its "lack of precise commitments," the *Times* paid tribute to the success of anti-sweatshop activists by observing that as recently as two years earlier the apparel industry would never have even considered some of the provisions it now agreed to follow. Although the *Times* applauded the task force's rejection of the idea of requiring a "living" rather than locally prevailing minimum wage, this only made its depiction of the agreement as "modest" more persuasive.[73]

The *Wall Street Journal's* April 15, 1997, story even more strongly incorporated opponents' criticisms of the accord. The *Journal's* lead paragraph stated that the agreement had "drawn quick criticism from a coalition of human-rights, labor and religious organizations." The second paragraph consisted entirely of criticism of the agreement and the third was devoted to Benjamin's assessment that "workers got a raw deal. It looks like a lousy deal to us." The *Journal* thus framed its coverage of the agreement in strongly negative terms and even quoted apparel industry representatives joining critics in questioning the appropriateness of accounting firms like Nike's Ernst & Young acting as independent monitors. When an article in an influential publication like the *Wall Street Journal* portrays industry and its usual critics on the same side, few readers are likely to conclude that both are wrong.[74]

I spoke to many activists after the announcement of the task force agreement and "No Sweat" plan and was surprised by the common belief in the likely success of the Clinton–apparel industry strategy to defuse the growing anti-sweatshop movement. Their main point was that activists would have to divert resources from proactive anti-sweatshop campaigns to fighting against the enshrinement of the task force proposals as the definitive, bipartisan anti-sweatshop strategy. The Clinton administration had previously created a "Trendsetters List," which provided public relations cover for garment manufacturers who supposedly did not use sweatshop labor but actually did; many activists foresaw even greater problems convincing the public that garments with a government-endorsed "No Sweat" label were in fact produced in sweatshops.

As a result of aggressive media advocacy by Global Exchange, little was heard about the task force or its prominent labeling plan in the months following the president's announcement. Phil Knight and Nike spokespersons continued to refer to the company's participation in the agreement as an example of its leadership in fighting sweatshops but subsequent stories about Nike's labor practices ignored the proposed accord. In contrast, Global Exchange's chief critique of the agreement, that it failed to assure a living wage, increasingly became the dominant media frame for assessing Nike's labor record. The most commonly highlighted defect in Andrew Young's report was thus its failure to address wages. The wage issue also put the campaign on a firmer footing than demands such as for independent monitoring. Nike could ultimately decide to select a monitor other than its own accounting firm, but if the workers continue to receive a subsistence wage, then the fundamental problem has not been addressed. The living wage focus also connected the anti-Nike campaign to related struggles focusing on this issue at home and abroad.

Once Global Exchange used its media prowess to reframe the presidential task force accord as a debate over wages, Nike was put in an untenable public posture. I heard a debate on Pacifica Radio's *Democracy Now* show between Eleanor Smeal and a Nike spokesperson on October 28, 1997, the date of the Women against Nike press conference, that demonstrated this. When the issue of independent monitoring was raised Nike's representative referred to the company's reliance on the "fairly credible" Ernst & Young, Price Waterhouse, and Andrew Young. Smeal pointed out that these entities were paid by and reported to Nike, but those not familiar with the need for truly neutral monitors could interpret "independent" to merely mean someone other than Nike. On the wage issue, however, Nike had no escape. After insisting that Nike paid a living wage—which showed how Nike had been forced to fight on its opponents' terms—the company representative was forced to concede that the wages for its Indonesian and Vietnamese work force were forty-five to fifty-six dollars per month. When Smeal quickly computed that this amounted to twenty cents per hour Nike's spokesperson suddenly shifted from talking about the company's high wages to repeatedly emphasizing that Nike "had to respect the economic scale of wages" in these countries. Whereas Nike's claim of relying on independent monitoring could fool some people, few see paying twenty cents an hour for a forty-eight-hour regular work week as anything but sweatshop labor.[75]

Nike called upon America's commander in chief to stem criticism of its labor practices; instead the Clinton task force created stronger momentum for the anti-Nike campaign.

Student and Campus Anti-Nike Activism

The fall of 1997 brought student and campus activists into the growing campaign against Nike's labor practices. As a result Nike faced the first sustained challenges to its often multimillion-dollar contracts with university athletic programs. These challenges were fueled by three factors. First, increased publicity about Nike's labor abuses since the end of the previous school year caused students, faculty, and staff

Doonesbury   BY GARRY TRUDEAU

to begin questioning campus links to Nike. Second, the AFL-CIO's "Union Summer" created a network of trained "Students against Sweatshops" activists capable of mobilizing on thirty campuses in the new school year. Third, the Campaign for Labor Rights began using e-mail and action packets to connect anti-Nike activists within and among campuses and to link students to the broader anti-Nike campaign.

The international Nike mobilization planned for October 18, 1997, gave campus activists an initial focal point for building student participation in the campaign. Students from more than twenty campuses participated in the protests. More than fifty students at the University of Michigan handed out flyers and held a huge banner at the school's football game that day; students at the University of New Mexico passed out anti-Nike leaflets at two shopping centers in Albuquerque and had people sign letters to Phil Knight; the University of North Carolina at Chapel Hill had a campus "speak-out" on November 7 to concide with a school football game, while more than sixty students protested at the University of Illinois at Urbana-Champaign.[76]

A common theme at the protests was a call for an end to universities' contractual relationships with Nike unless wages and working conditions for the company's overseas workers improved. Nike has such "partnerships" with more than two hundred colleges and universities. At Duke University the campus's "Students against Sweatshops" chapter sent a letter to Duke president Nan Keohane on September 12, 1997, requesting that she impose a policy that would guarantee Duke merchandise had no links to sweatshops. When she failed to respond the group organized a mass e-mailing to her from student organizations on October 3. Keohane then informed the group on October 7 that Duke had recently inserted a clause in its contract with the Collegiate Licensing Company that opposed labor abuses by licensees. The students subsequently met with administrators to develop a more detailed code of conduct requiring manufacturers of items bearing the institution's logo to disclose the working conditions of their employees. Duke adopted the tougher code, which includes independent monitoring, on March 6, 1998. As Duke student Ben Au noted, such codes of conduct focus on more than one country or company but "try to make sure the entire system is correct." Bruce Siegal, Collegiate Licensing Company's general counsel, observed that "when top schools such as Duke pay attention to this issue, I wouldn't be surprised if other colleges don't jump on the bandwagon." Students at Notre Dame, Michigan, and Illinois have also pushed for such codes of conduct and students at Arizona State University have organized to prevent their school from contracting to have all its athletic teams wear Nike gear.[77]

Students have learned that convincing college administrators to give up Nike's royalties will not be easy. Marion Traub-Werner helped organize a Nike Awareness Campaign at Michael Jordan's alma mater, the University of North Carolina at Chapel Hill. The school had agreed in July 1997 to a five-year, $7.1 million cash-and-clothes deal with Nike covering all its athletic teams. Although protests against Nike by Traub-Werner and her fellow students received coverage in the *New York Times* and other national media, university officials were not persuaded. When the students met with the school's former basketball coach, Dean Smith, he was fully informed from Nike's perspective and "didn't understand why we were questioning what they were doing in Asia." UNC chancellor Michael Hooker sought to defuse the issue by suggesting Nike underwrite a student-faculty tour of Nike's Asian factories to be covered by a reporter from the student newspaper, the *Daily Tar Heel.* Describing the media focus on Nike as "intellectually dishonest," Hooker stated that he had "read the Andrew Young report and I am satisfied that Nike is doing the best job it can."[78]

Fortunately, not all university presidents suffer from Hooker's brand of intellectual integrity. Stanford University president Gerhard Casper has publicly expressed concern over the commercialization of college athletics and has sought to reduce the university's dependence on corporate endorsements. All but a few of Stanford's thirty-three varsity athletic teams wear the Nike swoosh and the school's contract with Nike is worth $1 million. Stanford's Ad Hoc Committee on Nike has pushed Casper to renegotiate or cancel Stanford's Nike logo deal. As Tim Keown of the *San Francisco Chronicle* suggested in a column decrying the University of California at Berkeley's Nike deal, "Imagine the great press a university athletic director or coach could receive by calling a news conference to say, 'We've read the reports, and we're going to wear something else for a while.'"[79]

To forestall threats to its lucrative college endorsement deals and ensure continued loyalty among students exposed to information about its labor abuses Nike sent public relations staff to campuses around the country in October 1997. Nike hosted a conference call with college newspaper editors from across America, took out full-page ads in college newspapers, and visited several campuses. This was the first time Nike felt compelled to systematically respond to its campus critics and its strategy—no doubt developed by public relations rather than marketing staff—was curious. For example, two Nike representatives handed out "Informed Consumer Updates" near the student protest at the University of Michigan on October 18; Nike would seem to have more effective ways of responding than to show themselves outnumbered by their opponents by a ratio of more than twenty-five to one. Similarly, one set of publicity packets included an article by Jardine Fleming Research that highlighted Nike's role in leading the way for Asia's economic success. While the subsequent sharp decline in the Indonesian and other Asian economies have raised questions about Nike's purported economic development role, more significant was the image of itself the company used to counter its critics. The article stated that

Nike tends to favor strong governments. For example, Nike was a major producer in both Korea and Taiwan when these countries were largely under military rule. It currently favors China, where the communists and only two men have led the country since 1949, and Indonesia where President

Suharto has been in charge since 1967. The communist party is still very much alive in Vietnam. Likewise, Nike never did move into the Philippines in a big way in the 1980s, a period when democracy there flourished. Thailand's democracy movement of 1992 also corresponded to Nike's down-grading of production in that country. . . .

Nike management found that it was very hard to make sneakers in America, primarily because of much higher labour costs and more stringent labour laws.[80]

The article that Nike saw as a means of winning students to its side instead confirmed what Jeff Ballinger and others had argued about the company for years. Not surprisingly, such material failed to stem rising campus opposition to Nike's labor policies.

Knight's confidence in his ability to convince students that he and Nike have been unfairly maligned perhaps explains his decision to appear on camera with film maker Michael Moore. Moore's huge campus following must have convinced Knight that he could irrevocably halt student criticism by speaking directly to Moore's audience. Big mistake. Moore visited Nike headquarters and with cameras rolling asked Knight to move one of the companies factories from Asia to Flint, Michigan, Moore's hometown. Knight maintained that Americans do not want to work in shoe factories. Moore then cut to a group of unemployed persons in Flint chanting "We need jobs" and expressing an eagerness to make Nike shoes. Moore also asked Knight on camera how the CEO felt about fourteen-year-old girls manufacturing Nike shoes in Indonesia. Knight responded to Moore's question "Do you feel bad about it?" with a pithy "No, I don't." Such responses were unlikely to build support for Nike among the college-age viewers of Moore's film, *The Big One*. The movie skewers Borders and other corporations but Knight was the only corporate CEO willing to appear on camera. This gave Moore the opportunity to present Knight with two plane tickets to Indonesia so that he could inspect the labor problem firsthand. Knight hoped to use Moore to rebut critics' claims about Nike but instead reaffirmed these charges before a national moviegoing audience. Because people are more likely to be influenced by Knight's movie appearance than an article about Nike in a newspaper or magazine the CEO's public relations goal clearly backfired. To make matters worse, the weekly periodical *U.S. News & World*

Report used Moore's film as the backdrop for a major article on Nike's financial and public relations woes, further enhancing the campaign's momentum.[81]

Enlisting Sportswriters to Challenge Nike

Among the greatest challenges faced by the anti-Nike campaign was overcoming the pervasiveness of the Nike swoosh on the clothing and gear of amateur and professional athletes in nearly every field of sports. When sports fans observe every National Football League player and superstars like basketball's Michael Jordan, tennis's Pete Sampras, and baseball's Ken Griffey Jr. wearing the swoosh, Nike's identification with success rather than labor abuses is affirmed. David Meggyesy of the National Football League Players Association in a *Los Angeles Times* editorial called Nike's superstar endorsers "moral jellyfish" for disavowing responsibility for speaking out against Nike's labor practices. To undermine Nike's popular image among sports fans

Doonesbury   BY GARRY TRUDEAU

the anti-Nike campaign urged sportswriters to integrate the company's labor problems into their columns. Such a strategy was almost unprecedented for a social change campaign, as well as risky. The modern sports section typically avoids analyzing the relationship between sports and social problems and is even seen as practicing under entirely different journalistic rules than news departments. For example, when CBS News was widely criticized for having news reporters wear blazers with the Nike swoosh during the 1998 Winter Olympics, the network continued to require its sports reporters to wear Nike advertising on the grounds that this was "totally standard practice."[82]

The entry of the Nike labor issue into the sports page thus represented a major achievement of the anti-Nike campaign. Ira Berkow's July 12, 1996, *New York Times* column, "Jordan's Bunker View on Nike's Slave Labor," described Nike as an "international octopus" and noted the "brutal conditions" in which the makers of Nike shoes in Asia must work. Berkow quoted Jeff Ballinger of Press for Change in the column and succeeded in exposing those readers who focus intently on the sports page to the dark side of Michael Jordan's financiers. Nearly a year later Berkow's *Times* colleagues used the fiftieth anniversary of Jackie Robinson's breaking the color line in major league baseball to reflect on the changed values of modern sports stars. Harvey Araton's "Standing for More than a Logo," April 15, 1997, argued that unlike Robinson "today's players unlock many vaults but open few doors." He continued: "Maybe it is not Jordan's obligation to speak out, to take stands, choose sides, but it has been his choice to stand right in the middle, to offend no consumer. That is what Nike, champion of the third-world sweatshop, wants him to do." George Vecsey's column the following day, "A Role Model for the Ages Is Honored," observed:

What a different world today. The admirable Tiger Woods walks the fairways wearing a corporate brand over his forehead. The hostile Alonzo Mourning says he doesn't work for a basketball team, he works for Nike. The smooth Michael Jordan pushes cologne, stars in films, sells sporting goods, but does not feel the need to publicly address Nike's labor conditions in Asia. Jackie Robinson's successors must remember when one athlete stood for a cause, not a corporate emblem.[83]

Sportswriter Tim Cushman of the *San Diego Union-Tribune* used former basketball star and U.S. senator Bill Bradley as a contrast to Woods and Jordan. Cushman noted that Bradley had refused to do commercial endorsements while a member of the New York Knicks because he felt they were offered because he was the team's only white starting player; Bradley explained that "racial harmony on the team and in society became a compelling imperative for me." After citing Nike's labor abuses and quoting Medea Benjamin that Jordan's deal with Nike probably exceeds the annual salaries of Nike's workers in

Vietnam and Indonesia, Cushman asks, "Can one imagine Bill Bradley accepting a contract under these conditions?"[84]

Fittingly it was in a sports column that Nike icon Jordan gave a strong indication of the campaign's growing impact. After refusing to involve himself in the Nike labor controversy for years ("I play basketball; they make shoes"), Jordan told the *Times*'s Ira Berkow in November 1997 that he was "keeping on top of how Nike treats workers in Asia, though I think some of that is misunderstood." Jordan subsequently went even further and told Steve Marantz of the *Sporting News* that he had heard "a lot of different sides to the issue" and would "go to Asia and see" Nike's factories for himself in the summer of 1998. Jordan further stated that "if there are issues, [Nike executives] have to revise the situation. If it's an issue of slavery or sweat shops, they have to revise the situation." Garry Trudeau's *Doonesbury* comic strip satirized Jordan's plan by describing it as "the 1998 Michael Jordan Asian Sweatshop Tour." Sportswriter Carol Slezak from Jordan's hometown *Chicago Sun-Times* also questioned Jordan's motives, since he is under contract with Nike until 2013. As Slezak concluded, however, there are thousands of laborers in Asia who hope Jordan is serious about raising the wages for Nike's workers; she quoted Ballinger's claim that "Michael Jordan might be the only person Phil Knight would listen to." Few thought that Michael Jordan would ever feel compelled to express interest in Nike's labor abuses; the anti-Nike campaign found a vulnerable spot in the legend that rival teams could not locate.[85]

Sports columnists also criticized colleges' and universities' acceptance of Nike's money and athletic gear in exchange for turning their athletes and programs into advertisements for the company. Both Harvey Araton of the *New York Times* and Tim Keown of the *San Francisco Chronicle* used their columns to decry the "hypocrisy" and "shame" of Nike's ability to "purchase" the idealism and social conscience of such public universities as the University of North Carolina at Chapel Hill and the University of California at Berkeley. As Araton observed, when coaches like Georgetown's John Thompson own eighty thousand shares of Nike stock and options, schools cannot credibly debate their contracts with the company. Araton also reported that former North Carolina basketball coach Dean Smith told student Marion Traub-Werner, who founded a campus Nike Awareness Committee, that he believed Nike was the leader in labor practices. Smith's assessment, given soon after publicity about the damaging Ernst & Young report, was no doubt shaped by the $11 million in business Nike does with his school.[86]

By continually faxing articles and columns about Nike to sports columnists the anti-Nike campaign turned the sports section into a leading source of media criticism of Nike. Longtime journalist Nat Hentoff observed that while the sports pages were full of stories about Nike's labor relations, he had yet to come across any statements about Nike from such "moral leaders of our times as Bill Clinton, Hillary Clinton, Bill Bennett, Bill Graham, Rush Limbaugh, and Rudy Giuliani." Their silence was perhaps best explained in the sports pages, which noted that Nike's saturation of the airwaves with its "Ken Griffey Jr. for President" commercials could lead the company to put its resources and marketing savvy behind a real political candidate. No wonder President Clinton held two press conferences within a year with Phil Knight at his side.[87]

Rising Activism, Lower Profits

In the twelve-month period ending May 31, 1996, Nike's total sales jumped 36 percent to $6.47 billion. A stock analyst quoted in the *Oregonian* described Nike's economic performance as phenomenal and added that she did not know of another company its size outside of technology that has posted this kind of growth. Phil Knight described Nike's year as great. Jeff Manning's July 10, 1996, story on Nike's gold-medal year noted that the company had been criticized for its Asian labor practices but that the latest financial results and strong future orders showed that few retailers share those concerns. Knight predicted even greater gains in 1997 and financial analysts concurred with this projection. Nike's tremendous annual growth rate of 46 percent from 1986 to 1996 led *Fortune* magazine to place Knight on the cover of its June 23, 1997, issue as one of the world's great business innovators.[88]

The fiscal year ending May 31, 1996, preceded the widespread publicity about Nike's labor practices that largely began with the March

1996 *New York Times* story. The optimism generated by the company's 1996 earnings would prove short-lived. On April 8, 1997, Manning reported that Nike's stock had dropped 7 percent the preceding day due to reports that the company had instructed its Asian factories to cut back on expansion plans. Company officials were not fazed by the one-day loss of $1 billion in Nike's market value, claiming that future orders were up 34 percent. But the following month brought further bad news for Nike. In a story by Jeff Manning of the *Oregonian* that ran throughout the Newhouse newspaper chain and appeared on the Sunday, May 18, 1997, front page of such prominent papers as the *St. Louis Post-Dispatch*, the headline read, "Has the Air Gone Out of Nike? Price, Fashion, Politics Blamed for Slip in Sales." The story cited retailers seeing a decline in consumer demand for Nike products. The reason cited? According to the president of a Fleet Feet store in Sacramento, it is escalating prices and the bad publicity the company had been getting on its labor practices. The operator of a popular running store in Seattle told Manning that she hears from one or two customers a week who refuse to consider buying Nike's products because they don't like the company's politics. The article noted that some retailers, like the 480-store Footaction chain based in Dallas, Texas, found declining sales even though Nike's labor practices had not been an issue. Nevertheless the combination of political concerns and Nike's growing number of high-priced shoes led longtime company observer Manning to conclude that U.S. consumers appear to have sated their once insatiable demand for Nike shoes.[89]

Less than two weeks after Manning's nationally syndicated story Nike received further bad news. On May 30, 1997, the *New York Times* reported that Nike shares fell 13 percent the previous day after the company reported that its quarterly earnings would fall below expectations due to disappointing sales. While some stock analysts attributed the decline to Nike's inability to maintain its own unprecedented growth rates, the *Times* noted that some of the company's competitors enjoyed stronger sales even as the overall market was soft. A company that only one year earlier had predicted tremendous growth for itself in 1997 and that seemed invulnerable to normal market cycles was now described as potentially on a slippery slope of bad news. The *Wall Street Journal* echoed this theme on June 2, 1997, when it stated that after last week's stock decline Nike suddenly seemed vulnerable. The *Journal* story attributed Nike's problems to better marketing and lower-priced competition from Nike's rivals, and ignored any mention of the impact of publicity about Nike's labor practices.[90]

By the time of Nike's September 1997 annual meeting the *Oregonian* reported that the "euphoria" of the two previous years' events had been replaced by "a new cautious reality." Growth in Nike's U.S. footwear sales had "slowed considerably" and company officials warned stockholders that its domestic sneaker sales would continue to decline for at least the next three quarters. Nike's 1998 fiscal year, which ended June 30, subsequently showed a 49 percent drop in earnings from the previous year. This included $67.7 million in losses during the last quarter, Nike's first quarterly loss in thirteen years.[91]

Following the public emergence of a national anti-Nike campaign in the summer of 1996 the company's economic performance significantly declined. Nike stock fell 39 percent in 1997 while the market as a whole rose more than 20 percent. Financial analysts in 1998 saw the "fundamentals of the company deteriorating" with little positive in sight. Much of Nike's financial problems were caused by the dramatic overproduction of its sneakers from 1995 to 1997. Nike's sneaker production doubled during this period, creating pressure on subcontractors to engage in the worker abuse that brought the company such notoriety. While Nike was producing sneakers at record levels the market began declining in 1997, and with Asia's economic problems in 1998, the glut of Nike shoes steadily increased. But overproduction was not the only factor in Nike's decline. It is obvious from both anecdotal evidence and basic human psychology that many Americans stopped purchasing Nike shoes after learning of the company's Asian labor practices.[92]

The drop in American sales of Nike sneakers has been precipitous. Phil Knight has denied that the labor controversy has affected sales and his anger following Nike's successful 1995 performance demonstrates that the national pressure campaign's impact on Nike cannot be evaluated by simply looking at the bottom line. Knight and Nike have always been primarily influenced by public criticism of the company's morality, values, and vision of corporate behavior in the global economy. No multinational corporation has ever gone to the lengths Nike has to shroud itself in the image of virtue and sanctimony, and the company's carefully constructed image has been permanently besmirched by its adversaries. Nike's new image was perhaps best captured by late-night talk-show host Jay Leno after the birth of the McCaughey septuplets on November 19, 1997. Commenting on the donations of apple juice, diapers, and other supplies for the newborns, on November 20 Leno cracked that "Nike plants in Indonesia had offered them a job as soon as they turn six."[93]

Knight's eagerness to be seen as joining the ranks of sweatshop opponents, his two Rose Garden events with President Clinton announcing the task force creation and then its accord, his continued insistence that the company would and should do better, his stated willingness to consider some form of quasi-independent monitoring, and the company's putting its own employees into the factories to monitor conditions would have seemed unthinkable as late as February 1996. Nike also finally complied with minimum-wage laws in Indonesia and Vietnam and paid back wages owed to Vietnamese workers in 1997, although Nike's workers still do not receive a living wage. The company's perspective on economic globalization has been harshly criticized. Phil Knight has observed that "for whatever reason, we've been the poster boy on globalization." Activists challenging unfettered free trade and sweatshop labor throughout the world have all benefited from the anti-Nike campaign's challenge to the company whose globetrotting for lower labor costs and higher profits became the model for corporate behavior in the global economy.[94]

Nike Blinks

In recent times, Phillip Knight has been described as a corporate crook, the perfect corporate villain for these times. In addition, it has been said that Nike has single-handedly lowered the human rights standards for the sole purpose of maximizing profits. And Nike's product has become synonymous with slave wages, forced overtime, and arbitrary abuse. One columnist said Nike represents not only everything

*that's wrong with sports, but everything that's
wrong with the world.*

    *So, I figured that I'd just come out and let
you journalists have a look at the great Satan,
up close and personal.*

              —Phil Knight, in a speech to the
              National Press Club, May 12, 1998[95]

On May 12, 1998, Knight came as close as he ever had to publicly admitting that his critics had got the better of him. In a highly personal and often bitter address Knight pledged to significantly reform Nike's overseas labor practices. Knight promised to raise the minimum age for new workers at its shoe factories to eighteen, to improve worker health and safety conditions, and to allow labor and human rights groups to monitor working conditions in its factories. Although Knight failed to commit to raising workers' wages the company's New Labor Initiatives publicly affirmed that the campaign had significantly affected Nike's labor practices.

Activists responded to Knight's speech with a mixture of praise for his pledge to reform working conditions and concern over his refusal to raise wages. Jeff Ballinger applauded Nike's plans to improve working condition in factories and felt it would now be difficult for Nike to wiggle out of its commitment to truly independent monitoring. Medea Benjamin of Global Exchange focused on the gap in Knight's pledge, emphasizing that a sweatshop is still a sweatshop until you start paying a living wage. To ensure media coverage of the living wage issue Global Exchange had held a press briefing three hours prior to Knight's speech that featured Jeffrey Winters, professor of political economy at Northwestern University and a leading expert on Indonesia. Winters told reporters that the sharp decline in the value of Indonesian currency (the rupiah) meant that Nike could give a rupiah wage increase of more than 200 percent and still be paying the same wage in dollar terms as in July 1997. The currency devaluation, coupled with a worsening economic crisis in Indonesia, made Nike's refusal to increase wages even more untenable. By highlighting these facts Global Exchange facilitated the media's assessment that although progress had been made, the larger struggle to ensure Nike's workers a living wage was far from over.[96]

Knight's assertion that Nike was now synonymous with slave wages and that he was seen as the great Satan reflected an almost revolutionary shift in America's consciousness about Nike, the garment industry, and the global economy since 1992. When Jeff Ballinger first exposed Nike's labor practices in Indonesia, terms like *free trade* and *globalization* were little understood by most Americans. The debates over NAFTA and fast-track trade authority increased public understanding of the dangers posed by unfettered free trade, but activists lacked a strategy for addressing the seemingly inevitable rules of the global economy. The national corporate pressure campaign against Nike, the self-proclaimed model for corporate practice in the developing world, provided the necessary strategic vehicle. Nike was not the first corporation to increase profits by moving its plants overseas nor is it the only corporation that ruthlessly exploits third-world workers. Nike became the target of the most publicized national campaign against a company's global economic practices because of its unprecedented hypocrisy and its avowedly revolutionary vision of a world where sweatshops are seen as essential components to economic growth. In addition Nike's pervasive advertising campaigns linking the purchasing of the company's sneakers to one's sense of self-worth was seen as echoing the mind-control techniques of America's Cold War adversaries.

Anti-Nike activists have crystallized opposition to socially irresponsible economic globalization around an easily understood core idea: a living wage for all workers. This message has already proved a worthy adversary to the misleading but effective nostrum of free trade. A living wage does not mean, as free trade advocates often claim, that corporations must pay their overseas workers wages high enough to maintain a living standard equal to Americans'; it instead merely requires corporations profiting from economic globalization to ensure that their workers earn a living wage by their own society's standards. Medea Benjamin drove this point home when she challenged Phil Knight to raise the wages of Nike's overseas workers to three dollars per day; that Nike refused to pay what to most Americans is a paltry sum left the company on the defensive. The living-wage message clarifies what is at issue in the free trade debate and gives Americans a tool for seeing through media obfuscation around the battle. The anti-Nike campaign can help establish a global living wage because its target is wealthy and dependent on consumer loyalty; if activists can pressure Nike to pay living wages to its Asian factory workers the company would have an interest in using its vaunted marketing department to convince all corporations in the global economy to follow its lead.

The anti-Nike campaign will continue until Nike's overseas workers are assured a wage that enables them to lead decent lives in their home societies. Asian and women student groups on campuses are drawing highly motivated, energetic young activists into the anti-Nike effort. National women's groups including the National Organization for Women (NOW) have joined the fight on behalf of female sweatshop workers at home and abroad and can particularly influence the demographic groups whose sneaker purchases are steadily rising. Organized labor has increasingly recognized that, as Ray Quan, a San Francisco Bay Area leader of the Service Employees International Union, put it, "the Nike struggle is our struggle." Labor knows that raising workers' wages abroad creates a disincentive for the loss of union jobs through plant closures at home; unions now view the pitting of worker against worker as a counterproductive approach to addressing the global economy.[97]

From 1995 to May 1997 national activism against Nike increased and achieved tremendous results without a single full-time organizer. After Global Exchange hired Kim Miyoshi to organize full-time, the grassroots component of what had largely been a media-driven campaign has increased dramatically. The Campaign for Labor Rights (CLR), a project of the Nicaragua Network, saw its funding increase through 1997 sufficiently to hire an anti-sweatshop organizer. The Campaign's remarkably effective Labor Alerts/Labor News e-mail service expanded participation in the national struggle by linking anti-Nike student activists and sympathetic campus groups and by providing prompt information and even tactical assistance by phone or e-mail. As activists saw positive results from the efforts of groups like Global Exchange, Campaign for Labor Rights, Press for Change, and Justice! Do It Nike, the well-known bandwagon effect—present even in idealistic national social justice struggles—brought new resources and energy. Even elected officials have joined the anti-Nike effort, as seventy-five members of congress signed on to a resolution criticizing Nike circulated in October 1997 by Representatives Bernie Sanders (I-VT) and Marcy Kaptur (D-OH). National activism against Nike's labor abuses has thus realized the popular chant: if the people lead, the leaders will follow. The new national activism of the anti-Nike campaign is reclaiming America's progressive ideals by bringing living wages and greater social and economic fairness to the global economy in the twenty-first century.

Chapter 2

From Challenging American Sweatshops to a Movement for a Global Living Wage

At age eleven Lora Jo Foo joined her mother and older sisters working at a sewing factory in San Francisco's Chinatown district. Foo sewed for twelve hours a day, six days a week during the summer and whenever she was not in school to help pay the rent and put food on the table. Foo's mother would leave for work when her daughters left for school. After coming home to cook dinner she would return to the factory. Her workday did not end until after 10:00 P.M., long after her younger daughters were already asleep. Eventually Foo's mother worked this schedule on Sundays as well. Lora Jo Foo recalled that "we never saw much of Mom; the garment factory stole her from us."

By the time Foo graduated from high school her mother had found a decent-paying job as a seamstress outside of Chinatown. Upset about the illegal working conditions of her mother and other immigrant garment workers, after college Foo worked as a seamstress in a unionized factory so that she could help organize workers. After eight years as a seamstress and then as a hotel housekeeper representing Asian immigrant women as a shop steward, Foo went to law school. In 1992 she joined the Asian Law Caucus as its employment/labor attorney, and subsequently created Sweatshop Watch, a coalition of labor and community groups combating abuses in the garment industry.

Unfortunately, the number of families of immigrant women who

have been deprived of their mothers' love and care during their waking hours has dramatically grown since Lora Jo Foo's experience in
the 1960s. In America today more than 875,000 women work ten
hours a day, six days a week for at best minimum wage and without
overtime pay in garment sweatshops. In New York City, where sweatshops were virtually wiped out in the 1950s and 1960s, more than
fifty thousand of New York's garment workers work in conditions
that violate minimum wage and hour standards and/or occupational
health and safety requirements. Labor department inspections have
found such violations in 63 percent of the city's apparel shops. Southern California, the other major U.S. sweatshop center, has nearly one
hundred thousand sweatshop workers. Twice as many Californians
work in apparel industry sweatshops as in the state's vaunted computer manufacturing. The General Accounting Office estimates that
90 percent of Southern California's five thousand garment shops violate wage and hour laws. Sweatshops have also proliferated in the San
Francisco Bay Area, Texas, and Florida, areas whose large pool of immigrant workers made them ripe territory for those seeking to impose exploitative and substandard working conditions.[1]

The apparel industry's exporting of thousands of America's well-
paying manufacturing jobs and increasing economic globalization have
perhaps overshadowed the persistence of America's domestic garment
industry. While many apparel giants have moved much of their work
overseas and others threaten to do likewise in response to union organizing efforts, America's garment industry has continued because
smaller manufacturers lack sufficient volume to benefit from overseas work. In addition, the need for quick reorders for hot-selling
items requires a one- or two-week turnaround that only local producers can provide. The downside of America's preservation of garment
industry jobs, however, is that the domestic apparel industry remains
America's largest unorganized and economically exploited manufacturing sector. The shameful perpetuation of sweatshop labor in major
American cities has led many activists to mobilize nationally to unionize such workers or at least ensure them a living wage. Anti-sweatshop
campaigns not only can bring decent-paying blue-collar jobs back to
low-income communities; they have also become a powerful vehicle
for highlighting and redressing the nation's growing social and economic inequality.

As was demonstrated by Nike's compliance with an Indonesian minimum-wage law that left female workers malnourished, anti-sweatshop campaigns must seek a living wage rather than a minimum wage for garment workers. The drive for living wages for garment workers has raised public sympathy for the plight of all low-wage workers and bolstered local and national grassroots campaigns for living-wage laws. Since many Americans' parents or grandparents once worked in sweatshops, the public felt an emotional connection with immigrant garment workers that it did not feel toward other low-wage workers. Immigrant workers often provided the leadership and impetus for this country's previous great labor and economic justice struggles; national anti-sweatshop campaigns can reclaim America's progressive ideals by uniting diverse constituencies into a national movement for garment workers' justice and a living wage for all.

This chapter explores what are likely the two most prominent domestic anti-sweatshop campaigns of the 1990s: the three-year struggle led by activists of the Asian Immigrant Women Advocates (AIWA) against Jessica McClintock, Inc., and the battle by the labor union UNITE and its activist supporters to unionize Southern California sweatshops producing apparel for the Guess jeans company. AIWA's campaign offers an organizing model for national anti-sweatshop campaigns that could be replicated by a broader living-wage movement; UNITE's struggle shows the extra hurdles involved when the goal is achieving union representation of domestic sweatshop workers. These campaigns, along with the anti-Nike struggle and others, provide opportunities for citizen activists to channel popular opposition to sweatshop wages toward support for the creation of a global living wage. The expansion of anti-sweatshop activism from specific corporate campaigns to a national grassroots movement pressuring all employers to pay a living wage holds the greatest promise for reclaiming a fair deal for workers at the dawn of a new century.

Jessica McClintock—"Let Them Eat Lace"

From April 1991 through February 1992 twelve Chinese immigrant women worked for Lucky Sewing Company in Oakland, California, ten hours a day, six days a week without overtime pay, health benefits, or even the minimum wage. Such labor conditions were nothing unusual for America's garment industry, and the twelve workers had dutifully performed in this way for ten years. Lucky Sewing Company was a subcontractor for Jessica McClintock, Inc. Known for its stylish fashions and wedding dresses, the McClintock Company grossed $145 million in 1992 and company president McClintock is frequently described as a role model for women.

Under normal circumstances the twelve workers would have collectively received wages that amounted to five dollars for each dress being sold in McClintock's San Francisco boutique for $175–200. When Lucky Sewing Company filed for bankruptcy in February 1992, however, the twelve women were left holding bad checks amounting to fifteen thousand dollars in back pay for several months of labor. Because Lucky Sewing was an independent contractor, the ultimate beneficiary of the women's work, Jessica McClintock, Inc., was not legally responsible for covering Lucky Sewing's debts. It seemed that the women would simply be the latest victims in the long history of the fashion industry's mistreatment of its workers.

The women, however, sought the assistance of Asian Immigrant Women Advocates (AIWA), a community organization established in 1983 to assist low-wage immigrant workers. AIWA used the workers' plight to launch a "Garment Workers' Justice Campaign." By engaging labor unions, religious groups, students, and the media and using creative strategies and tactics, AIWA transformed what could have remained a short-term, losing local campaign into a national campaign the success of which provides a road map for future economic justice struggles.

AIWA began its campaign on September 29, 1992, by writing a letter to company president Jessica McClintock requesting compensation for the workers. Rather than simply sending a check for fifteen thousand dollars and thus resolving the matter, Ms. McClintock refused the request. She responded by fax on October 1, 1992, that her company did "not exercise any control over contractors," who were "independent business people" whose internal operations were not McClintock's concern.[2] AIWA then joined the workers in visiting McClintock headquarters to discuss the dispute, but the group was rebuffed.

In response to McClintock's position AIWA issued a press release on October 7, 1992, announcing that on October 13 it would hold a rally and press conference at the San Francisco headquarters of McClintock, Inc. According to the release these events would "launch a national campaign to make clothing manufacturers responsible for contractors' working conditions." Speakers would include the head of the San Francisco Labor Council, a representative from the International Ladies Garment Workers Union (ILGWU), Asian community leaders, and the coordinator of La Mujer Obrera, a workers' advocacy group based in El Paso, Texas.[3] Only six days after McClintock's rejection of the offer, AIWA responded by showing it was supported by prominent labor and community leaders and declared its intention to wage a national campaign over the dispute. AIWA had clearly prepared its response in advance of McClintock's denial, displaying the tactical smarts that would typify its campaign. Although AIWA was primarily a service provider for Asian women immigrants in the San Francisco Bay Area, it recognized that obtaining justice for the Lucky Sewing workers required advocacy on a national scale. As Young Shin, AIWA's executive director, observed, "Since McClintock sells her sweatshop goods nationally, we've got to go national too."[4]

In order to transform a dispute at one shop into a national campaign AIWA used the October 13 events to launch a national Garment Workers' Justice Campaign against sweatshop labor. In urging support for the campaign AIWA emphasized the link between the seamstresses' failure to get paid and the trend of McClintock, Inc., and other companies to move garment work offshore to lower-wage countries. Carma I. Dominguez, coordinator of the El Paso, Texas, workers' advocacy group, La Mujer Obrera, signaled the potential breadth of AIWA's campaign when she told the rally, "San Francisco is only one of many cities where workers are cruelly exploited." At an October 20, 1992, rally at McClintock's Union Square boutique AIWA escalated its pressure by calling for a national boycott of McClintock until the workers were compensated and given a two-year contract to sew Jessica McClintock's dresses.

A well-attended rally, even one that includes representatives of groups throughout the country, does not make a national campaign. All too often groups attempting to nationalize their issues never get beyond the initial publicity burst accompanying their pledge to take their struggle nationwide. To establish the credibility of its national aspirations AIWA followed its campaign launching by quickly taking two significant actions.

First, on October 26, 1992, AIWA took out a full-page advertisement in the West Coast edition of the *New York Times*. The ad pictured an older Asian woman holding a large wedding dress and was titled "Jessica McClintock Says: 'Let Them Eat Lace.'" The ad contrasted the sweatshop wages and working conditions of those sewing McClintock's dresses with their high price tags, the company's $145 million annual gross income, and McClintock's own use of romantic images of feminine fragility to sell the product of hard-working and exploited female labor. The *Times* ad reached a target audience of West Coast opinion makers and conveyed the message that AIWA was mobilizing for a major campaign.

AIWA's ad was so hard-hitting that McClintock took out a full-page *Times* ad of her own on November 2, 1992. Headlined "Jessica McClintock Says 'I Will Not Tolerate Intimidation or a Blatant Shakedown,'" the ad provided a spirited defense of McClintock's position and of her "personal sadness" about the "abhorrent" working conditions alleged to exist by the twelve women workers. The pro and con full-page ads raised public awareness of a dispute that in only its first few weeks had already expanded beyond any sweatshop dispute in recent times.

AIWA's second strategy to transform its conflict into a true national campaign was to hold simultaneous demonstrations against McClintock on October 31, 1992, in Beverly Hills, Chicago, Denver, Houston, Portland, and San Jose, and in New York City on October 30. Synchronized protests are an excellent measure of a campaign's national stature; unlike a press conference using national figures, simultaneous protests require sufficient supporters in each city to create a successful event. Less than a month into its campaign AIWA had already achieved a sufficient base to hold such rallies. AIWA accomplished this by accessing resources commonly available to similar-sized advocacy and service organizations. In AIWA's case this included the various groups with which AIWA participated in networks or informal working relationships, Asian-American groups, women's groups, and the broad coalition of labor unions, churches, workers' rights organizations, and broad-based progressive organizations that have traditionally supported national movements for economic fairness. AIWA conducted a major outreach effort to colleges, a strategy equally available to other citizen activist organizations considering national campaigns. AIWA's successful mobilization of local organizations and citizen activists created the base necessary for a national campaign and required AIWA to maintain activists' participation, carrying out a constant stream of highly creative and effective activities.[5]

AIWA followed the October 31 nationwide protests with weekly leafleting in several cities. This activity further expanded the base for a second round of simultaneous protests on the day after Thanksgiving—the year's busiest shopping day. AIWA then took out another full-page *Times* ad on December 2, 1992. Titled "Fantasy v. Reality," the ad contrasted the corporate image of McClintock apparel with the sweatshop conditions of garment workers. The ad urged McClintock to pay the twelve women during the holiday season and, sticking with this theme, AIWA ended the year with a Christmas season caroling protest at McClintock's posh San Francisco boutique.

Within three months of its initial letter to McClintock AIWA had staged two days of national demonstrations, placed two full-page *Times* ads, held innumerable protests, and begun ongoing weekly literature distribution in several cities. AIWA accomplished this with four full-time staff and a $200,000 annual budget. Many organizations would not even think of beginning a national corporate accountability campaign on a budget of more than ten times that amount; because AIWA understood the strategies and tactics necessary to prevail, it was not deterred by its financial limitations.

AIWA's recognition that national campaigns require constant visibility and outreach to maintain activist interest and that this one needed to keep the pressure on the still-recalcitrant McClintock led to a staggering array of actions in 1993. On January 8, 1993, the Urban-Rural Mission (URM), a global network for justice of the World Council of Churches, joined with the Korean Immigrant Workers Advocates (KIWA) in picketing McClintock's Beverly Hills boutique. Further support for the faith-based community came on March 16, 1993, when the division of public ministries of the American Baptist Church of the West, comprising 217 churches, sent a letter to McClintock, Inc., announcing its vote to support AIWA's boycott.

AIWA expanded its religious support throughout the campaign, bringing the United Methodist Voluntary Services and other groups to the picket lines during their annual conventions in Los Angeles and the San Francisco Bay Area. AIWA used a similar tactic when its close ally, the Oakland, California–based Center for Third World Organizing (CTWO) held a national gathering of women organizers. While in San Francisco, the group led a "Shopping District Protest Tour" to coincide with International Women's Day. The event further invested the organizers in AIWA's struggle and sent a powerful message by linking AIWA's campaign to a day commemorating the death of Jewish immigrant seamstresses at the Triangle Shirtwaist Factory in New York in 1911.

Like all great organizers, AIWA realized that it could pretty much follow the cues from the calendar to sustain enthusiasm for its campaign. In addition to staging protests related to Christmas and International Women's Day, AIWA staged a "Jessie Have a Heart" Valentine Day's picket in front of Jessica McClintock's lavish Victorian home. On Mother's Day a lesbian and bisexual Asian/Pacific group picketed McClintock's San Francisco store, chanting, "We're queer, we're Asian, we're not going shopping!" To celebrate the start of the June 1993 wedding season, AIWA's "We've Got the Unpaid/Wedding Day Blues" protests occurred both at Jessica McClintock's home and at her flagship store. Perhaps concerned that the media needed an unusually creative event to justify continued coverage, AIWA, "in the spirit of the season," held a mock wedding ceremony at both locations. Unlike the traditional wedding ceremonies portrayed in McClintock catalogues, AIWA's event featured a cross-dressed bride and groom; the former shed his McClintock gown in protest of the company's mistreatment of workers.

On October 30, 1993, AIWA held a series of national protests at McClintock boutiques locally organized by an essential but all too often neglected resource for national action: college students. In Atlanta students from Emory University's Students in Alliance for Asian American Concerns picketed McClintock's boutiques at the Perimeter Mall. Boston's protest at Copley Place included supporters from Harvard's Asian-American Association, Cornell students held an all-day campus teach-in on October 29, students from the University of Washington and Evergreen College led the Seattle protest, and the San Francisco event included supporters from Asian student groups at the

University of California at Berkeley. In Los Angeles the Korean Immigrant Workers Advocates (KIWA), which was leading the campaign in that sweatshop-laden city, joined with Korean student groups on October 30 and throughout the holiday season to protest at McClintock's Beverly Hills store. These events often saw local union members and church and community activists joining the students in an all too rare display of unity.

Although recent history shows that campus activism is essential for successful national campaigns, contemporary organizations fighting the good fight in the national arena do not conduct the outreach necessary to harness student power. This strategic omission is perhaps attributable to inaccurate stereotypes of today's students as either too overburdened by tuition costs to pursue activism or more concerned with exploring their personal identities than addressing broader social problems. AIWA ignored these stereotypes and found that Asian-American and women students were particularly motivated to join the campaign.

AIWA's use of "identity politics" to build its economic justice campaign enabled the struggle to reach many communities and a consumer base that would otherwise have been missed. As is also evident from the participation of Vietnamese-American students in the anti-Nike campaign, students who organize themselves around race, ethnicity, gender, or sexual orientation have not ignored economic justice activism. On the contrary, members of these groups have been in the forefront of such campaigns. Critics who blame what they perceive as the misguided priorities of such students for the decline in campus activism addressing social and economic inequality have, curiously enough, not found fault with the inaction of tenured professors or other college students. Both the anti-Nike and McClintock campaigns show that the plight of predominantly female Asian or Latina sweatshop workers has created a powerful emotional connection with students of the same gender and/or ethnic background. Established campus organizations focused on the needs of these constituencies facilitate student activism in such struggles.

AIWA created its college links without first having campus chapters, an infrastructure that might appear to be a precondition for student participation in an off-campus national campaign. AIWA instead simply did what any organization with a potentially popular cause can do: it worked closely with the students it knew and then used its allies to build support on as many campuses as they could reach. By the start of the fall semester of 1993 AIWA's student outreach had resulted in twenty-two campus support chapters for its campaign. Although AIWA was the immediate beneficiary of the students' involvement, the training, leadership skills, and off-campus contacts that the campaign brought to the students will facilitate their future participation in other activist campaigns.

AIWA's nationwide protests on October 30, 1993, were soon followed by the passage of NAFTA. The national debate over NAFTA demonstrated widespread public anger toward "free-trade" policies that accelerate job flight and weaken workers' rights. AIWA connected NAFTA's passage to its own struggle, arguing that its McClintock campaign was a critical test for holding corporations accountable in the post-NAFTA world. AIWA scheduled "Post-NAFTA National Holiday Season Protests" in several cities, again to take place on the day after Thanksgiving. AIWA gave those angry at NAFTA's passage an immediate outlet for their energy, and AIWA's holiday season protests continued weekly through Christmas.

Why would a savvy businesswoman like Jessica McClintock endure personal attacks, protests outside her home, and a second year of a national boycott over a fifteen-thousand-dollar dispute? AIWA contended that the real issue for McClintock was manufacturers' practice of hiding behind contractors like Lucky Sewing so that they could profit from sweatshops without legal responsibility to the workers. McClintock's intransigence confirmed her recognition of the larger stakes, but it was becoming increasingly clear that she sought resolution. On December 17, 1993, McClintock offered to resolve the dispute by making a "charitable contribution" to the twelve workers through a Chinese garment association. McClintock's offer was conditional upon each worker's written acknowledgment that the money was a donation, not wages, that she was not owed wages by McClintock, and that she was never a McClintock employee. Under tremendous pressure, five workers accepted the offer; the seven who refused had their names published in *Sing Tao*, the Chinese-language daily, which essentially prevented their future employment in the industry.

While claiming victory in winning the five workers the pay they had long sought, AIWA trumpeted the refusal of seven to accept the conditions of McClintock's "gift." Escalating its original demands, AIWA's executive director, Young Shin, now insisted that the boycott would continue until McClintock guaranteed an end to sweatshop wages and working conditions for those who sewed her dresses.

Having failed to end the boycott, McClintock promptly intensified the conflict. In addition to using the Chinese press to blacklist the remaining seven workers, the company hired an Asian public relations firm, which brought Asian students to counterleaflet at McClintock's San Francisco and Los Angeles locations. Rising to the challenge, AIWA attacked McClintock's "charity" in a February 14, 1994, *New York Times* ad and moved forward on yet another creative strategy: a series of "Prom and Wedding Season" protests. Jessica McClintock rose to fame as a designer of such attire, and the contrast between the expensive wear and its sweatshop origins could not be greater. AIWA then initiated a new wave of simultaneous nationwide protests on February 19, 1994, and followed this on April 21 with "Time to Pay Up, Jessica" National Actions in thirteen cities, with students again playing significant roles.

A boycott of prom dresses requires outreach to the chief market for such attire: high school girls. Starting with its personal contacts, AIWA contacted Bay Area Asian and women's high school groups and enlisted their help. The students responded by leafleting on campus, discussing the boycott at school assemblies, and by sending letters and petitions to fashion magazines. As discussed in chapter 1, high school students are often an important market for sweatshop goods, so anti-sweatshop campaigns must invoke strategies for reaching pre-college youths. As AIWA's rallies and protests continued, McClintock, Inc., continued to fight back. Court rulings limited picketing at Jessica McClintock's home, and McClintock, Inc., filed National Labor Relations Board charges claiming that AIWA's boycott was illegal because the organization was a de facto labor union under federal law. AIWA's supporters responded to the picketing injunction by wearing gags in their mouths outside McClintock's San Francisco mansion to symbolize the attempt by McClintock, Inc., to "strangle immigrant garment workers' free speech rights."[6] McClintock even wrote letters to Greenpeace and other environmental groups supporting the boycott, saying, "Shame on you—we expected better from your organization."[7]

As 1995 began both sides had reason to reach a settlement. AIWA's boycott had succeeded in reducing McClintock's sales and the clothing giant feared its continuation would jeopardize its position on the labor department's newly created "Trendsetter List." Labor Secretary Reich had established the Trendsetter List to highlight clothiers that agreed to monitor the working conditions of their subcontractors. The inclusion on the list of Nike, Guess, and other companies charged with profiting from sweatshops has raised doubts about its accuracy. Further, as Labor Party activist Tony Mazzochi has observed, the list gives a government award to companies simply for not ruthlessly exploiting workers, which is like giving people a medal for not mugging someone on the way to work. Despite the list's shortcomings, it was created to immunize apparel makers from criticism; the exclusion of McClintock, Inc., because of the AIWA dispute would have injured the company's image as a model for the industry.

For its part AIWA had spent more than three years on the McClintock campaign and needed to return to addressing other critical immigrant workers' rights struggles. The campaign's persistence also represented a festering problem for the Clinton administration, which needed to secure organized labor's active support for the 1996 election despite Clinton's support of NAFTA. AIWA was constantly reminding the public of "free trade's" hard realities at a time when Clinton was emphasizing NAFTA's benefits for his reelection campaign. The labor department thus sought to mediate the conflict and after lengthy, confidential negotiations announced a signed agreement between AIWA and Jessica McClintock, Inc., on March 21, 1996.

The agreement called for "cooperative efforts" between the parties, including money for the remaining seven Lucky Sewing workers, establishment of a garment workers' education fund, scholarships for students and garment workers, and two all-free bilingual hot lines for McClintock contractor employees to enhance compliance with wage and hour laws. The hot lines would be maintained by the labor department.

Although AIWA was limited by a confidentiality agreement from widely publicizing the agreement, the accord and the entire campaign represented an unprecedented triumph for the organization. In tangible terms, the individual workers received their back pay and many other garment workers would receive financial benefits. The hot lines would enable garment workers to anonymously report sweatshop abuses, eliminating the requirement that workers jeopardize their jobs by personally reporting wage and other violations. Although AIWA did not succeed in forcing McClintock, Inc., to accept legal responsibility for its contractors' wages and working conditions, this ambitious goal would most likely require state or federal legislation affecting all manufacturers and could not have been won by continuing the McClintock campaign. The California legislature actually passed such legislation in 1990, 1992, and 1994, only to have it vetoed each time by Republican governor Pete Wilson.

AIWA's greatest strategic accomplishment was the massive publicity it generated about the plight of garment workers in contemporary America. AIWA's constant rallies, protests, and leafleting generated a sustained level of national and local coverage to enable millions of Americans to learn how working conditions that victimized young girls in nineteenth-century Massachusetts mills had returned to modern America. More important, AIWA gave people a strategy for addressing the problem, to boycott clothing made in sweatshops. AIWA always emphasized that the back pay owed to the twelve women was simply evidence of a systemic and widespread injustice; its campaign was the first sustained assault upon American sweatshops since they became common in America in the 1970s after a forty-year period during which they were unusual.

AIWA's campaign also enhanced the prospects for national activism by creating a replicable model for integrating local organizations into broader campaigns. The various grassroots, students, labor, and religious-based organizations that comprised AIWA's national base did not sacrifice their autonomy; nor was their role limited to implementing decisions made in AIWA's Oakland, California, office. Rather, individual groups determined the scope of their participation and the means for mobilizing their constituencies. The national campaign's decentralized structure encouraged local initiative and fostered new organizational relationships that could benefit participating groups' future struggles. Media coverage of the rallies and protests focused on the local group's activities, so that participation in national activism bolstered the group's public presence and enabled local groups to claim credit for the campaign's eventual success.

An unfortunate legacy of the 1960s was the feeling that the period's national campaigns disempowered citizen activists working at the community level, discouraged rather than fostered the growth of grassroots groups, ceded local decision making to distant, unaccountable national leadership, and fundamentally diminished the power and influence of those whose familial and/or work responsibilities restricted their activities to cities and towns other than Washington, D.C. The successful movements for local control and community self-reliance since the 1970s have created thousands of local organizations and grassroots leaders who will not join national campaigns if it means sacrificing their hard-won local media presence, power, and political relevance.

Both the McClintock and anti-Nike campaigns demonstrate that citizen activists and their organizations can act nationally without jeopardizing their influence or stature. These campaigns also show that local groups can take ownership of national struggles. The concept of ownership reflects the need for organizations to sustain themselves by making an issue or campaign their own. While diverse organizations may chant that they are waging the "same struggle, same fight," funding, media coverage, and organizational stature are usually awarded to the group most identified with the particular issue. This leads many groups to focus on issues in which they are the lead group rather than join campaigns where their participation would be helpful but their role would be subordinate. For example, no doubt there were groups that supported AIWA's struggle but did not participate because it was AIWA's issue and AIWA, not their organization, would get the primary credit for success. The ability of AIWA's campaign to create local and national publicity opportunities for grassroots groups joining the struggle should help dispel the ownership obstacle to increased national activism. If Global Exchange had followed the approach of working exclusively on campaigns it controlled, the organization would never have joined an anti-Nike struggle presumably owned by Jeff Ballinger and the Portland activists in Justice! Do It Nike. Both national and local campaigns can be structured to ensure meaningful involvement by citizen activists and their organizations; when a national campaign reduces people and groups to mere cogs in a centralized machine, blame should be attributed to the campaign's leadership, not the inherent nature of national activism.

In launching a formal boycott against McClintock, Inc., instead of relying exclusively on a corporate pressure campaign, AIWA demonstrated how the boycott strategy can still be an effective tool in national campaigns if strategically implemented. Boycotts have fallen into disfavor even among activists familiar with the successful grape boycott by the United Farm Workers in the 1960s, the J. P. Stevens boycott by the American Clothing and Textile Workers Union (ACTWU) in the 1970s, and the South Africa divestment movement of the 1980s. The problem with launching boycotts is that, as anti-Nike activist Max White puts it, they are hard to get going and even harder to stop. National boycotts against powerful corporations require organizations to expend significant resources on an intense struggle with no clear end and where victory is far from assured. Boycotts have all of the pressure of the month before an election, except that this high level of intensity and commitment must be maintained for years. Unlike pressure campaigns, formal boycotts have typically required formal endings; this has often required groups to reach agreements that are heralded as victories but bring few tangible results. Boycotts that have achieved significant benefits, such as Nestle's agreement to stop marketing infant formula in the third world, could not be restarted after the corporation sidestepped its obligations. Boycotts are a high-risk strategy that can divide organizations over the meaning of success and leave once-committed activists skeptical of joining future national campaigns.

Further, most boycotts fail to achieve their stated goals. A major reason for their low success rate is the predominance of boycotts unaccompanied by grassroots campaigns. Even the most committed political activist is likely unaware of the huge number of boycotts included in such publications as the *Boycott Quarterly*. Some of the targets, such as the ABC television network, would require millions of Americans to completely stop watching one of the nation's three leading broadcast outlets; the goal may be noble, but absent a multimillion-dollar campaign, the strategy can only fail. Constituencies increasingly call for boycotts as an alternative to grassroots corporate pressure campaigns, rather than as a tactic within a broader campaign. When consumers see boycotts indiscriminately launched or learn that they have innocently purchased products that for reasons unknown to them are on a boycott list, they are less likely to honor boycotts. Organizations that seize on media stories about a corporation's deficiencies to

announce boycotts and then quickly call them off once they have received a contract for "monitoring" or for distributing the company's
products have also harmed the boycott's once pristine image.

During a visit to my office by Stanford students participating in Alternative Spring Break in 1997, we had a lengthy discussion of the
boycott strategy. None of the students, whose social consciousness led
them to be in my Tenderloin office rather than at the beach, felt boycotts could succeed. Their view was that people are weary of thinking
about everything they consume or purchase, that there are so many
boycotts that people cannot keep track, and that it is too hard to convince people to penalize a particular company when nearly all major
corporations are guilty of some wrongdoing.

After reaching consensus that boycotts are doomed I discussed
AIWA's McClintock campaign. The students felt that it had succeeded
because the boycott was accompanied by an active grassroots campaign that enabled the public to differentiate McClintock from other
garment companies. They also felt that exposure to the personal testimony of sweatshop workers created the emotional connection necessary for the boycott to succeed. The students still saw an obstacle in
persuading people that the labor practices of McClintock, Inc., were
sufficiently worse than its competitors to justify not buying its products. Jessica McClintock no doubt shared the students' analysis of
her comparative innocence, for she maintained throughout AIWA's
campaign that she was being blamed for practices customary in the
industry. AIWA, however, had used Jessica McClintock's reputation
for social responsibility to attack her hypocrisy on this issue. Although
Nike's Phil Knight lacked McClintock's personal commitment to social causes, the anti-Nike campaign also succeeded by challenging the
company to live up to its claim to be a positive global model for corporate behavior. AIWA's successful targeting of one of the most socially responsible manufacturers demonstrates that a campaign that
has an active grassroots presence and makes an emotional connection
to the public through personal testimony of corporate victims can convince the public to boycott a particular wrongdoer despite its competitors' wrongdoing.

AIWA's boycott strategy made sense because it focused on a very
specific, winnable objective: reimbursement of wages for the Lucky

Sewing workers. Although McClintock, Inc., vigorously contested the workers' claims, the actual cost of paying the women was never the issue. AIWA successfully reasoned that at some point McClintock, Inc., would find the economic cost of continuing to fight greater than the expense of settlement. In campaigns to organize domestic sweatshop workers into unions, however, employers have a strong economic motive to defeat organizing campaigns. Further, the boycott strategy is typically not available to such campaigns because federal law prohibits unions from boycotting goods made by a company that is not the target of union organizing efforts. The same legal fiction that immunized McClintock, Inc., from paying its subcontractors debts prevents unions from boycotting a garment company's goods because the workers making the products are technically employed by the subcontractor. Despite the difficulties of organizing domestic sweatshop workers into unions, such campaigns are crucial for reversing growing social and economic inequality both in America and throughout the world.

Guess: An American Sweatshop Tradition

The Guess Jeans Company is perhaps best known for raunchy ads portraying women, as *Fortune* magazine described, in "a jailbait-on-heroin" look. Founded by the Algerian-born Marciano brothers, Guess went from selling twenty-four pairs of pants in 1981 to sales of $487 million in 1995. Guess's dramatic growth has been accompanied by flagrant violations of garment workers' rights. Unlike Jessica McClintock, who contributed to AIDS programs and had a reputation as one of the more enlightened manufacturers, the Marcianos are virtual poster boys for inequitable American economic policies and the damage to workers caused by global "free trade."

The breadth of Guess's wrongful conduct is impressive. Starting in 1990 the Department of Labor found Guess's contracting shops guilty of several violations of the Fair Labor Standards Act, including child labor, illegal homework, nonpayment of minimum wage and overtime, and false record keeping. To avoid legal action Guess agreed in August 1992 to monitor its contractors for labor law violations. By subsequently agreeing in writing to a "Compliance Program Agreement" with the labor department Guess became the first major manufacturer to sign such an agreement and was placed on Labor Secretary Robert Reich's "Trendsetter List" as an industry leader in the battle against sweatshops.

Despite Guess's compliance agreement, in July 1996 California investigators raided fifteen sites where illegal homework was being conducted. Guess work was being performed in a majority of the sites and all of the homework contractors did work for Guess. Homework has been banned for decades in America, primarily because it encourages child labor and wages and working conditions cannot be monitored. As the headline in the *Los Angeles Times* coverage of the raids stated, the "discovery casts doubt over effectiveness of Sweatshop Program."[8] The ability of Guess, Southern California's biggest garment manufacturing company, to evade its own agreement while drawing praise as a "trendsetter" seemed to reveal both Guess and the labor department as liars and hypocrites. Guess insisted it had complied with federal laws and Secretary Reich claimed Guess *could* (!) be removed from the Trendsetters List if the changes were confirmed.

A week following the raid a group of Guess workers filed a class action lawsuit on behalf of about two thousand workers employed in sixteen contracting shops working for Guess. The suit alleged widespread illegal practices, including falsification of time cards, below minimum wages, and forced homework. Guess retained Daniel Petrocelli, the attorney for the Goldman family in the O. J. Simpson civil case, to defend it against the charges. But the Marciano brothers were not satisfied to allow the legal process to potentially vindicate them. Instead, Guess responded to the charges by firing nearly twenty workers who had attempted to organize. Guess then followed this act of intimidation by filing a lawsuit against Sweatshop Watch, the Korean Immigrant Worker Advocates (KIWA), and Common Threads, a women's organization seeking improved labor conditions at Guess. The suit even charged, among other claims, that a September 8, 1996, poetry reading at Santa Monica's Midnight Special bookstore constituted libel and slander against Guess.

Guess saved its most destructive—and most politically significant—action for 1997. In response to UNITE's growing unionization drive and historic community opposition Guess announced in January 1997 that it was relocating 40 percent of its production work to Mexico and South America, leaving just 35 percent of its overall work in Los Angeles. Guess's plans reflected industry's increased use of the relocation threat to stifle worker organizing following the enactment of NAFTA. Its strategy also spotlights the central issue surrounding anti-sweatshop campaigns: if companies can respond by relocating to regions or nations where sweatshops are tolerated and even encouraged, activists must pressure corporations to pay living wages worldwide. According to Lora Jo Foo of Sweatshop Watch, "Guess is sending a message that it is okay to close factories and move overseas in response to union organizing drives and to efforts to force wealthy clothing manufacturers and retailers to end sweatshop conditions for their workforce. If they can get away with this, it could set a precedent that will devastate efforts to improve working conditions and wages for American workers." Foo recalls working with immigrant sweatshop workers in the 1970s making goods in the San Francisco Bay Area for the clothing giant Esprit, whose unionization drive led the company to relocate to Hong Kong. Two decades later, at the 1996 United Nations Fourth World Conference on Women in Beijing, Esprit gave Foo and the other thirty-eight thousand women in attendance canvas bags with the motto "Look at the world through women's eyes." Guess may be looking for its relocation to similarly refurbish its image. Steve Nutter, Los Angeles vice president of UNITE, shares Foo's concern over the national implication of Guess's action. According to Nutter, "UNITE will fight Guess's attempt to run from its obligations to workers who sew their clothing. I think it particularly significant that Guess is planning to move to Chile, whereas there is a push nationally to expand NAFTA to include that nation."[9]

Labor advocates are not alone in recognizing the national implications of Guess's conduct. The *Los Angeles Times* article on Guess's move stated that "manufacturers privately say that stepped-up enforcement of labor laws by federal and state regulators in the Southland's abuse-ridden garment industry have pushed them to leave."[10] In other words, an industry making multimillion-dollar profits from American consumers is throwing down the gauntlet to UNITE and anti-sweatshop activists: Either let us run sweatshops at home or we'll simply relocate abroad. Guess's plan is the flip side of Nike's departure to Indonesia after the South Korean makers of its shoes organized and won higher wages. Nike spokesperson Jim Small warned that the April 1997 increase in Indonesia's minimum wage could price the country "out of the market"; Guess and its domestic apparel industry colleagues have sent a similar message connecting workers' demands for improved wages and working conditions with plant shutdowns and the loss of jobs.[11]

Guess's scheme to shift work overseas bolstered its industry image. Once viewed as something of a rogue apparel maker, Guess suddenly became a hero in such publications as the *California Apparel News* and *Women's Wear Daily*. In April 1997 Guess president Maurice Marciano was named Man of the Year by the Fashion Industries Guild of Cedars-Sinai Medical Center. The Guild's president denied a political motive to the selection, claiming that Marciano was "very giving" and had the support of all of his industry peers. Both industry publications gave extremely favorable coverage to Guess's tactic on June 18, 1997, of having more than five hundred of its subcontractors' workers protest against UNITE. Although the employers provided bus transportation to the protests and paid the workers attending the event, the apparel industry saw the anti-UNITE rally as evidence of "anti-union fervor." Marciano, who was present at the event, denied that management had a role in planning the march, a claim that was consistent with a stream of industry articles quoting worker opposition to unions. A UNITE spokesperson was briefly quoted in one article noting that workers who had publicly supported unionization efforts had been fired, with Guess only agreeing to reinstatement to avoid a National Labor Relations Board unfair labor practices charge. But the tone of the industry-backed publications reflected the conviction that if Guess could beat back UNITE's efforts, the historic tradition of American sweatshops in the garment industry could be preserved into a new century.

A week prior to the pro-Guess rally more than two hundred activists, including UNITE's president, Jay Mazur, and Rich Trumka, the AFL-CIO's secretary-treasurer, demonstrated in front of a Dilliard's clothing store in Las Vegas in order to pressure the retailer to demand that Guess stop relying on sweatshop labor. Trumka's participation reflected the AFL-CIO's increased commitment toward organizing low-wage workers that would become a national story during the August 1997 Teamsters strike against UPS. Trumka was a fixture at low-wage-sector organizing drives ranging from the warehouse workers who sort fruit to the farmworkers who pick it. His support for the Guess campaign is consistent with what Trumka describes as the AFL-CIO's "whole new attitude about organizing. We're reaching out to everyone from the top to the bottom."[12]

The election of John Sweeney to the AFL-CIO presidency in October 1995 also changed organized labor's attitude toward cross-border organizing drives. The AFL-CIO publicly supported general strikes in Brazil and South Korea in 1997 and has devoted critical resources to campaigns against sweatshops in Central America and Haiti. Such steps would have been extremely unlikely under the labor organization's previous nationalistic and protectionist approach to international worker issues. Organized labor's cooperation with Central American unions and their American-based solidarity groups quickly paid dividends. For example, in September 1996 a campaign for a labor contract was launched by a Guatemala union representing Phillip Van Heusen workers producing garments for American export. The campaign drew the strong backing of UNITE, the International Textile, Garment and Leather Workers Federation, and such American solidarity groups as Witness for Peace, Nicaragua Network, the Resource Center for the Americas, and the U.S./Guatemala Labor Education Project (US/GLEP). The coalition's pressure helped convince Phillip Van Heusen to enter contract negotiations with the union in March 1997. US/GLEP subsequently assembled a similarly broad coalition of labor and solidarity groups to improve wages and working conditions for Starbucks coffee workers in Guatemala.

In January 1998 AFL-CIO president Sweeney visited Mexico to encourage Mexican and American unions to help each other in cross-border organizing. It was the first trip to Mexico by any president of the American labor movement since Samuel Gompers visited in 1924. With twenty-six thousand American garment jobs having been transferred to Mexico during the mid 1990s alone and with Guess shifting an additional thousand workers south of the border to avoid UNITE's organizing drive, Sweeney emphasized that organized labor sought to develop "coordinated cross-border organizing and bargaining strategies." Such strategies would challenge the ability of Guess and other employers to operate Mexican sweatshops in response to American worker organizing drives. They would also reduce the economic incentive for companies to shift American jobs to Mexico. The AFL-CIO has focused on the country's smaller and more militant independent unions rather than the weak government-controlled labor groups to ensure that the unionization of Mexican garment workers results in higher wages and better conditions. In a powerful assertion of cross-border solidarity Sweeney told an audience of Mexican labor leaders, "We may live in different nations, but we face the same adversaries and fight the same battles. We are at the very beginning of a renewed freedom struggle."[13] This struggle will affect Guess, the Southern California garment industry, and the future of sweatshops in the region.

Religious Groups and Students Battle Guess

Although Guess's base in traditionally anti-union Southern California has increased the campaign's difficulty, the area's garment workers have found two important allies: religious groups and students. Religious organizations have traditionally supported union organizing drives, but anti-sweatshop struggles have galvanized faith-based groups to an extent not seen since Cesar Chavez's United Farm Workers' struggle of the 1960s. In Los Angeles both the Catholic and the Jewish communities have played vital roles in supporting the Guess organizing drive. When Guess fired the workers leading the union organizing drive in 1996 three regional bishops of the Catholic archdiocese appeared at a press conference to support UNITE's campaign. The bishops defended the right of the Guess workers to organize and proclaimed that workers' rights are central to Catholic social teaching.[14] As the Guess struggle grew, representatives of Catholic archdiocese in such diverse cities as Austin, Newark, Albany, and Hartford publicly lent their support.

The nation's Jewish community has felt a special obligation to combat sweatshops. Jewish immigrants worked in garment industry sweatshops in the early twentieth century and the notorious fire at the Triangle Shirtwaist Factory (March 25, 1911) in New York City claimed the lives of 146 Jewish women. Organizations such as the American Jewish Congress, the Union of American Hebrew Congregations, the

Pacific Southwest Council, and the Jewish Coalition in Support of Garment Workers strongly backed the struggle for justice by Guess workers. These groups linked Jewish traditions to the cause of Guess's overwhelmingly Catholic work force by holding a "Dignity Seder" at a center for garment workers and their children in downtown Los Angeles. Other Jewish groups, including the Sholem Community and the Workmen's Circle/Arbeter Ring, distributed flyers declaring "Children and Grandchildren of Jewish Garment Workers Say: No More Sweatshops. Protest Guess!" to publicize a demonstration against the company. Los Angeles–area rabbis were instrumental in the Union of American Hebrew Congregations' adoption of a set of strong anti-sweatshop resolutions at its biennial meeting in 1997. The resolutions, passed almost unanimously by delegates representing the nation's Reform Jewish congregations, endorsed congregational awareness campaigns around sweatshops and urged participation in coalitions and actions that seek to end such abuses.[15]

In addition to Catholic and Jewish organizations, the Guess struggle won public support from the bishops of several Episcopal diocese and from the United Methodist Church. Achieving such broad faith-based support for workers' rights and union organizing can prove critical for building the public sympathy necessary for successful anti-sweatshop campaigns. In order to facilitate such support, leaders of eighteen denominations have formed the National Interfaith Committee for Worker Justice. Headed by Kim Bobo, one of the country's most skilled community organizers, the Chicago-based group could bolster support for anti-sweatshop efforts and for struggles to ensure workers a living wage.[16]

The Guess campaign has also won strong support from student activists. The AFL-CIO's Union Summer program created the necessary links between students sympathetic to labor struggles and ongoing anti-sweatshop campaigns. Joe Goldman of Vassar College observed that Union Summer gave students training in organizing that they could then put to use in their own campus projects. These projects included the campus codes of conduct governing purchasing adopted by Duke University (discussed in chapter 1) as well as student-generated actions designed to highlight sweatshop campaigns. At Vassar, Goldman and his colleagues held a "Dare to Bare" night at which students were encouraged to wear no clothing made in sweatshops.

This left many students with little to wear, which made the event both popular and political. Goldman also led a delegation of students to a protest at a Guess store in New York City and is working with students at Wesleyan and other schools lacking big-time athletic programs to develop purchasing codes of conduct that better apply to their schools.[17]

The largest student project spawned by Union Summer was the creation of Students Stop Sweatshops, a coalition of student groups from more than fifty campuses nationwide. The coalition started the school year in fall 1997 with a "Back-to-School Boycott" of Guess. The student campaign was launched the week of August 17, 1997, with demonstrations in fourteen cities at Guess retail outlets and major department stores selling Guess clothing. These protests were followed by a National Day of Action against Guess on September 13, 1997. As protests continued and student participation has grown, rock stars like Tom Morello of Rage against the Machine joined the struggle. Morello's arrest at a protest against Guess on December 13, 1997, brought widespread publicity for the cause. By the fall of 1998 activities against Guess occurred on nearly two hundred campuses. Since Guess's marketing is directed to college students and teenage consumers, Students Stop Sweatshops's participation in the campaign has proved invaluable to its success.[18]

Guess Feels the Heat

The involvement of students and religious organizations helped transform a Los Angeles–area labor dispute into a national struggle for justice for garment workers against Guess. When Charles Kernaghan of the National Labor Committee stood in front of a new Guess store in New York City to promote the 1997 "Holiday of Conscience" effort for workers' rights, the campaign had clearly hit the big time. As public opposition to its labor practices grew, Guess suffered a series of reversals. In November 1997 the National Labor Relations Board issued a formal complaint affirming UNITE's charges that Guess fired employees and coerced others in order to deter the union's organizing drive. Although Guess vigorously denied the allegations, the company agreed to pay $113,000 in back wages to the fired workers in

April 1998. Guess also reported in November 1997 that its third-quarter net income fell 20 percent from a year earlier. Relying on its practice of going on the offensive in response to negative publicity, during the first week of December Guess took out ads in major newspapers claiming that its sewing contractors were "100 percent guaranteed sweatshop free." It also placed similar promotional tags on its jeans and other garments. Guess then distributed flyers to shoppers erroneously claiming that the company was on the labor department's "Trendsetter List" (the company remained indefinitely suspended from the list). The labor department was not pleased by such misrepresentations and, in what was described as "an unusual move," publicly released a letter strongly criticizing the company's "no-sweat" claims. California's labor commissioner, appointed by a governor hostile to unions, also objected to Guess's contention that it was in compliance with fair labor standard laws.[19]

The capacity to maintain union or living wages depends on raising wages throughout the industry. This means that activists cannot allow certain communities, states, or regions to become safe zones for the continuation of sweatshop labor. The discovery in 1995 of seventy undocumented Thai immigrants working as slaves in an El Monte, Los Angeles County, factory making clothes for major apparel makers demonstrated that for all its tinsel and glamour, Southern California has among the nation's worst labor conditions. The enslavement of the Thai sweatshop workers became an exhibit in the Smithsonian Institution; activists can create a more positive historical precedent for Los Angeles–area garment workers by winning justice for those sewing clothing for Guess.[20]

From Campaign to Movement

The campaigns against Nike, McClintock, and Guess involved local grassroots activists; immigrants', civil, workers', and human rights organizations; organized labor; religious institutions; sympathetic media; students; educators; women's groups; and sweatshop workers. Although anti-sweatshop campaigns have drawn the participation of constituencies long involved in national activism, the specific struggles have not blossomed into an economic justice movement because each struggle's participants, organizational leadership, specific goals, corporate targets, sweatshop location, and worker ethnicity and nationality appear unconnected. As a result even the most sympathetic media stories about a particular anti-sweatshop campaign fail to reference similar struggles.[21] This omission reflects the insufficient connection between anti-sweatshop groups, the absence of an umbrella coordinating institution, and most significantly the lack of a widely promoted common theme and specific, implementable agenda. Improving communication among campaigns and creating an umbrella structure can be readily accomplished; the Campaign for Labor Rights already provides up-to-the minute e-mail updates on all major sweatshop campaigns and the leaders know each other well enough to create the necessary coordinating structure. More critical is the adoption of a unified message. The movements for civil rights, women's rights, and gay and lesbian rights, and against nuclear power and American intervention in Southeast Asia and Central America lacked extensive formal communication vehicles, were loosely structured, and included activists with wildly different strategies, tactics, and visions of the world—but each of these movements had a broad, commonly accepted agenda that could be explained on a bumper sticker. To successfully overcome corporate adversaries whose global economic agenda—free trade—sounds sensible at first hearing and fits neatly on the rear of a car, activists fighting against sweatshops and for greater social and economic fairness must build a national movement around an even more powerful message: a living wage.

The living-wage agenda has already captivated the diverse strands of citizen activism toward greater economic justice; the agenda simply awaits becoming the emblem for a movement. The Nike, McClintock, and Guess campaigns were fundamentally driven by the demand that apparel workers at home and abroad receive a wage that is sufficient for them to live decently according to local living standards. The 1990s has seen the emergence of broad coalitions of community groups, labor unions, and faith-based organizations mobilizing for the passage of municipal laws requiring private employers contracting with the city to pay their employees a living wage. Such ordinances were enacted in major cities such as Los Angeles, St. Paul, Oakland, Milwaukee, New York City, Baltimore, Portland, and Chicago, and are under consideration in others. Creating a national living-wage campaign would immediately connect the grassroots activists working at the local level to broader struggles. The living-wage agenda is already the centerpiece of such nascent political vehicles as the New Party, which has played a leading role in local living-wage campaigns, and Labor Party Advocates, which is organizing in support of a constitutional amendment mandating a living wage.

The living-wage agenda is the best strategy for connecting America's blue-collar work force to the interests of foreign sweatshop workers; a movement demanding a global living wage can lead American workers to view overseas laborers not as competitors but as victims of the same free trade nostrums that have caused economic inequality to increase as the wages of unskilled workers drop worldwide.[22] Americans are more likely to support corporate pressure campaigns and become actively involved in fighting third-world sweatshops if they view raising workers' wages abroad as diminishing the corporate incentive for exporting domestic jobs. A national living-wage movement would also reframe the global economy debate and put the proponents of unrestricted free trade on the defensive; instead of getting away with championing free trade policies as a boon to third-world workers, multinational corporations would have to justify their reliance on sweatshops and their refusal to pay a living wage to the makers of their goods. At the same time, the negative connotations of being an opponent of free trade would be replaced with the positive image of being a proponent of a global living wage. A national living wage movement can rewrite the rules of global trade and bring new activists and organizations into campaigns against sweatshops in the United States, Indonesia, Vietnam, Latin America, China, and elsewhere.

The idea of a national movement for a global living wage may strike some as no less fanciful than calls early in the twentieth century for the workers of the world to unite. But the rapid growth of anti-sweatshop campaigns, broad consumer opposition to purchasing sweatshop goods, the electorate's overwhelming support for increasing the federal and various state minimum wages in 1996, organized labor's shift toward greater support of labor movements around the world, public disaffection with NAFTA's failure to bring promised economic benefits, and the increasing number of activists and organizations long involved in Central America issues who are now working to end sweatshops in the region all show the potential for channeling anti-sweatshop sentiment into a national movement for a living wage. Moreover, activists and organizations propelled sweatshops into the popular culture and consciousness with relatively minimal resources. The potential activist and financial resources for building a national living-wage movement remain largely untapped.

Just how untapped is evidenced by anti-sweatshop campaigns' capacity to succeed with far fewer resources than is contributed to a major candidate in a congressional race. For example, the US/Guatemalan Labor Education Project (US/GLEP) is a coalition of labor, human rights, and religious organizations focused on improving workers' rights in Guatemala. The coalition used a corporate pressure campaign and demonstrations in thirty American cities to support Guatemalan worker struggles against shirtmaker giant Phillips Van Heusen and against Starbucks Coffee. But the success of its campaigns has not won US/GLEP new funding from major foundations. The group's budget has remained at about $100,000 a year, enough for only 2.5 staff members. US/GLEP staffer Steve Coats and other activists working on sweatshop campaigns could accomplish much more if they had additional resources.[23]

Many anti-sweatshop activists have achieved significant results while working in less than a full-time capacity. Larry Weiss, coordinator of the Labor and Global Economy Project of the Resource Center of the Americas, used the two and one-half days a week he had available during 1995 and 1996 to speak and present a *Zoned for Slavery* video to more than eight thousand high school students in Minneapolis–St. Paul, Minnesota. Weiss's presentation shows "how the clothes we all buy and wear are made," thus personalizing students' connection to sweatshop labor and the global economy. Weiss also coordinates the Clean Clothes Campaign, which mobilizes area students and activists in support of all of the prominent garment worker struggles. Despite Weiss's ability to work only half-time on school outreach, the video and presentation resulted in more than seventeen hundred students signing up to receive regular updates about sweatshop campaigns. Imagine what a few full-time staff could accomplish! Weiss believes that teachers around the country would love to have similar presentations, but there is a need for a staffperson to train speakers and coordinate appearances for the project. Bill Bigelow, a high school social studies teacher in Portland, Oregon, uses his nonwork time to produce materials about sweatshops and the global economy for use in classrooms. Bigelow, who writes for the educational reform magazine *Rethinking Schools*, echoed Weiss in observing that "teachers are very receptive to activists coming in to talk about sweatshops. I wish more activists would make the effort." Both Bigelow and Weiss lament that although high school students are a major market for sweatshop goods, anti-sweatshop campaigns typically lack the full-time staff who could seize on schools' desire to expose students to the sweatshop issue and coordinate activists' presentations.

Staff necessary to further mobilize college students against sweatshops and for a global living wage has also been lacking. Ginny Coughlin of UNITE helped spawn the campus-based Stop Sweatshops Campaign and has been the only full-time staffperson in the country focused entirely on student anti-sweatshop mobilizing. Working with the network of student activists from the AFL-CIO's Union Summer internships, Coughlin has assisted students organizing rallies against sweatshops on campuses throughout the Northeast. Coughlin and campus activists like Patricia Campos, cofounder of Students Stop Sweatshops, have greatly increased student participation in the anti-Guess struggle and in developing the campus codes of conduct regulating the purchases of college sweatshirts, graduation gowns, and athletic jerseys made with sweatshop labor. In July 1998 student anti-sweatshop activists from dozens of universities formed the United Students Against Sweatshops to ensure enforcement of codes of conduct and to push for a living wage. Staff support could quickly double the number of campus chapters, creating the vehicles necessary to broaden national student activism against sweatshops.

The Campaign for Labor Rights (CLR) has done a remarkable job of connecting campus anti-sweatshop activists and providing students with critical advice and information; CLR has accomplished this without a field organizer. Kim Miyoshi of Global Exchange has been the country's only full-time anti-Nike organizer. Her campus mobilizing has focused on California but she has flown across the country on numerous occasions for weekend speaking engagements at colleges. Miyoshi joined University of Michigan students in handing out flyers about Nike's labor practices at the school's annual climactic game against archrival Ohio State; she then hopped on a return flight and was back organizing other constituencies the next day. Miyoshi has done the work of ten, but a full-time campus organizer for the Nike campaign would increase the extent and visibility of student anti-sweatshop activism. Campus anti-sweatshop organizers would also foster student participation in a national living wage movement.

Despite these great accomplishments with limited resources, a lack of staffing has delayed vehicles for uniting local-oriented, grassroots activists and organizations to a national living-wage movement. For example, in February 1997 the town of North Olmstead, Ohio, enacted legislation that prevented the city from purchasing or leasing goods made in sweatshops. North Olmstead mayor Ed Boyle conceived the measure to prevent his city from participating in worker exploitation, as he observed that "whether it's children making soccer balls in Pakistan or women making Gap T-shirts in Guatemala, our democracy must not support those inhumane practices. And the best way is not to buy from sweatshops."[24] Susan Cowell, an international vice president of UNITE, attended the signing ceremony for the ordinance and expressed hope that the legislation would become a national model. Lora Jo Foo of Sweatshop Watch sees the passage of such ordinances as imperative. Foo notes that the elimination of tariffs under NAFTA in 2003 and of quotas on garment imports in 2005 pursuant to GATT threatens the future of American garment manufacturing. Public entities, barred from purchasing sweatshop goods, would provide important markets for domestic producers that comply with wage and hour laws.

A critical opportunity exists to mobilize activists nationally to pass municipal anti-sweatshop ordinances. Grassroots organizing in support of laws barring cities and other public institutions from doing business in South Africa helped build the national anti-apartheid movement in the 1980s, and citizen activism on behalf of measures restricting sweatshop purchasing could have a similar impact for a national movement for a living wage. Foo sees the lack of resources as the key obstacle to a national anti-sweatshop/pro-living-wage movement: "The coalition of groups is already there, and we could run a city-by-city national pressure campaign on AIWA's model with as little as $100,000 for full-time staff. What we need is the resources to organize a worker leadership team committed to fighting a national campaign."[25] Sweatshop Watch is working to make San Francisco the first major city to adopt a purchasing restriction on sweatshops, and activists in Austin, Chicago, and other cities have expressed interest. The ability to mobilize local activists around purchasing restriction measures, however, is dependent upon new resources for staff to coordinate such struggles.

The lack of resources to capitalize on growing public opposition to sweatshops and support for greater economic fairness reflects the emergence of the global sweatshop issue seemingly overnight in the mid 1990s. The anti-Nike campaign percolated in relative quiet for more than three years before bursting into the spotlight in the summer of 1996. Even after Charles Kernaghan of the National Labor Committee exposed that Honduran sweatshops produced clothing for the Kathie Lee Gifford label, few could have foreseen that *U.S. News & World Report* would ask on its December 16, 1996, cover, "Sweatshop Christmas—Nice gift, but was it made by kids or exploited workers?" Sweatshops were suddenly no longer seen as a relic of America's past, and the Smithsonian Institution seized on the new public interest by installing an exhibit discussing "American Sweatshops from 1820 to the Present." The multiplicity of grassroots anti-sweatshop campaigns and their nonstop action so quickly broadened public awareness that the usual processes for securing resources simply could not keep up with the pace.

As organized labor's commitment to raising workers' wages worldwide continues to grow and groups formerly focused on other campaigns, such as Central America, turn toward sweatshops, the staffing for a national living-wage movement should catch up to the demand. Continued publicity about sweatshop abuses will help the movement grow. The emergence of anti-sweatshop and living-wage activism in the 1990s represents the decade's greatest contribution to the building of a new national progressive movement. The challenge is whether the historically slow process of building such a movement can overcome public and media pressure for instantaneous results as validation of a social-change activism's success. Anti-sweatshop activism as a strategy for rewriting the rules of the global economy achieved tremendous strides in a relatively brief time. Such activism contributed to the unprecedented defeat of fast-track trade authority in 1997 and has irrevocably changed public attitudes toward the Nike swoosh. These gains came more rapidly than those achieved by civil rights activists in the wake of the 1955 Montgomery bus boycott, but neither the activists nor the general public of that earlier era expected the passage of federal civil rights laws overnight. Rather the assumption was that when long-standing historical forces are challenged, the struggle can be painfully slow and rife with disappointment but activists must continue to build the base necessary for success. If today's mentality had prevailed, the civil rights movement would likely have been seen as having failed for not achieving equal rights by 1958. Activists must not become impatient for a national movement for a global living wage to emerge or succeed, but must keep working to create the base necessary for the struggle. Reclaiming America requires activists focused on local issues to join with national organizations in building this base; ensuring living wages is the best strategy for addressing the growing social and economic inequality that undermines the fabric of community life.

Part Two

Reclaiming America
through the Political Process

National Environmental Activism
and the Pentagon Redirection Campaign

Chapter 3

The New National Environmental Activism

On a beautiful June afternoon, about fifty people were crammed into the hot, airless second-floor office of the California Public Interest Research Group (CALPIRG) in downtown Berkeley. The predominantly under-thirty group included diverse races and ethnicities and was equally split between genders. Seemingly oblivious to their uncomfortable surroundings, people were involved in highly animated activities from practicing canvassing speeches to gathering literature that stood in piles throughout the office. Several were making media calls to follow up on a press conference held that morning. The event at a child care center in nearby Contra Costa County featured local child care providers urging the district's as yet uncommitted congressional representative to protect kids' health by endorsing stronger federal clean air standards. Others in the room were planning a media event for the upcoming U.S. Conference of Mayors meeting in San Francisco to urge support for stronger Clean Air Act provisions. A photograph of the activity in the office that day, which closely resembled the backstage preparations of dancers prior to performance, might have been titled "Environmentalists Acting Nationally."

The scene I witnessed at the CALPIRG office in June 1997 was repeated throughout the first six months of that year by state and campus PIRG organizations throughout the country. Sierra Club chapters were similarly involved in the day-to-day organizing tasks of phoning, outreach, meeting with editorial boards, and planning of media events. All of this effort was necessary to force the ever-wavering and untrustworthy Clinton administration to maintain its previous commitment to stronger Clean Air Act standards. From Environmental Protection Agency (EPA) chief Carol Browner's announcement of the proposed new Clean Air Act guidelines on November 27, 1996, to President Clinton's announced support for the regulations on June 25, 1997, the nation's two largest grassroots environmental groups, the PIRGs and the Sierra Club, engaged in the most impressive display of affirmative national environmental activism in recent history. Both groups successfully mobilized citizen activists previously disconnected from national environmental debates. This alienation, which translated into either inaction or exclusive focus on local issues, had prevented national environmental groups from achieving the affirmative goals expected to be implemented early in President Clinton's first term. The two groups' reliance on a national grassroots mobilizing strategy for the Clean Air Act battle was a clear break from the past and offers great hope for the movement's future.

In building national environmentalist power through field operations in local communities rather than continuing to rely on backroom deals with Beltway politicians, the PIRGs and the Sierra Club brought the confrontational tactics and people power associated with grassroots fights to the White House and Capitol Hill. National politicians were unaccustomed to seeing environmental groups use methods generally only seen in the capital when Frank Capra's 1939 film, *Mr. Smith Goes to Washington*, plays in a local theater. Critics of national organizations' overreliance on Capitol Hill lobbying were likely even more surprised to see the Clean Air Act fight fought in the field by citizen activists and organizations largely disconnected from prior national campaigns. The framing of the national campaign as a vehicle for solving local problems forged links between national and local activists that had not emerged in years. The PIRGs' and the Sierra Club's commitment to fighting the Clean Air campaign through national grassroots mobilizing won the immediate battle and created a successful new model for national environmentalism's future struggles.

The PIRGs and the Sierra Club created what I describe as the "new national environmental activism" following such activism's virtual disappearance by the early 1990s. Both groups accomplished this by pursuing strategies that fostered grassroots participation in national environmental campaigns. This participation was demonstrated during the landmark national grassroots mobilizing campaign to strengthen the Clean Air Act. While other organizations, particularly the National Environmental Trust and the American Lung Association, significantly contributed to the winning campaign, success in the national political arena requires social-change organizations to build field operations for exerting local pressure on federal officeholders. The PIRGs and the Sierra Club are the national multi-issue environmental organizations with the largest field operations and were the prime organizational vehicles for linking local activists and groups to the national Clean Air Act campaign. These two groups' capacity to mobilize people in the field was pivotal to if not determinative of the Clean Air Act victory. By creating the infrastructure necessary for reconnecting local-focused activists and organizations to the national arena, the Sierra Club and the PIRGs have built a model for national activism that can be applied to other struggles to reclaim America's progressive ideals.

Disappearing National Environmental Activism in the 1990s

During the 1980s national environmental groups saw rising membership and funding in response to public fears about the Reagan administration's anti-environmental agenda. Although attacks on environmental laws declined during the Bush presidency, it was not until the election of the Clinton-Gore ticket in 1992 that national environmental groups saw their first opening in more than a decade to proactively implement a progressive environmental agenda. Unfortunately, for reasons I detail in The Activist's Handbook, 1993 did not bring the anticipated dawning of a new environmental era. One reason was national environmental groups' failure to adopt what I describe as a "fear and loathing approach" to President Clinton and self-professed environmentalist Vice President Al Gore. When the Clinton administration began breaking its promises to environmentalists soon after inauguration day, the national groups whose membership had supported the Democratic ticket refused to publicly denounce their alleged allies or take other steps necessary to hold them accountable. Many perceived the national groups' silence as sacrificing the environmental agenda for their leadership's continued personal access to Gore and other administration officials.

The personal opportunism and reliance on inside deal making by many national environmental leaders clearly hampered the movement's progress during Clinton's first two years. But these factors obscured a deeper, systemic weakness: the national environmental groups lacked the national grassroots mobilizing base necessary to hold the Clinton administration accountable. Among what is commonly viewed as the nation's dozen top environmental groups in 1995 only the Sierra Club and the Audubon Society had an active grassroots membership base. (The PIRGs are not included on this list because of their nonexclusive environmental focus.) The remaining organizations' "membership" existed only as responses to direct mail appeals. Although Greenpeace maintained a strong field presence through its staff's participation in local struggles, the other national groups had little connection to grassroots activists or their organizations. Most national groups relied on their leadership's relationship with lawmakers and the belief that they knew what was best for the environmental movement. As a result the national environmental agenda through the Reagan, Bush, and early Clinton years was heavily dependent on close alliances between the national groups and key Democratic congressional leaders. The risks of relying on a coterie of skilled Washington lobbyists to fight environmental battles in the national political arena were obscured by the insiders' success during the strictly defensive struggles of the 1980s. When Clinton's election opened the door for affirmative national environmental campaigns, the holes in this inside-the-Beltway strategy became clear.

Some critics argued that the solution to environmentalists' national political failures lay in killing off the national groups and relying exclusively on local activists. Grassroots environmental groups were more confrontational, uncompromising, and ethnically and economically diverse than their national counterparts. But although these groups were extraordinarily effective in defeating proposed incinerators and toxic dumps in their communities, they lacked the resources and national base to win the federal environmental protections upon which their local struggles often relied. Rather than destroy the existing national environmental infrastructure, a better solution was to transform the national groups into effective grassroots mobilizing vehicles for federal campaigns.

Advocates for national environmental groups reinventing themselves as grassroots mobilizers found an unexpected ally in House Speaker Newt Gingrich. Gingrich's 1995 legislative agenda failed to achieve a Republican revolution but its anti-environment components awakened national groups from their lethargy and frustration of the two preceding years. Gingrich's program ignited fears that had arisen after the Republicans' unanticipated seizure of congress in November 1994 saw environmental groups' longtime congressional allies either defeated or losing control of committees to anti-enviro Republicans. With hostile Republicans now the insiders, the national groups' strategy had to change. Newt Gingrich had a broad social-change agenda, but one of his greatest impacts was forcing environmentalists to create a more effective and sustainable strategy for national success.

The initial impulse toward the creation of such an organizing base was manifested when the Sierra Club, the PIRGs, and other national environmental groups created the grassroots pressure necessary to defeat nearly all of the Republicans' anti-environmental legislation in 1995 and 1996. Although this effort was tremendous, it simply preserved an environmental status quo that the national groups viewed as untenable during Clinton's 1992 campaign. The question remained whether this newfound national mobilizing capacity could be used to implement a proactive agenda. The campaign to strengthen the Clean Air Act thus became a critical test.

The PIRGs: Mobilizing a New Generation of National Environmental Activists

Minnesota senator Paul Wellstone, one of the few activists to reach such high office, has observed, "I think to a certain extent that a good many of us in the progressive community have forgotten the importance of good grassroots organizing. We're going to have to do it over again."[1] No organization working on national environmental issues does a better job of the nuts and bolts of organizing and outreach than the network of local and state Public Interest Research Groups, commonly known as the PIRGs. Created in 1971 by Ralph Nader, the

PIRGs may well represent the broadest secular institutional network of national social-change organizations outside the AFL-CIO. The PIRGs consist of twenty-two state organizations that are usually based on college campuses. The student PIRGs cover eighty-four chapters in fourteen states and range in size from MASSPIRG, which includes twenty-eight campus chapters, to Florida PIRG, MoPIRG, INPIRG, and OhioPIRG, each of which includes only one. It is no coincidence that the states where environmental activism is most prevalent, Massachusetts, California, New Jersey, New York, Wisconsin, Oregon, and Washington, have the strongest PIRGs. In 1983 the state organizations saw a need to expand their national presence and created the Washington, D.C.–based U.S. PIRG. Unlike most social-change organizations with a national agenda, the PIRGs' power rests with the state and local affiliates. The national office implements the national agenda of the local and state chapters rather than directing from above. The national office also organizes a PIRG presence where no state chapter exists; PIRG staff mobilizes on national issues in forty states and 350 congressional districts and will cover every state by the end of the year 2000. The PIRGs work simultaneously on local, state, and national campaigns. The organization applies the same hard-hitting pressure tactics in each arena, refuting the common notion that the state and national political spheres require a nonconfrontational approach.[2]

The PIRGs are routinely excluded from commentary on national environmental politics and from rosters of national environmental organizations. This omission is perhaps attributable to the PIRGs' focus on such issues as campaign finance reform, consumer protection, and homelessness in addition to their primary emphasis on the environment. The PIRGs may also be excluded because they fail to satisfy the negative stereotypes often attributed to national environmental groups. For example, the PIRGs have no affiliated political action committee that makes candidate endorsements or campaign contributions to politicians. The group has thus never closely aligned itself with Democratic Party officeholders and is zealously nonpartisan. The PIRGs strongly opposed NAFTA, GATT, and related free trade agreements, and their staffs receive none of the high salaries and lavish benefits that have drawn criticism to other national organizations. The PIRGs are also the only national environmental group that is primarily composed of student activists. This automatically leads some to discount their influence in the rough, tough, and purportedly adult world of the Beltway. Finally, the PIRGs have consistently demonstrated that grassroots activists are eager to work on national issues if the proper vehicle exists. The PIRGs have become this vehicle for thousands of activists, thus undermining critics who view organizations working on national campaigns as hopelessly wedded to insider rather than grass-roots politics.

The PIRGs have contributed to building national environmentalism's new grassroots mobilizing capacity in three key ways. First, the PIRGs lead all groups in recruiting new environmental activists. Second, the PIRGs are the chief providers of training and skills for environmental activists and continuously groom new generations of environmental leadership. Third, the PIRGs have consistently demonstrated the abil-ity to mobilize their base. The PIRGs' base not only provides the large number of postcards, phone calls, and letters necessary to influence state and federal officials, but after graduation their campus activists become part of the national constituency that will mobilize to hold presidents and other politicians accountable for their commitments on environmental issues.

Activist Recruitment

A national grassroots environmental campaign requires broad activist participation. College campuses are among the best places to recruit new activists and the PIRGs' campus chapters provide the perfect ve-hicle for attracting activists to environmental causes. Gene Karpinski, executive director of U.S. PIRG since its formation in 1984, has ob-served that "students are particularly receptive to the environment, and their interest has become more intense" over the years. Because most students at four-year universities have little connection to polit-ical struggles in the surrounding community, there is often great in-terest in helping national campaigns. Maureen Kirk of OSPIRG (Ore-gon's PIRG) observed that her chapter's student volunteers "want to make history in some way. They are interested in working on issues discussed on the front page of the *New York Times*."

The PIRGs clearly do the best job of any national social-change organization in providing students with a means of entering the activist world. They accomplish this in four ways. First, their campus chapters are accessible to students. Second, the PIRGs are continually involved in a variety of local, state, and national campaigns. These struggles offer students the immediate opportunity to directly participate in an activist struggle. Despite politicians' rhetorical calls for increased volunteerism, it is often difficult for social-change groups to productively use volunteers. Effectively harnessing volunteer resources requires close staff supervision and the development of work plans that involve specific tasks so participants can have a sense of accomplishment. The PIRGs offer students such diverse opportunities as working on state ballot measures, distributing and coordinating petition drives, and planning and carrying out creative media events. These activities are necessary to sustain the volunteer participation of college students, who have many other demands on their time.

The campus chapters recruit potential environmental activists by holding General Interest Meetings (GIMS) at the start of each semester. Organizers make a major effort to build the buzz on campus by widespread leafleting, tabling, and by inviting a prominent speaker; for example, CALPIRG's winter 1997 meeting at UCLA featured former Democratic Party presidential nominee Michael Dukakis. During the GIMS for winter/spring 1997 most chapters attracted forty to seventy attendees, with as many as ninety-one at the Indiana University event. These initial information meetings ultimately produced fifteen to thirty core volunteers per chapter. When the PIRG core volunteer total is added for all chapters, the early 1997 recruitment drive nationally produced more than four hundred new volunteers. Any social-change organization would be thrilled to have such a large infusion of new activists. The PIRGs' success at campus recruitment should lead other national social-change campaigns to commit resources to campus outreach. Cesar Chavez's United Farm Workers movement maintained a daily information and recruitment table on campuses through the 1970s and attracted students to both volunteer and become full-time organizers for the cause. One of the first innovations of the AFL-CIO's new leadership team was to enroll interested students in the Union Summer organizing program. When the students returned to school they built campus support for anti-sweatshop campaigns and other union issues. Both labor and peace activists lamented their movements' earlier failure to use the campuses to recruit new generations of activists. The PIRGs are ensuring that the national environmental movement does not make a similar mistake.

Finally, the PIRGs provide activist opportunities for students who must earn money rather than volunteer. The PIRGs' canvassing program, as the omnipresent posters on telephone poles suggest, enables students to earn money working for the environment. Canvassing programs are an excellent method of distributing campaign information and often represent an important share of an organization's budget. In addition to enhancing student recruitment, the PIRGs canvassing operation identifies supporters in the target areas who are then called upon to contact legislators or otherwise support campaigns. The PIRGs' ability to mobilize these supporters, known in PIRG terms as citizen activists, demonstrates how student participation in social-change campaigns also expands the struggles' off-campus base.

To measure canvassing's role as an activist recruitment vehicle I surveyed twenty-nine new canvassers for CALPIRG's summer 1997 Campaign to Save the Environment program. Only six reported previous activity in an environmental group but nearly all expressed interest in working on local, state, and national environmental campaigns. When asked about the effectiveness of environmental groups, many saw grassroots mobilizing as essential for environmentalists to overcome their big-money opposition. Responses included: "The effectiveness of the campaign depends on how well the voice of the voters outweighs special-interest money"; "if an organized portion of the public speaks, the government must listen"; and "if no environmental groups pushed politicians, nothing would get done." Not a single response identified lobbying as an effective strategy for environmentalists. The survey, along with my interviews with PIRG staff, demonstrated that the PIRGs' canvassing operation provides a critical point of entry for new environmental activists. It also instills in canvassers the recognition that grassroots mobilizing is the key to success. PIRG has more than a thousand canvassers nationally each summer and many PIRG staff members started working on environmental issues through canvassing. Unlike direct mail, which many national environmental groups use to raise money, canvassing is a fundraising tool that also builds a national grassroots mobilizing base for environmental campaigns.[3]

Training and Developing
New Environmental Leadership

In addition to recruiting new environmental activists, the PIRGs also
train and develop environmental leaders. The PIRGs likely spend more
time than any other organization in providing students with skills in
organizing, outreach, and political strategy. Skilled activists are valued
in any campaign and are at a premium when mobilizing citizen activists and organizations in national struggles. As was discussed in chapters 1 and 2, the decentralized models for national activism evidenced
in the anti-Nike and McClintock campaigns give grassroots activists
broad responsibility for carrying out campaign tasks. This requires
grassroots activists and leaders to operate without outside supervision
and to make the smart, spontaneous judgments endemic to activist
campaigns. By teaching students how to be effective activists the PIRGs
greatly increase the prospects for successful grassroots mobilizing for
national environmental campaigns.

The PIRGs develop new environmental leadership by creating
employment opportunities that enable the experienced activists they
have trained to continue environmental advocacy after graduation.
PIRG leaders have typically risen through the group's ranks. Maureen Kirk, executive director of OSPIRG, began as a campus volunteer and was a staff member prior to assuming her current job. She
noted that it is "remarkable how many students I have worked with
who have gone on to do environmental or other social-change work."
Seth Levin of WASHPIRG has worked for the organization in five
different states on a wide range of state and national environmental
issues. Andy MacDonald became a canvasser with COPIRG after
graduating from college, moved on to a job as a student organizer for
MASSPIRG, and subsequently became its executive director. U.S.
PIRG's national field director, Margie Alt, followed a similar route before reaching her current position, and national campus organizing
director Andre Delattre had his initial political involvement as a volunteer with the PIRGs. The PIRGs offer such a wide variety of jobs—
trainers, field managers, lead field managers, canvass directors, telephone outreach project directors, and many more—that the organizations can retain top student volunteers interested in a permanent
PIRG position.

The PIRGs have created a broad pool of experienced environmental activists capable of mobilizing local activists and their organizations. In the many states and critical congressional districts where no PIRG chapter exists the organization uses roving field directors to help mobilize grassroots pressure. By developing the leadership necessary to mobilize the infrastructure of local and state groups in much of the country the PIRGs enable the Sierra Club and other groups to target their resources in the remaining areas. This coordination makes a huge difference in struggles like the Clean Air Act campaign where environmentalists face particularly well financed, nationwide opposition.

The PIRGs Can Mobilize Their Base

In addition to actively recruiting new environmental activists, providing necessary training and organizing skills, and creating a nearly national base of environmental leadership, the PIRGs play a vital role in national grassroots environmental campaigns because of their demonstrated ability to mobilize their base. A mobilizable constituency base is essential for a social-change struggle to prevail in the national political arena. Although grassroots pressure does not guarantee victory, its absence ensures defeat. Unfortunately, the power of money to influence politics obscures this critical point. Beltway lobbying and big-money campaigns have led many citizen activists and organizations to flee the national political arena on the assumption that money will prevail regardless of grassroots pressure. In some cases money does guarantee victory. In many others, however, it does not. It is the latter cases that have caused Minnesota senator Paul Wellstone and other elected officials to openly lament the lack of grassroots organizing by progressives on national issues in the 1990s.

The PIRGs have consistently demonstrated the capacity to create grassroots pressure around local, state, and national issues. Their ability to organize and mobilize diverse constituencies is evidenced by their grassroots organizing achievements during the first three months of 1997, when their top priority was the Clean Air Act campaign. During a period of frenetic activity on the Clean Air campaign, the PIRGs' mobilizing capacity enabled the group to also: gather forty thousand postcards to congressmembers urging support for PIRG-initiated federal toxic Right-to-Know legislation; arrange a national lobby day on which PIRG staff and students visited more than 270 congressional offices; organize a coalition of more than four hundred labor, health, and community groups to endorse the Right-to-Know measure; collect more than 12,500 signatures and sixty legislative co-sponsors for a MASSPIRG-drafted state Citizens' Right-to-Know measure, and obtain a majority of the legislature's endorsement for MASSPIRG's Updated Bottle Bill; submit 1,000 postcards and 150 personal letters from citizen activists to the Colorado legislature opposing anti-environment bills, and organize opposition to industry efforts to weaken COPIRG's victorious November 1996 ballot initiative protecting three million acres of Public Trust Lands; win passage of a PIRG-drafted radon testing law in New Jersey (NJPIRG); lead the effort to maintain a state tax that funds pesticide education in California (CALPIRG); send a delegation headed by WISPIRG to the House Education Committee to successfully derail a proposed campus gag rule designed to limit PIRG advocacy; and use such creative tactics as a mock toxic spill to generate more than twelve hundred postcards supporting the federal toxic Right-to-Know measure (OSPIRG). When these and other activities are added to the PIRGs' tremendous organizing and outreach efforts on the Clean Air Act during the same period, the organization's capacity to mobilize people in support of national environmental campaigns is clear.

Two features somewhat unique to the PIRGs have enhanced their staff's connection to their volunteer base and hence the groups' mobilizing capacity. First, the campus PIRGs are funded by a per-student fee added to the cost of tuition. The PIRGs' funding is then conditioned upon their retaining at least majority support in campuswide votes by their constituency. If PIRGs are failing to attract students or are working on issues students do not care about, the chapter— particularly in an era of ever-rising tuition costs—will lose majority support for continued funding. The PIRGs thus have a strong interest in ensuring that their student base is motivated and energized; such students mobilize and often convince others to get involved. I expressed concern to PIRG's national field director, Margie Alt, that the PIRG funding plebiscites forced the groups to divert resources from activist campaigns to winning campus elections. Alt thought the PIRGs greatly benefited from the plebiscites because they showed that students supported the groups' work and helped ensure that the PIRGs paid close attention to their constituencies' needs. Based on the PIRGs' success, such strict constituency accountability would likely enhance the mobilizing capacity of most social-change organizations.

The second unusual feature of the PIRGs that facilitates their national mobilizing capacity is their unified approach to local, state, and national environmental issues. The PIRGs fuse local, state, and national activism in two key ways. First, each state PIRG divides its work program into a number of national, state, and local campaigns. The relative emphasis is determined by a state's political context. Seth Levin, who has worked for PIRGs in five states, found that the Colorado chapter (COPIRG) faced so many major state fights that only about 5 percent of its activities focused on national campaigns. In Levin's prior experience with WASHPIRG, however, the lack of state development fights and the enormous rate of toxic pollution generated by Washington's pulp and paper industry made national campaigns to strengthen federal toxic Right-to-Know and Clean Air standards the top priorities. Oregon's OSPIRG operates where state ballot measures are common, so its work is slightly more focused at the local and state level; MASSPIRG's large number of campus chapters and its success with the state's legislature have made it and NYPIRG (whose successful campaign to defeat a proposed Brooklyn incinerator was detailed in *The Activist's Handbook*) probably the most state-focused of the PIRGs.

When a PIRG chapter is primarily focusing on local or state issues, these struggles do not separate or disconnect activists from national environmental campaigns. On the contrary, as Andre Delattre, the PIRGs' national campus organizing director, observed, regardless of the arena where they end up focusing "many students are motivated to join the PIRGs because we are part of a national network." An OSPIRG activist working in Eugene, Oregon, on a local toxic right-to-know initiative will also become active in the PIRGs campaign for a federal right-to-know law. CALPIRG focuses on many state issues but its canvassers provide those contacted with their congressional representatives' and senators' PIRG voting scorecard and a list of their votes on key environmental issues. A canvasser for WASHPIRG found himself in Bellingham, Washington, talking to a person who was very concerned about the need for federal right-to-know legislation. Instead of ignoring the conversation because WASHPIRG was primarily focused on other issues at the time, the canvasser gave the citizen activist's name to PIRG staff. A meeting was then arranged between the activist and an aide to district congressperson Jack Metcalf, who had yet to endorse the measure. PIRG canvassers regularly identify citizen activists during doorway conversations who then become active in national campaigns.

In addition to mounting simultaneous local, state, and national campaigns, the PIRGs encourage national activism by emphasizing the local impacts of national struggles. After years mobilizing environmental activists, PIRG's national field director, Margie Alt, believes that people have to see how their concern about a local problem requires a national solution before they will become active in a broader campaign. One reason that environmental activists and organizations have become disconnected from national political struggles is their belief that such efforts do not affect their own backyard. When grassroots environmental justice campaigns prevail the assumption is that national organizations played no role. But in many cases local struggles rely on federal regulations or laws won by groups like the Sierra Club in the national arena. The influence of national legislation on environmentalists' ability to prevail locally is easily overlooked. The PIRGs' unifying of environmental struggles facilitates recognition of their interconnectedness; the groups consciously explore the local impacts of national campaigns in assessing what issues and campaigns to pursue.

Building national environmental campaigns as solutions to local problems has become the chief strategic approach for many national environmental groups. This strategy best applies when an issue, like clean air or water, directly affects almost everybody. It can even be used where only a specific geographic area is involved. For example, a national campaign developed to prevent Pacific Lumber Company from clear-cutting northern California's Headwaters Forest, the world's last stand of privately owned ancient redwoods. Spurred by the late forest activist Judi Bari, Earth First! and local groups such as the Environmental Protection Information Center launched a campaign to save the ancient forest. Bari saw the potential for making Headwaters a national issue and activists throughout the country conducted protests, wrote letters, and in other ways mobilized to preserve Headwaters. The national campaign put sufficient pressure on the Clinton administration in 1996 to prevent the forest's imminent clear-cutting. The pressure forced a deal that preserved seventy-five hundred of the sixty thousand acres surrounding Headwaters, and the battle to save the remainder continues.

On the other hand, when people cannot identify with a specific geographic dispute, national grassroots mobilizing becomes quite difficult. I surveyed several PIRG staff and volunteers about the prospects for a national grassroots campaign to overturn continued threats to Western lands posed by the fiscally and environmentally destructive 1872 Mining Law. This law, which subsidizes private mining on public lands, affects Western states and areas where the PIRGs and other national groups have a weaker constituency base. The lands lack the postcard quality of Headwaters and the historic meaning and uniqueness of an ancient redwood grove. PIRG National Field Director Alt echoed other staff in wishing that a national grassroots campaign could be launched but saw this as difficult in light of the lack of direct local impacts in most PIRG jurisdictions. My survey of CALPIRG's summer 1997 canvassers confirmed this view; respondents expressed little interest in making the abolition of the 1872 law a top priority. The difficulty of mobilizing sufficiently to overturn the law on a single-issue basis has led the PIRGs to join with twenty other environmental groups in packaging the law with a total of $36 billion in similar environmentally destructive boondoggles. The bunching of environmental issues, each insufficient by itself to generate national mobilizing, under a national campaign theme, in this case the "green scissors," appears the best strategy for creating the broad citizen activist pressure necessary to prevail.

The PIRGs' New Challenge: Mobilizing Alumni

The PIRGs have created an effective national infrastructure for mobilizing students and citizen activists to overcome well-funded industry opposition and hold national politicians accountable. In 1997 the PIRGs moved to harness the skills and resources of their former students by creating a new alumni group, the State PIRG Alumni (SPAN). The group began with a list of more than one thousand former PIRG activists, and alumni events held around the country were well attended. Alumni could not only become potential donors but could become part of the PIRGs' and the environmental movement's local, state, and national mobilizing base. In the survey I conducted of the CALPIRG canvassers, twenty-two of twenty-three responded yes to the question, "After leaving school, would you be interested in engaging in environmental activism by joining a Citizens CALPIRG [i.e., nonstudent] chapter, or a similar PIRG-affiliated chapter in your home state?" There can never be too many vehicles to enlist citizen activists in national campaigns and the PIRGs' capacity to mobilize its former volunteers in national grassroots struggles should prove enormously beneficial.

The Sierra Club:
The Mainstreaming of National Activism

Unlike the PIRGs, the Sierra Club's emphasis on building a field operation that can mobilize grassroots activism represents a shift from its recent past. The nation's oldest and probably most influential national environmental organization, the 600,000-member Sierra Club went along with its national allies' strategic reliance on inside-the-Beltway deal making even after this approach failed during Clinton's first two years. As a member of the Big Ten national environmental groups, however, the Sierra Club was often unfairly associated with these groups' most elitist and politically conservative features. For example, while their Washington or New York City headquarters came to symbolize the national groups' distance from any grassroots base, the Sierra Club has long been based in San Francisco. In fact, until 1997 the Club was lodged a few blocks from my own office in the city's low-income, very grassroots Tenderloin district. Similarly, while the Natural Resources Defense Council's vocal support for the environmentally harmful NAFTA led critics of free trade to castigate the Big Ten's alleged support for the measure, the Sierra Club officially opposed NAFTA, GATT, and subsequent efforts to expand these treaties. While the national groups were continually attacked for being unaccountable to grassroots environmentalists, the Sierra Club's

democratically-elected board provided a vehicle for staff accountability to the Club's membership.

Unfortunately, the Sierra Club's more progressive politics did not
prevent it from de-emphasizing the maintaining of a strong national
field operation necessary for mobilizing its base. Until the cataclysmic
election results of November 1994 caused a shift in the group's approach, the Sierra Club relied on building connections in Washington as the route to legislative success. Unlike groups like Greenpeace,
Earth First!, or the PIRGs, the Sierra Club was closely identified with
Democratic Party officeholders and reluctant to engage in the fear and
loathing tactics against the Clinton administration that were essential
for success. Much of this may be attributable to the Club's use of an
affiliated but separate political action committee (PAC) that endorsed
candidates and solicited and made campaign contributions. On the
positive side, the Sierra Club PAC plays a critical role in supporting
proenvironment candidates and defeating those hostile to the Club's
agenda. The downside is the creation of cozy relationships with those
endorsed that inhibit public criticism of their performance.

Unlike its national colleagues, the Sierra Club had a large membership base and sixty-five local chapters that could potentially be enlisted
in national grassroots mobilizing campaigns. It took Newt Gingrich
to convince the Club to make this a priority. As the Sierra Club's national organizing director, Bob Bingaman, described it, Newt taught
us the importance of raising hell out in the states and communities.
We had walked the halls of Congress for over a decade and it wasn't
enough. The Sierra Club's official and public shift from lobbying politicians in Washington to mobilizing citizens in communities across
America is one of the most significant if largely unreported political
developments of recent times.[4]

Mobilizing Chapters for National Campaigns

How does a hundred-year-old organization shift its strategic approach?
By first addressing its problems in the field. The first step was an organizational restructuring to increase coordination between national
staff and the local chapters/membership. This was followed by Project ACT, designed to strengthen the Club's grassroots mobilizing capacity. Initiated by former Club president Robbie Cox, Project ACT

began by focusing on enhancing the organizing and base-building capabilities of six chapters and groups. The Atlantic chapter, which had difficulty uniting its urban and rural groups, began a process of developing common work programs and goals. The Mississippi chapter and El Paso group of the Rio Grande chapter focused on outreach to African-American and Latino communities that were underrepresented in the Club. The San Diego chapter's project was to better integrate its outings and conservation programs through stronger connections among the leaders of both areas. Finally, the Delaware chapter and the East River group of the South Dakota chapter were given assistance in organizational development to bolster the Club in two states where its influence was weak. Project ACT thus addressed many of the problems that had limited the Club's capacity to broaden and mobilize its grassroots base: the lack of connection between urban and rural agendas, inadequate minority participation, a split between members primarily concerned with recreation as opposed to conservation, and the lack of Club influence in various states and regions that would hinder national struggles unless remedied.

The Club's inability to fulfill its chapters' national mobilizing potential was also based on three other factors. First, unlike the PIRGs, Sierra Club chapters operated largely autonomously from national staff. This fostered independence but could also cause problems. For example, individuals more intent on self-aggrandizement than environmental protection could try to use the chapter leadership to pursue their own agendas. Or as occurred during the internal Club controversy over its stance toward commercial logging on public lands, chapters might take positions on issues that differed from those of the national organization. Such conflicts can emerge in all national groups but the Sierra Club's lack of national/local coordination increased the prospects for serious division. By increasing the connection between local chapters and groups and the national organization the Club enhanced its national mobilizing capacity.

The Club's national activism has also been hampered by the organization's political diversity. A 600,000-member organization cannot expect to have everyone agree on all issues but the Sierra Club membership has traditionally exhibited a degree of internal political differences beyond that of other environmental and social-change groups. The Club's elections of its board of directors have come to reflect these differences, as candidates nominated by the incumbent boards square off against those endorsed by a grassroots network of Club leaders organized as the John Muir Sierrans. The latter group's message—that the incumbent board preferred talk to action and compromise over strong advocacy—was countered by board members who felt that their opponents were too extreme and politically naive. Ironically, the Club's political differences are also its strength: a diverse membership base that includes both socially and culturally conservative sportsmen whose primary concern is preserving hunting and fishing habitat, and vegetarian deep ecologists who oppose the notion that humans have greater environmental rights than other species. The diversity of opinion within the membership has forced the Club to divert badly needed resources from fulfilling its mission to addressing internal conflicts.

Even when members share the same goal, the means for accomplishing it can create debate. For example, an article by Ted Williams in the Club's September/October 1996 *Sierra* magazine urged environmentalists to create coalitions with fishing and hunting groups. Noting that sportsmen assisted the creation of the Gate of the Arctic National Park, backed the wilderness status of the Adirondack Mountains, and contributed to dozens of other environmental victories, Williams concluded that "if only hunters, anglers and environmentalists would stop taking potshots at each other, they'd be an invincible force for wildlands protection." But Williams's call for unity between environmentalists and sportsmen's groups like Trout Unlimited and the Izaak Walton League brought angry responses from many Club members. The letters page of the following issue included missives from environmentalists horrified by the idea of aligning themselves with animal killers. Although the Club's membership includes more than one hundred thousand active hunters and anglers and the Club has developed an outreach campaign to sportsmen's groups in several states to bolster its clean water and habitat preservation campaigns, its tactical alliance remains controversial. Similarly, although the Club's board unanimously opposed adoption of an anti-immigration platform, dissenters among the membership forced a high-profile Club plebiscite on the issue in 1998. Although the measure failed, the controversy generated negative publicity, squandered resources, and showed that Club members often had vastly differing world views.[5]

During the early 1990s the Club's political divergences caused particularly serious unrest. The disputes centered on some chapters and
activists urging the Club to endorse far greater restrictions on commercial logging on public lands. Underlying the battle between those
supporting the "zero cut" policy and the official Club position allow-
ing restricted but continued logging was a dispute over the vision of
the organization. Many Chapter activists felt the Club should adopt
the ideal policy and use uncompromising, confrontational grassroots
mobilizing to sway the public and lawmakers to their side.

The national leadership, which was dealing with Capitol Hill on a
daily basis, was oriented toward working within the current political
reality. Club leaders and national staff were concerned that adopting
policies like "zero cut" sacrificed the Club's credibility because its Beltway allies saw such positions as politically unreasonable. The dispute
over logging policy and the Club's vision steadily intensified. Chapters
took out newspaper ads criticizing the parent organization and local
leaders were threatened with suspension for acting in conflict with Club
policies. The conflict was not resolved until two Club referendums (the
first failed) moved the membership in 1996 to adopt by a two-to-one
margin the proposed ban on commercial logging in national forests
as official Sierra Club policy. Chad Hansen, who spearheaded the winning referendum, was elected one year later to the Club board along
with two of his allies, Michael Dorsey and Betsy Gaines. Their presence on the board sent a message to grassroots forest activists that
their voice was being expressed and heard by the Club's national leadership. Although political differences among Sierra Club members remain, the Club's chapters and national office agree that grassroots mobilizing is the most effective route to realizing its goals.

Finally, until the Club shifted to its grassroots mobilizing orientation, chapters were not given adequate resources to participate in national struggles. Many chapters have a paid staffperson but their duties
are primarily administrative. Few chapters can afford to hire organizers or to produce the informational materials for national campaigns.
The Club addressed this obstacle to chapter mobilizing in two ways.
First, national staff work more closely with chapters, becoming quasi
supervisors for local and regional organizing efforts. For example, in
the Clean Air Act campaign, Kathryn Hohmann of the national staff
did not simply provide guidance from her office in Washington, D.C.;

rather, she traveled to the Northeast to work with area field staff in coordinating letters to the editor and holding a series of meetings with newspaper editorial boards. The national office also produced informational materials for chapters linking local air-quality issues to the national struggle. Chapters' receipt of technical assistance from skilled national organizers like Hohmann and of high-quality publicity materials facilitates the participation of local-oriented activists in national efforts.

The Club's national staff now regularly provides training and assistance to chapter leaders and the Club has developed literature that is specifically designed to educate and mobilize local environmentalists for national campaigns. For example, in the fall of 1997 the Club printed 300,000 postcards for a public education campaign directed toward defeating congressional legislation that would weaken the Endangered Species Act. One side of the postcard contained a standardized message. The other side included twenty different local messages targeted toward local endangered species put at risk by the legislative proposals. The Sierra Club's Florida chapter could use the materials for tabling and outreach to convince people to act to protect the local panther; Maryland residents were urged to protect the endangered bog turtle, and Minnesotans the timber wolf. By producing high-quality literature for local chapters to enlist support for national campaigns and to recruit new members, the Club's national office is fostering both local and national environmental activism. In addition, the Club's eight regional field offices and ten smaller offices now spend the greatest part of their time assisting volunteers with priority regional conservation efforts. As long as the Sierra Club's national and regional leadership is seen as assisting the growth and development of its chapters, local-oriented activists will increasingly join national campaigns.

A New Club President

The Sierra Club's shift to an outside-the-Beltway grassroots mobilizing strategy was also facilitated by the election of twenty-two-year-old Adam Werbach to the Club presidency in 1996. The election of a young, energetic activist to the leadership of the nation's largest and most influential national environmental group was covered by *News-week*, MTV, *People*, the *New York Times*, the *Los Angeles Times*, and hundreds of other media outlets. Werbach even appeared on the David Letterman show. Werbach was elected to the Club's board in 1994 after a career in grassroots activism that began with his leading a Sierra Club–sponsored James Watt recall petition drive while in the second grade. He went on to found the Sierra Student Coalition, where he spread the Club's message over the Internet and used media-savvy strategies such as selling black snow cones at fairs and concerts to publicize oil industry threats to the Arctic National Wildlife Refuge.

Actively supported for the presidency by fellow board member David Brower, Werbach's election reflected the membership's desire to return to the grassroots, principled approach to environmental protection that Brower had pioneered thirty years earlier while he was the Club's executive director. Although careful to avoid criticizing the Club's previous overreliance on Beltway lobbying, Werbach emphasized "getting people—especially young people—to understand that they can act on their beliefs and then vote." The Club must also "ensure that we can deliver hundreds of thousands of votes, hundreds of thousands of letters on a dime." To these ends Werbach enlisted rock stars from the Beastie Boys to the Red Hot Chili Peppers to build the sense of fun and excitement that is often necessary to move young people from apathy to activism. He has also been an important behind-the-scenes force pushing the Club toward devoting greater resources to fieldwork and public visibility. Werbach transformed the Club's previous image as the environmental group for the over-forty set and catalyzed young people's participation in both the Club and environmental activism. The Club's enhanced grassroots mobilizing during Werbach's tenure also confirms the importance of recruiting and developing new generations of leadership to enlist young people in national campaigns.[6]

The Planet: *Chronicling Activism*

A grassroots organization must communicate the success of its activism to its members. Prior to 1994 the Sierra Club produced a *Na-*

tional News Report of legislative updates every two weeks. The graphically dull *Report* was sent by first-class mail to members who paid a subscription fee. Although such updates motivated some members to call their congressional representatives, the *Report* was an expensive reflection of the Club's focus on Washington lobbying over mobilizing at the grassroots. Because of both budget restraints and a desire to increase the Club's activist focus, the *Report* was replaced in June 1994 by *The Planet*. Published ten times a year and available to Club members by request, *The Planet* is first and foremost a mobilizing vehicle. It highlights the daily activism that proves the difference between victory and defeat yet is little publicized either in the media or in most organizational newsletters. *The Planet's* typical headlines have included "How Club's Grassroots Activism Hit Political Paydirt," "Hounding the Opposition: Club Bird-Dogs Flush Out Eco-Frauds," "Club Flexes Grassroots Muscle on Election Day," and "Public Outrage Stalls Congress' Wildlands Grab." The newspaper offers frontline reports on the Club's grassroots struggles and details—with names, phone and fax numbers, and e-mail addresses—the ways in which readers can assist local, state, and national campaigns. Most important, *The Planet* is readable. Its photos, short paragraphs, punchy action alerts, organizing tips, and creative, two-color design gives it the accessibility of *People* magazine rather than the dense and boring tone of the typical organizational newsletter.

Why is such a publication the exception rather than the rule for social-change organizations? As I discuss in the context of nonprofit newsletters in chapter 5, internal publications are the easiest means of mobilizing a group's membership. Organizations have total control of their message and their membership is presumably the audience most interested in assisting the group's campaigns. Activists frustrated by the lack of media coverage of a campaign or issue often forget that their newsletters and magazines are a form of media; but to have an impact such organizational materials should echo the punchier, reader-friendly formats used by the popular press to attract readers. Instead, environmental groups are particularly inclined to long feature articles about their work. These are the pieces that make members feel guilty over never quite getting the time to read. Groups that have proved successful in mobilizing their members, such as People for the Ethical Treatment of Animals (PETA), whose magazine regularly profiles celebrity activists, as well as the Sierra Club, have demonstrated the benefits of inviting, activist-oriented publications.

The Planet fulfills another critical function for grassroots mobilizing campaigns by confirming that activists' local protests are the essential components of national struggles. Imagine if the protests in small towns and communities during the Vietnam anti-war movement or Central American anti-intervention campaign received no broader media coverage. This blackout could have left the activists involved with the erroneous impression that their actions made no difference and that only anti-war activities in major cities or Washington, D.C., made an impact. Activists and grassroots organizations working at the community level as part of national and even global environmental struggles also need validation that their contributions are essential. Otherwise they will stick to working exclusively on local issues such as urban sprawl, on which their influence may be greater. Because neither the mainstream nor the progressive press provides much coverage of grassroots activism, organizations must use their publications to chronicle the participation of their members in national campaigns.

The Planet's comprehensive, headlined coverage of Club members' activism in support of strengthening the Clean Air Act validated and confirmed the value of local-oriented activists to the national struggle. *The Planet* fulfills this role for all of the Club's national campaigns. In addition virtually every issue of *The Planet* includes photos of Club activists holding signs at a rally or protest. Photos of activists with canoes blocking the Minnesota state capitol to protest proposed congressional bills to expand motorized recreation, of a child holding a teddy bear whose button reads "Clean Air for Kids," and of volunteers from the Pisgah group in North Carolina tabling to gather signatures show people that their contributions are appreciated and recognized as vital to the success of nationwide campaigns. As conventional media coverage of activism has diminished, its role as validator of the efficacy and legitimacy of grassroots action must be taken up by an organization's own publications.

Finally, *The Planet* shows how the Club's local and national environmental activism has truly become national. It regularly covers struggles in states such as Texas, North Carolina, and Iowa that are not often identified with environmental campaigns. Although the Club's national membership can reflect the disagreement and dissension of any large democracy, *The Planet* shows that the flip side is an organization with a broad enough geographical base to prevail in national struggles.

Although *The Planet* represents a powerful national mobilizing tool, the Club's funding problems that began in the early 1990s have prevented the newspaper from being regularly sent to all members. According to Sierra Club executive director Carl Pope, the organization still cannot afford to send out *The Planet* other than by request. More than 20,000 of the Club's 600,000 members regularly received the newspaper, with the Club being able to distribute as many as fifty thousand copies four times a year. The Club recognizes *The Planet*'s value and in 1998 began offering subscriptions as a premium to new members to expand circulation. If an issue were mailed to all members so that people can see what they have been missing, requests for *The Planet* would rise along with an increase in Club membership likely sufficient to cover mailing costs. Best of all, Sierra Club activism would be enhanced.[7]

Forging Nontraditional Alliances

In 1996 the Sierra Club sought to broaden its grassroots base by forging nontraditional alliances. As I discuss in *The Activist's Handbook*, coalition activism increasingly requires the rounding up of the unusual suspects; working with longtime adversaries on an issue of common concern is often critical to success. The Sierra Club has sought to forge nontraditional alliances both to win local campaigns and to enlist new resources for national campaigns. In North Carolina Kathie Dixon, the Club's Clean Water Project coordinator, spent a year working with fishing and hunting groups around the region's problem with hog and poultry waste lagoon overflows. Dixon regularly attended angling "expos" where she had the opportunity to inform people about the link between their concerns and the proposed weakening of the federal Clean Water and Safe Drinking Water Acts. The result? Anglers sent more than seven hundred postcards to their governor and won a commitment of $50 million in river cleanup funds. The Club also won new allies for its national clean water campaigns.

The Club is pursuing a similar strategy with the ranchers, Native American communities, and independent prospectors of Nevada's

Great Basin. This region is directly affected by the 1872 Mining Law discussed earlier, as rivers and springs continue to dry up as the government issues permits to mining corporations eager to profit from the Law's generous subsidies. Ranchers have frequently opposed Club proposals in the West but have aligned with environmentalists to push for national mining reform. Once again the Club's willingness to work with nontraditional allies on local issues is helping to create the broad mobilizing base needed for a successful national campaign. Other potential alliances, such as working with small woodlot owners to oppose federally subsidized logging on public lands (such logging unfairly competes with private holdings), will also help end congressional support for such anti-environment policies. Marge Hanselman, conservation chair for the Lone Star chapter's Houston group, and other Club members even worked with the National Rifle Association to prevent the Katy Prairie wetland from being turned into an airport. As Ken Midkiff of the Club's Ozark chapter puts it, "The key is working with local folks to identify shared issues. Based on our experience, the more we help, the more we are sought by others being assaulted by corporate opponents. After a while, 'their' agenda and 'our' agenda become the same."[8]

Both the Sierra Club and the PIRGs have found that mobilizing local-oriented activists occurs most readily when local problems clearly require a national solution. Improving air quality is particularly difficult to address locally, as evidenced by the harm caused to New England lakes by air pollution from Midwestern power plants. The Clean Air Act campaign of 1996–97 thus became the perfect test of both groups' capacity to reconnect citizen activists to national environmental campaigns.

The Clean Air Act Campaign:
Test-Case for the New National Activism

When the Clean Air Act was amended in 1990 the Environmental Protection Agency (EPA) was required to recommend new standards for two specific forms of air pollution, ozone (smog) and particulates (soot), every five years. As it has on many other occasions involving federal regulations protecting environmental health, the EPA failed to meet the five-year deadline. The American Lung Association then sued the EPA and the court ordered the agency to act. On November 27, 1996, with the national elections now safely past, EPA chief Carol Browner announced the long-awaited new standards to protect the public from breathing smog and soot. Browner and the Clinton administration had so frequently disappointed environmentalists over the past four years that few expected new standards worth fighting for. But Browner surprised her critics by issuing new standards that although not as strong as environmentalists would ideally seek were far more stringent than anticipated. The most significant impacts of Browner's proposed standards were twofold. First, they would put hundreds of counties out of compliance with the Clean Air Act. This meant that opponents could use the time-honored claim that the regulations were yet another example of Washington meddling in local affairs. Second, the new standards would force states to impose controls on power plants whose burning of fuels caused the emissions of ozone and fine chemical particles. This would raise charges that the standards would choke off economic growth in the Midwest and other regions where such plants operated.

The Clean Air Act standards became a battle over framing the issue. If the public saw the new standards as a health issue environmentalists would prevail. Industry would win if, as in the health care debate, it could define its campaign as trying to stop Big Government from hampering the private sector's ability to improve people's lives. The campaign would revisit the philosophical battleground where corporate America had increasingly prevailed in the past decade. Whether environmentalists' new emphasis on national grassroots mobilizing would change this would soon be seen.

Winning by the EPA's Rules

Carol Browner's proposal began rather than culminated the EPA's decision making process. It would be followed by both public hearings to solicit input and a written comment period. Although these procedures simply provided cover for what would ultimately be a political decision, the Clinton administration would watch the public process to assess what action its EPA chief should ultimately take. The Sierra Club and PIRGs thus began their campaign for the new standards by seeking to mobilize citizen activists to attend four public hearings scheduled to begin on January 15. Since one of the hearings was in Boston, MASSPIRG took time out from its statewide campaigns both to testify and to get people to turn out. Although the Boston hearing occurred on a chilly winter day, MASSPIRG and Sierra Student Coalition activists, some of whom wore gas masks, combined for an outside rally prior to the event. Staff from U.S. PIRG testified at the hearings held in Chicago, Salt Lake City, and Durham, North Carolina. PIRG national field director Margie Alt also launched the organization's campaign to overwhelm the EPA with public comments supporting the standards.

The Sierra Club's national membership base put the group in the perfect position to mobilize its chapters and dominate attendance at the hearings. The Club's Illinois chapter made sure that its members arrived early for the Chicago hearing, so that twelve of the first fifteen speakers favored the new standards; by the time opponents began to speak, the media had gotten their story and left. The Club wisely emphasized speakers who personally suffered from the ill effects of dirty air. Eight-year-old Kyle Danitz told the EPA panel that he suffered from severe asthma and had to go to the hospital if he went outside on an ozone warning day. "I hate going to the hospital," he said. "They poke tubes in you. I get shots. I can't play outside. I don't understand why people pollute." Kyle's mother, Maureen, stated that her son's treatment had cost the family $75,000 in medical costs, countering industry claims that the new standards would be too expensive. In Salt Lake City, Club attendees wore blue stickers urging "Clean Air for Our Kids." Aerobics instructor Amy Spector testified with her two children, one of whom suffered from respiratory problems. She stated that "if we are going to balance costs and benefits, let us not forget all the costs attributable to breathing polluted air, such as the health care costs, absences from work and school, and shortened life spans." Howard Peterson, a member of the U.S. Olympic Ski Team, argued that poor air quality could pose a risk to athletes' health during the city's 2002 Winter Olympics. At Durham, not commonly known as an environmentalist hotbed, supporters outnumbered opponents by nearly three to one. The press only stayed for the first ten speakers, all of whom supported the new standards.[9]

The tactics of outnumbering opponents at hearings, speaking early to win media attention, wearing stickers, and relying upon people's personal stories rather than the opinions of experts or professional activists are normally associated with local, grassroots campaigns. Their use in the national Clean Air Act campaign not only proved persuasive but created the ideal counterpoint to the slick public relations campaigns of opponents. To defeat the new standards the National Association of Manufacturers organized a five-hundred-member industry coalition named the Air Quality Standards Coalition. The American Petroleum Institute hired a firm to run a scientific think tank called the Foundation for Clean Air Progress; not surprisingly, none of the scientists involved saw a need for new standards. The oil industry also created Citizens for a Sound Economy, which became widely known through its twenty-city radio blitz in March 1997 attributing increased rates of childhood asthma to "the humidity, or Mother Nature's pollen."

The January EPA hearings showed that opponents needed time for their multimillion-dollar public relations campaign to match environmentalists' grassroots support. On February 1, 1997, EPA chief Browner decided to give industry extra time by stating that the agency would ask the federal court for a two-month extension of its deadline for reviewing the standards. Browner claimed that the delay was necessary for a "thorough, fair and informed public debate." Paul Billings of the American Lung Association, whose suit had forced the standards, saw it differently, noting that "the purpose of this delay is not to invite more public participation; it is meant to increase the amount of time available for bad inside politics."[10]

While seeking to extend the comment period from mid February to mid April and the final decision until August could seem insignificant, the Clinton universal health care campaign of 1994 showed how opponents of proposals invariably benefit from delay. Campaigns relying on mobilizing people rather than media advertising especially need time to coordinate individual and organizational schedules. Delaying reform also makes it easier to convince people to retain the status quo. Recognizing that environmentalists would see the delay as

giving industry more time to shift momentum, a "White House official" told the *New York Times* that those who favor the rules "could
use the extra time to educate the public about the health benefits" at
stake. The court ultimately rejected Browner's request and granted
a delay of only a few weeks. The greatest impact of the request for a
longer delay was to remind environmentalists that their national grassroots mobilizing had to target the White House, which clearly was calling the shots.

The Sierra Club, the PIRGs, and other environmental groups thus
prepared for a long pressure campaign. Congressional hearings on the
EPA proposal began soon after Browner's request for a delay and the
Republican committee leadership was not about to let environmentalists outnumber or outorganize their industry opponents. Several committees, such as the Clean Air subcommittee of the Environment and
Public Works Committee, chaired by Oklahoma senator James Imhofe
(author of the unsuccessful "gag rule" amendment that sought to bar
any lobbying by nonprofits receiving federal funds), held hearings
dominated by industry-funded scientists and economists opposed to
the new standards. Imhofe and Representative David McIntosh (R-
Indiana) sought to use the hearings to advocate reopening the Clean
Air Act to weaken the EPA's authority to set new standards. At the
initial hearing on February 19 Carol Browner testified before a senate committee and forcefully cited the more than 270 health studies
supporting tougher clean air standards. Browner was grilled for eight
hours at the last house hearing in May and faced similar hostile opposition throughout the congressional hearing process.

The restricted, often one-sided nature of federal hearings can dis-
courage national activism. People working on local issues are accustomed to lengthy public hearings where everyone has the opportunity
to speak. The testimony may have little effect on decision makers but
people like the idea that their voices have been heard. In congress
and in many state legislatures, however, this exercise in participatory
democracy is bypassed. Environmental and public health groups were
shut out of every congressional hearing on the new clean air standards, leaving Browner to fend for herself. Rather than flee national
struggles in response to such events, activists must recognize that most
congressional hearings are simply political theater to impress the chair's

constituents or funders. The best approach is to follow the lead of activists like the Sierra Club's Illinois chapter director, Jack Darin, who
used such industry-slanted testimony to frame the campaign as a "battle of the real doctors versus the spin doctors." National campaigns
can also use video footage of opponents' conduct and assertions at
these show hearings to turn a potentially demobilizing event into a
spur to action.[11]

Congress had a potentially critical role in the clean air campaign because a 1996 law gave it the power to reject Browner's regulations by
a majority vote in both the house and the senate. President Clinton
could veto this rejection and congress could then override this veto
by the customary two-thirds vote. Although clean air opponents would
be unlikely to muster sufficient votes to override, even the prospect
of congressional majorities opposing the regulations would cause Clinton to preemptively weaken them. Environmentalists thus had to both
pressure the White House and win commitments of support for the
new standards in congress.

By the end of February opponents' arguments against the standards had become so absurd that their quotations became central to
environmentalists' own mobilizing strategy. One of the most widely
used quotations originally appeared in the February 3 *Washington
Post*, in which an oil industry lobbyist claimed "people can protect
themselves. They can avoid jogging. Asthmatic kids need not go out
and ride their bicycles." Another favorite was from a spokesperson
for the American Automobile Manufacturers Association, who claimed
when the standards were announced that "the effects of ozone are
not that serious. A temporary loss in lung function of 20 to 30 percent
is not really a health effect." The greatest inspiration for supporters,
however, came from the Citizens for a Sound Economy radio ads run
on eighty stations in twenty cities. The ads were a response to Sierra
Club radio spots and the one run in Chicago typified opponents' attacks on the proposed regulations:

Voice 1:   Hey, Dad!

Voice 2:   Hi, son. How's the new job?

Voice 1:   I'm worried. It's the impact those EPA air quality regulations
            will have on my job. You're a doctor. What do you make of the
            health claims of the EPA?

Voice 2:   Son, they just don't have the science to back 'em up. Even EPA's own Science Advisory Committee admits that. And the EPA won't make public its data.

Voice 1:   Really?

Voice 2:   I'm a pediatrician. Kids with asthma? Most of it's caused by bad indoor air. You know, dust mites, stuff like that.

Voice 1:   Sounds like the bureaucrats in Washington are scheming to keep their jobs.

Voice 2:   Son, air quality has been getting better the way it is. I guess they gotta have something new to work on.

Voice 1:   Well, these new regulations would drive up the price of cars, force people into carpooling, maybe even end up banning things like barbecue grills and lawnmowers.

Voice 2:   Force us to change the way we live, huh?

Voice 1:   I read in the *Sun-Times* where it could cost Chicagoans seventeen billion!

Voice 2:   Amazing, since it can't be justified for health reasons.

An announcer then gives a toll-free number for listeners to tell congress that they oppose the new regulations "because the need just isn't there."[12]

After protests from Sierra Club Illinois representative Darin and the American Lung Association against the false attribution to the *Chicago Sun-Times* (which was simply quoting an industry study claiming the $17 billion figure), one of the two Chicago stations running the ad pulled it. It turned out, however, that the ads helped the PIRGs and the Sierra Club to galvanize their constituency bases. Kathryn Hohmann, the Sierra Club's director of environmental quality, told the Club's activists through *The Planet* that "such exaggerated claims are likely to continue, so we have to keep voicing our support for new standards." Environmental groups highlighted industry lies through full-page newspaper ads picturing a man with a long nose who was identified as Pinocchio. Titled "It's the Same Old Fairy Tale . . . ," the ads highlighted the history of "polluter exaggerations and halftruths," and concluded with the theme that "Air Pollution Kills. And that's no fairy tale."[13] The PIRGs' monthly publication for their staff and core volunteers, the *News*, repeatedly urged chapters to overcome the "Dirty Air Lobby" by "setting the record straight." The PIRGs door-to-door canvassing materials surrounded generous quotations

from industry denying the health impacts of soot and smog with pic-
tures of bellowing smokestacks. The PIRGs' state focus came in handy
when industry sought to build the opposition's momentum by winning
state legislative resolutions against the clean air standards proposal.
NMPIRG director Jeanne Bassett organized doctors and health officials
to defeat such a measure in New Mexico, and although MOPIRG's
similar organizing proved unsuccessful in Missouri, the effort also
brought more local-focused activists into the national campaign.

CALPIRG, based in the nation's smoggiest state, joined with a coalition of celebrities and environmentalists in a "Hearses on the High-
way" event to focus attention on the health risks of smog and soot.
Using a caravan of a hearse, five limousines, and an electric car during morning rush hour, the event received widespread television and
radio coverage. In a brilliant twist I have not previously encountered,
the coalition got two hosts to conduct their morning radio shows from
inside the limos. Every national social-change campaign could probably
figure out an event that would attract the typical "merry prankster"–
type morning show host to provide lengthy and sympathetic coverage
of the cause. The hearse became an even more apt metaphor when
it was learned soon after the event that the National Association of
Manufacturers had found a new ally in its battle to defeat the new
standards—coffin makers.

During the spring the campaign had two major phases. The first
was generating postcards and letters for the EPA public comment period. Environmentalists not only succeeded in producing far more responses than their opponents did but EPA's Carol Browner told Gene
Karpinski of U.S. PIRG that the Clean Air Act campaign generated
"more public comments than anytime in history." Like the EPA public hearing process, the public comment period largely functioned as
another cover for what would ultimately be a political decision directed
from the White House. But environmentalists had little choice but to
actively garner support for both administrative procedures. The Clinton administration would have responded to their failure to get people to turn out at the hearings or submit massive numbers of public
comments by severely weakening if not killing the regulations. By prevailing in the EPA's administrative processes environmental groups deprived the president of his easiest escape route.

Capitalizing on Earth Day/Mother's Day

The campaign's second objective during the spring was to build public pressure for the new standards. Three critical strategies were used.
First, both the Sierra Club and the PIRGs capitalized on the media's
heightened interest in environmental issues as part of its May Earth
Day coverage. The Sierra Club's strategy was based on the distribution of thousands of double postcards at Earth Day events. The theme
of the cards was "Let's Protect Our Kids' Health and Natural Heri-
tage." One card was addressed to President Clinton and urged him to
stand up to industry pressure and adopt the new clean air standards.
The other card was to a local official and in most of the country also
focused on clean air except where a particular pressing local issue was
at stake, such as cleaning up San Diego beaches or improving hog farm
regulation in Oklahoma. As previously described in the context of the
Club's Endangered Species postcards, the materials represented the
Club's effort to mobilize grassroots activists in national campaigns by
also assisting local fights. Sierra Club members in Los Angeles collected five hundred postcards to Clinton and California governor Pete
Wilson at a booth during the pre–Earth Day Eco-Expo. Two hundred
Utahns held an Earth Day rally on the steps of the state capitol and
the chapter soon presented five thousand postcards to the state's governor urging him to support the new standards. In Aberdeen, South
Dakota, Club members recruited forty-five volunteers who delivered
eight thousand postcards supporting cleaner air. The Club's New York
City chapter joined with a South Bronx environmental health children's group to bring fifty kids to enjoy a New York Mets double-
header and advertise support for cleaner air. Wearing shirts with the
message "Clean Air for Our Kids" and holding Sierra Club banners,
the kids took the field between games to be photographed with the
team's mascot, Mr. Met. Hundreds of fans signed postcards while thousands in the stands saw the clear connection between children's health
and cleaner air. In April and May Club members in more than fifty
cities distributed more than a quarter million of the postcards and the
Club supplemented this effort by running pre–Earth Day radio ads
in twelve cities.

Sierra Club activists who spent the weekend tabling at supermarkets or in front of hardware stores, who attended rallies and hearings, or who spent hours on the phone recruiting other volunteers found their efforts chronicled and highlighted in *The Planet*. From January to September 1997 every issue of *The Planet* focused on the Club's clean air campaign and the individual activists and chapters who make such efforts succeed. Club members reading *The Planet* were continually provided with phone numbers to call, addresses to write to, and a list of events throughout the country where their participation was crucial. *The Planet* covered the clean air struggle like a political campaign, only the actors were not politicians but Club activists and staff members. Since the national media was not covering local actions, *The Planet* enabled activists to see their individual labor as part of a coordinated national struggle. *The Planet* clearly became the newspaper not of an organization but of a movement, and its advancement of the clean air story in every issue fostered the local/national connection that was at the heart of the campaign.

The PIRGs' combination Mother's Day/Earth Day events coincided with the State PIRGs' May 5 launching of their Summer of 1997 Clear the Air campaign. On Mother's Day (May 11) U.S. PIRG and the Sierra Club coordinated a news conference across from the White House. The event featured mothers of children with asthma and the signing and delivery of a five-by-seven foot Mother's Day card to the White House. The card was signed by mothers and kids urging the President to support the clean air standards and was accompanied by fifty thousand Clean the Air postcards collected by the PIRGs. The PIRGs and the Sierra Club collected more than one hundred thousand such postcards using the type of grassroots activism seldom seen in national campaigns. For example, OhioPIRG's Earth Day events included a Clean Air for Kids day at a Cleveland elementary school. Not only did every child in the school write a letter to the president urging him to support cleaner air but the students had all created homemade Clear the Air posters for a parade. The parade was headed by a gigantic OhioPIRG banner, and cheers included the innovative "two bits four bits six bits, a dollar. All for clean air stand up and holler!" Showing how federal elected officials can facilitate grassroots participation in national campaigns, U.S. PIRG had filmed a video of area representatives Dennis Kucinich and Lewis Stokes commending the students on their efforts. During the filming Kucinich agreed to author a letter to President Clinton urging him to support the new standards; urging other representatives to sign on to Kucinich's letter became the chief goal of the PIRG's congressional pressure campaign.[14]

Tombstones, Barbecues, and the PIRG Canvass

The campaign's second goal was visually demonstrating the groundswell of public support for clean air. The PIRGs' May media events included press conferences in front of gas stations and other corporate offices with people dressed up with Pinocchio noses, sparklers, and barbecue skewers. The events not only highlighted industry lies but spoofed opponents' claims that the new regulations would make barbecues a crime in America. As anti–clean air forces sought to highlight this issue by having the Michigan legislature pass a resolution in support of local barbecues, the Austin, Texas, U.S. PIRG staff held a barbecue media event in front of talk-show host Jim Hightower's radio station. The message: Texas is the barbecue capitol of the world and people here see no threat in the clean air rules. The PIRGs also helped kick off the "Tombstone Tour" sponsored by the National Environmental Trust. The ten-foot-tall tombstone symbolized the tens of thousands of Americans who die prematurely because of smog and soot air pollution, and is the type of innovative prop increasingly essential for winning television news coverage. MaryPIRG and other clean air supporters achieved major coverage at the tour's start in Annapolis, Maryland, and the PennPIRG tombstone event won a front-page story and photo. The tour's other stops in Virginia, North Carolina, New Jersey, New York, and Connecticut amply demonstrated that this was truly a national campaign requiring the participation of grassroots environmental activists in virtually every state.

The initial tombstone tour proved so successful that it became a confrontational as well as media coverage– and crowd-generating tactic. It was used by U.S. PIRG, the Sierra Club, and the National Environmental Trust to protest outside a Washington, D.C., hotel where President Clinton was addressing the Business Roundtable. Its appearance next to House Speaker Newt Gingrich's Atlanta, Georgia, office brought an article in Gingrich's hometown paper—the *Marietta Daily Journal*—with a picture of PIRG's Atlanta canvassing director standing beside the tombstone. When the tombstone appeared at CALPIRG's protest during Vice President Al Gore's speech to the U.S. Conference of Mayors meeting in San Francisco, the event received both national television coverage and a story in the *Los Angeles Times*. The *Times* described the protest as the largest at the conference.[15]

On May 22 U.S. PIRG coordinated a national lobbying day for the clean air standards. After PIRG members met with staff in more than forty offices, the activists learned that congressional staff were hearing more from industry opponents than from constituents favoring the standards. The reason for this disparity was that multiple industries were contacting representatives daily about the issue. Big business, small business, the farm bureau, and the petroleum and pollution-creating industries whose front-groups were discussed above had all made defeating the regulations a top priority. Congressional staff reported that it was critical for activists to directly contact representatives while they were home for the two-week Memorial Day recess. As it turned out, sentiment outside the Beltway was so strong for the new standards that some representatives contacted PIRG chapters to set up meetings to discuss clean air. In Tallahassee, Florida, where Florida PIRG had made Representative Allan Boyd a prime target of canvassing and leafleting, the congressman invited PIRG staff to a meeting and urged them to bring "as many people as you'd like." A Michigan representative visited the PIRG canvas office on her first day home. In Connecticut two ConnPIRG canvass directors were handing out Clean the Air flyers at a Memorial Day parade when they noticed Republican representative Chris Shays on the route. The activists tracked him down as he exited the grandstands and asked him what they should tell his constituents about his stand on the issue. Shays responded that they should tell them that "they won't be able to drive their cars"; Shays subsequently agreed to support the new standards minutes before a tombstone tour press conference in front of his office was about to begin.[16]

The period beginning with the Memorial Day recess truly showed the great value of canvassing in mobilizing national grassroots campaigns. PIRG canvassers were perfectly positioned to criticize a congressmember's clean air stance to hundreds of that member's constituents every night, and representatives understood and often resented the PIRGs' power to spread the word. Representatives often learned about the PIRGs' canvassing message in unconventional ways. In Montana MontPIRG canvassers signed up Senator Max Baucus's (D-MT) mother as a member; she promised to call her son and tell him to support clean air. Florida PIRG's canvassers signed up Representative Bill Young's (R-FL) cousin, who promised to urge cousin Bill to support the new standards. Senator Carol Mosely-Braun of Illinois came home for dinner one night and found her son at the table with material dropped off earlier by an Illinois PIRG canvasser. The senator praised the PIRG's creativity for lobbying her son to lobby his mother. But the best canvassing success was achieved by MaryPIRG's Baltimore field manager, Lisa Dalsimer. While canvassing in Takoma Park, Maryland, Dalsimer was greeted at one door by EPA chief Carol Browner. Browner joined MaryPIRG and told Dalsimer that "it's all about you guys in the field. You're the ones who are really making a difference."[17]

Browner's comments were not simple political flattery. National grassroots mobilizing is not only effective because it puts the fear of electoral retaliation in the hearts of politicians. In addition such mobilizing enables elected officials to explain to their funders why they have no choice but to subordinate campaign contributions to the popular will. Since most federal elected officials will side with money whenever feasible, grassroots mobilizing makes it unfeasible. Politicians acknowledge this. OhioPIRG did a huge tombstone press conference in front of Representative Sherrod Brown's (D-OH) district office. A PIRG canvasser built a big wooden fence and a skit was performed in which the figure playing Brown was shown "on the fence" while canvassers dressed as industry lobbyists in three-piece suits stood on one side of the fence and others with face masks and asthma inhalers were on the other side. Brown's staff responded to this display by saying that this show of grassroots support was exactly what the congressmember needed to see; she expressed regret that Brown did not witness it firsthand. Senator Jack Reed (D-RI), a strong clean air supporter, implored PIRG canvassers to keep working despite hot weather and often discouraging campaign developments, since "without your work, this fight would have been lost a long time ago." Several other congressmembers emphasized that industry's $20 million opposition campaign could only be overcome by visible national grassroots outreach and mobilizing.[18]

A Truly National Campaign

In addition to capitalizing on media interest in Earth Day and generating visible grassroots support for the new standards, the campaign's third objective was to establish truly national support for the new standards. This can prove an insurmountable obstacle for national grassroots campaigns, as it requires outreach and organizing in southern and rural areas where social-change organizations are less present and have fewer resources. Establishing that the clean air standards had nationwide support was particularly important to offset opponents' charges that the proposals were elitist attacks on American values. To bolster the campaign's southern support, the PIRGs' peripatetic national field director Margie Alt visited the region in early June. Both Alt and PIRG southern states field organizer Robert Pregulman focused on Al Gore's home state of Tennessee. PIRG's Nashville canvassers used a letter-writing campaign to state daily newspapers to get their message out, and Pregulman had an op-ed published in the *Chattanooga Times*.

As soon as such letters or editorials appeared, as they did in papers across the nation, the PIRG field network immediately sent them to U.S. PIRG, which instantly hand-delivered the clippings to every Capitol Hill office and all White House decision makers. By heavily emphasizing Tennessee, Florida, and quasi-southern states such as Virginia and Texas, the PIRGs demonstrated to Washington decision makers that the clean air standards had strong support outside the Northeast and West Coast. When Ohio's Republican governor, George Voinovich, became a leading opponent of the standards, the PIRGs countered by asking Ohio representative Dennis Kucinich to be the first signer of the congressional letter to Clinton urging support for the EPA proposal. OhioPIRG and the Clean Air Trust also announced at a May 20 press conference that a poll found 80 percent of Ohioans supporting stricter clean air standards. The results undermined the governor's opposition to the standards, leaving him to claim that he "doesn't make decisions by polls."[19]

Winning rural America's support for stricter clean air standards would seem easy. Farming areas do not include the pollution-spewing plants targeted by the new standards but have suffered environmental damage from these health-endangering facilities. But industry opponents of social change can cleverly distort even the most obvious issue. Citizens for a Sound Economy radio ads run in North Dakota, Montana, rural Pennsylvania, and agricultural regions in other states stated that it "used to be that a farmer's worst enemy was the weather. But these days it seems to be the Environmental Protection Agency." The reason? The new standards seek to reduce "fugitive dust," which comes from "unpaved roads, agriculture, Mother Nature herself. . . . I suppose the EPA's gonna tell us that we can't plow on dry, windy days. Or that we have to pave every road." Such ads helped to undermine clean air support in areas that so distrusted Big Government that even the effort to reduce pollution became part of a nefarious plot. In the Amish country of western Pennsylvania, the PIRG's Philadelphia office had succeeded in winning support for the standards from the local 4-H Clubs. The 4-H Club coordinator ran a story on PennPIRG's campaign in the group's newsletter and included a sample letter to the local congressperson urging him to support the standards. After the newsletter was distributed, 4-H Clubs from around the state made angry calls to the coordinator for supporting EPA's attempt to regulate dust and plowing. The coordinator asked PennPIRG why they had not told her how "agriculturally unfriendly" the Clean Air Act was. Although PIRG staff tried to convince the coordinator that the radio ads were lies, she insisted that the 4-H Clubs be removed from the list of clean air supporters.[20]

Environmental groups tried to counter the misreading rural ads by holding a Capitol Hill press conference with congressmembers and two North Dakota farmers. This strategy was limited, however, by the groups' lack of access to rural residents. Because the low density of farming areas makes a PIRG canvass unfeasible and environmental groups lacked the resources to run rural-oriented ads of their own, rural Americans got most of their information about the Clean Air Act from industry. As a result potential allies for stricter standards became staunch opponents. Many rural congressmembers were conservative Republicans whose anti-environmental records could have led them to oppose the standards under any circumstances. But industry's $20 million campaign was clearly beginning to pay benefits. With Clinton and Gore still silent on the standards and EPA chief Browner left on her own to battle against virtually every other agency in the administration, environmental groups had two courses of action: first, to continue winning support from every congressmember's district and hometown newspaper in the country, and second, to raise the political stakes so that traditional supporters of the environment would not remain cowed into silence by the industry campaign. The PIRGs' *Electric Update*, its weekly campaign report for the internal use of field organizers and canvassers, reported on May 30 that the polluter lobby representatives were said to be "icing the champagne in anticipation of a major cave-in (crafted to look like a 'win-win compromise,' of course) by the White House with little congressional opposition." With the Clean Air Act standards in jeopardy environmental groups focused on the politician whose silence had proved most significant. The time had come for Vice President Al Gore to learn that if the new standards were going down, they would be joined by his presidential aspirations.

Where's Al Gore?

It is disappointing but not surprising that the broadest affirmative national grassroots environmental mobilizing in over a decade had failed through the end of May to convince President Clinton to publicly approve Browner's signing the new standards. But powerful Democratic Party interests, ranging from organized labor to Democratic mayors and governors in the Midwest, did not want the new regulations adopted. These interests influenced both Democratic house majority leader and potential presidential aspirant Dick Gephardt and the leading contender for the Democratic presidential nomination in the year 2000, Vice President Al Gore. Both of these key Democratic leaders had remained silent on the new clean air rules despite their party's use of environmental issues to win money and votes during election campaigns. Gephardt's strongest support came from organized labor, and advocating for the new standards would have antagonized

a key ally. Gore, however, had long claimed to be an environmentalist. His personal relationships with many national environmental leaders had protected the Clinton administration from attack despite repeated betrayals of environmentalists during much of its first term.
These national leaders' sacrifice of their constituencies' interests for
continuing invitations to the monthly Al Gore power breakfast came
to symbolize the inside-the-Beltway approach to national politics that
the new grassroots mobilizing strategy was designed to replace. With
Gore strangely silent over regulations that would enhance air quality,
the final exam for national environmentalists had been reached. Would
the Sierra Club and other groups follow the "fear and loathing" route
of grassroots activists and make Gore publicly responsible for the regulations or would they return to the "don't blame Al, he's our friend"
approach that brought failure in the past?

The answer was soon revealed. A May 30, 1997, unbylined news
brief in the *Wall Street Journal* claimed that pressure was mounting
on the EPA to "ease proposed antipollutant rules." Stating that the
White House "privately ordered EPA head Browner not to sign the
tough regulations until weaker measures got another look," the brief
added that "environmental groups complain Browner hasn't gotten
support from Gore, her former boss." The article then quoted U.S.
PIRG's Gene Karpinski, who noted "the silence from Gore on this
one is deafening." Karpinski's strategic targeting of Gore became the
opening salvo in what then became proponents' leading line of attack. If the White House and Gore backers downplayed Karpinski's
comments as coming from a person and group that were not close
allies, the same could not be said a few days later. On June 3 Kathryn Hohmann, the Sierra Club's director of environmental quality,
launched the Club's "Where's Al?" Northeast tour. Speaking from New
Hampshire, the site of the first primary for Gore's expected presidential bid, Hohmann told Reuters News Service that "We're here to say
'come out, come out wherever you are.' Our goal is not to bash someone, but there are some very large shoes he needs to fill" in leading
environmental causes.[21] This message from a group whose executive
director, Carl Pope, has been described by critics as an "intimate" of
Gore showed as much as anything that the Sierra Club had made a
clean break with the past. If the White House and Gore missed this

point, Hohmann and the Club would make it even more emphatically in the days ahead.

Hohmann's strategy for the "Where's Al?" tour had two goals. The first was to send a message to the presidential aspirant that his environmental credentials were on the line in the clean air campaign. With Dick Gephardt, Gore's main rival for the nomination, closely aligned with organized labor, the vice president's candidacy could be in deep trouble if he lost his environmental support. This is why the Club accompanied Hohmann's Northeast tour with radio and television commercials in New Hampshire and Iowa, the first two primary states, urging Clinton and Gore to "stand up to special interests." Hohmann's second aim was to use the Club's Northeast chapters to build local media pressure on the region's politicians to formally endorse the new standards.[22]

The "Where's Al?" tour went from May 26 to June 6. Hohmann, with the assistance of Mark Bettinger of the Club's Northeast office, joined with local Club activists in attending editorial board meetings throughout the region. In Maine the state's two Republican senators wanted to avoid taking a stand on the issue. The Sierra Club delegation, led by Susan Sargent of its Maine chapter, convinced the editorial boards of Maine's seven daily newspapers to come out in favor of the new standards. The resulting editorials in papers such as the *Portland Press Herald* on June 5 and the *Morning Sentinel* on June 11 spoke of Maine's legacy of leadership on clean air and challenged the Clinton administration and the state's undecided senators to strongly support the standards. Hohmann has noted that "congressmembers and senators read and are particularly influenced by their hometown papers." Soon after the editorials both senators endorsed cleaner air. The *Providence Journal-Bulletin* on June 5 described Hohmann's visit on the "Where's Al?" tour and quoted her as questioning why the vice president had not spoken out. The Rhode Island paper quoted numerous people criticizing the state's Senator John Chafee for seeking a weaker "compromise position" and linked the senator's future reelection chances to his support for the new standards. New Hampshire's *Manchester Union Leader* titled its June 4 story "Sierra Club Sounds Warning on the High Cost of Ignoring." The story in the prominent conservative daily exclusively quoted Hohmann's view of the clean air issue, including her criticism of New England politicians whose traditional support for environmental reforms had given way to their "playing a waiting game." Hohmann and her local Vermont delegation had similar success and moved the state's Senator James Jeffords to become the first Republican senator to formally endorse the new standards.

Hohmann's "Where's Al?" tour, which also included dozens of radio appearances and a visit to New York, fostered the national media's framing of the clean air debate as centered around Gore. The lead story in the Sunday, June 1, *New York Times*, "Top EPA Official Not Backing Down on Air Standards," had the subhead "Gore's Voice Could Be Pivotal in Contentious Battle over Tighter Pollution Rules." Noting that Gore would play a "major role—probably the decisive one—in deciding whether to back up Ms. Browner," the article reaffirmed Hohmann's argument that the clean air outcome would affect "how enthusiastically environmentalists support his presidential effort in 2000." Gene Karpinski of U.S. PIRG was given the front page of the most widely read edition of the nation's most influential newspaper to state: "Since this is the top priority issue for the national environmental community at this time, any weakening of public health protection by the White House would certainly be a huge negative for Vice President Gore that would not be forgotten." Karpinski's powerful challenge to Gore was bolstered by the *Times*'s identification of him as chairman of the Green Group, a committee of leaders of national environmental organizations. Although Karpinski did not intend to speak, and was in fact not speaking, for the Group, his quotation sent a message to the White House and millions of readers that environmentalists were united in holding Gore accountable for the outcome of the clean air fight.

The June 5 *USA Today* story on clean air, which also not coincidentally ran during Hohmann's tour, stated in its second paragraph that "what officials eventually decide could have far-reaching political repercussions, particularly for Vice President Gore." The article noted that Gore "has been particularly conspicuous in his low-key role," and quoted Paul Billings of the American Lung Association that "the silence from the White House has been deafening. There's a Gore watch out. We can't find Al."[23]

On June 22 a front-page, unbylined story in the Sunday *New York Times*, "Environmental Groups Say Gore Has Not Measured Up to the Job," further explored the issue. The article stated that "organizations that have sided with the vice president throughout his public career are now using extraordinarily blunt language to warn that 'green' voters might abandon him in the Democratic primaries in 2000 unless he delivers now." Deborah Callahan of the League of Conservation voters, who volunteered for Gore's 1988 presidential bid, found it "perplexing" that the vice president would "step back from providing the leadership" that she and her colleagues expected. Phillip Clapp of the National Environmental Trust, a group established to enhance environmentalists' national advocacy efforts, told the *Times* that "the failure of the White House to provide any leadership on the clean air standards raises real questions about what real environmental progress Vice President Gore can point to in claiming the mantle of the environmental candidate in the year 2000." The article noted that complaints about "Al Gore's silent spring" had recently moved Gore to act "behind the scenes" to ensure that the clean air decision would satisfy environmentalists. It also quoted Browner and John Adams of the Natural Resources Defense Council (NRDC) as praising Gore. Adams said, "people are angry and are upset and they want to win here, but I want to have a relationship based on the total record. This is a good man who cares about the environment—and he is a good man to have on our side."

The contrast between environmental groups' inside-the-Beltway strategy of the past and the new national grassroots activism is perfectly captured in the *Times* article on the "Where's Al?" tour. The story and tour showed that the Sierra Club, the PIRGs, and other national environmental groups have adopted the "fear and loathing" relationship to elected officials that has commonly brought success in local struggles. This approach was a sharp departure from most national group's previous approach to the vice president. In *The Activist's Handbook* I discuss how Al Gore promised during the 1992 campaign that if elected the Clinton-Gore team would prevent the issuance of a permit for an incinerator in East Liverpool, Ohio. When the administration issued the permit within three months after taking office, the only national group seeking to hold Gore accountable for the promise was Greenpeace. Greenpeace and local activists led by Terri Swearingen, who won the 1997 Goldman Environmentalist Award for North America for her work in the campaign, launched a bus tour parodying the Clinton-Gore pledge to put people first. But no other environmental group would touch the issue, presumably to avoid jeopardizing their leaders' personal relationships with Gore and what they thought would be a productive relationship with his administration. Environmental groups largely took the opposite approach toward Gore four years later, having learned that most politicians are motivated by fear of retaliation, not friendship.

But the *Times* article also showed that some national groups remained wedded to the failed strategies of the past. With Gore backed in a corner and victory in the clean air campaign near, John Adams of the NRDC threw the vice president a life raft and told the world that it made no difference if Gore sold out to industry on the clean air standards because "he is a good man" and we need to look at the "total record." Adams's view of Gore's responsibility could have undermined the Gore-focused strategy of the Sierra Club, the PIRGs, and other organizations leading the fight. Adams and the NRDC had previously adopted policies and stances opposed by other environmental groups, most prominently when the NRDC vocally supported NAFTA. Adams's apparent craving to be loved rather than feared by those in power enabled the Clinton administration and other politicians to use the NRDC for its own advantage. Because Adams and similar-minded leaders believe that their access to powerful politicians, rather than grassroots mobilizing, is the key to environmentalists' success, they look for opportunities such as the *Times* article to prove their loyalty. The new national environmental activism clearly undermines the capacity of the NRDC and like-minded Washington-based groups to broker insider deals on environmental issues.

On the same weekend as the *Times* story on Gore, opponents of cleaner air used their own tactics to pressure the Clinton administration into weakening the standards. On June 21 at its annual meeting in San Francisco, the U.S. Conference of Mayors passed a resolution opposing the new regulations. The mayor of Richmond, California, a minority community dominated by oil refineries and toxic hazards across the Bay from San Francisco, was the only official in attendance

who opposed the resolution. Many mayors did not attend the conference and some suggested that the overwhelming antiregulation vote
reflected the mayors' desire to avoid a divisive fight on a legally meaningless resolution. The vote, however, lent credence to opponents'
claims that urban America did not support and could not afford the
new standards. In a full-page "Memo to the Mayors" in the June 22
San Francisco Examiner clean air opponents warned of the EPA's "plan
to impose a $60 billion a year penalty (White House estimate) on
your constituents and economies." The ad claimed that "the EPA's not
listening to you or the thousands of others who think the plan is a
bad idea" and urged readers to tell President Clinton "to call off the
EPA. Today." CALPIRG's rally at the conference with the ten-foot-
tall tombstone representing the fifteen thousand Americans scientists claim would die from air pollution in 1997 failed to sway urban
mayors such as Detroit's Dennis Archer, who strongly opposed the
standards.

"I Think Kids Ought to Be Healthy"

On June 25 President Clinton announced his approval of virtually
every aspect of Browner's original proposal. Ironically, while the president was making his announcement at a fundraising dinner, three
members of the PIRG's Nashville canvass were outside wearing go-
rilla suits and holding signs saying "See the smog," "Hear the EPA,"
and "Speak up for Clean Air." When the organizers learned that Clinton had used the Nashville event to announce support for the standards, they changed their messages and were shown on television with
a sign reading "Thank you, Mr. President." Calling Clinton's action
"one of the most important environmental decisions of the decade,"
the *New York Times* stated that the administration credited the intervention of Al Gore, "after lobbying by environmental groups," for
resolving the "fierce behind-the-scenes battle" over the standards. Environmentalists aggressive targeting of the vice president had clearly
paid off and it was no coincidence that Gore was present for the
president's announcement and that it occurred in the presidential
aspirant's home state.

While expressing appreciation for Clinton's decision, environmentalists wisely continued to frame the administration's action as mandated by the promises Clinton-Gore made to environmentalists during their 1996 reelection drive. The national groups sent the message that they would use the same aggressive tactics to ensure that promises would also be kept involving other aspects of the environmental agenda. Environmentalists were also telling the Clinton administration that they expected assistance should congressional clean air opponents try either to overrule the EPA or to seek to block funding for implementing the standards. Both of these tactics and others were clearly on the minds of very angry clean air opponents in the aftermath of Clinton's June 25 decision. The American Petroleum Institute described the standards as "a new form of capital punishment." Rush Limbaugh interrupted his radio show to announce, "I was just handed this urgent update moments ago. President Clinton has just given in to the eco-terrorist underworld by supporting EPA's new clean air standards." Michigan representative John Dingell, the chief opponent of the 1990 Clean Air Act amendments, vowed he would "go to war" against the standards. But the angry denunciations of industry and its apologists soon gave way to political reality. The Sierra Club and the PIRGs had built such a strong national grassroots base for cleaner air that when congress returned from its August recess, neither the house nor senate leadership included the issue as a priority for the fall. Congressmembers had learned during their month at home that the public wanted the standards and that the Sierra Club, the PIRGs, the National Environmental Trust, the American Lung Association, and others had successfully overcome their opponents' $20 million advertising blitz.[24]

Reading Defeat in Victory

Some environmentalists have become so accustomed to losing in the national political arena that they find defeat in even the largest victories. In a column widely circulated in the progressive media, Jeffrey St. Clair and Alexander Cockburn argued that the new clean air standards were simply the same "smoke and mirrors" environmentalists should expect from the Clinton-Gore administration. The critics focused on two changes made to Browner's original proposal. The first was the loosening of requirements for measuring daily smog levels while the same annual smog restriction was retained. The second was giving cities and states until 2003 for smog and 2008 for soot to comply with the tougher standards prior to facing penalties. These revisions allegedly rendered the new standards the "bare minimum" required by law.

This critique has three problems. First, environmentalists always assumed that the new standards would be implemented to provide ample flexibility and sufficient time for cities and states to comply. Gene Karpinski of U.S. PIRG saw the timetables in the final proposal as "consistent with the EPA's practices in the setting of tough new standards."[25] Assume that instead of providing flexibility, President Clinton had announced on June 25 that cities and states were required to comply with the new standards within one, two, or even three years or face fines. Industry would have loved this. The short, inflexible timetable would have ensured a congressional override of the standards, resulted in a court striking down the schedule and perhaps throwing out the standards entirely, and convinced millions of Americans that the national environmental groups were the elitists that industry had portrayed. A slightly shorter timetable for the new standards would have been better but such a de minimis change to a proposal that remained essentially intact despite powerful opposition forces hardly reduces the standards to merely meeting the minimum legal requirement.

Second, St. Clair and Cockburn ascribed the environmentalists' alleged "self-spiking" of the standards to a desire to protect Gore. They support this conclusion by citing the NRDC's Adams's statement defending Gore set forth in the June 22 New York Times article previously discussed. It is clear, however, not only that Adams was alone in Gore's defense but that the Sierra Club, the PIRGs, and most other groups were prepared to destroy Gore's presidential aspirations over the clean air issue. The PIRGs have long proved unwilling to accept weak reforms, as evidenced by their opposition to the widely-supported 1997 McCain-Feingold federal campaign finance bill and other moderate state and federal campaign spending measures. The PIRGs are hardly in ideological sync with Vice President Gore, and would be the last group to claim a phony victory for clean air to help his presidential prospects.

Finally, the few critics of the clean air result ignore political reality. The final clean air standards were enacted while Republicans controlled congress and a weak, corporate-oriented Democratic president occupied the White House. The EPA estimated that compliance with the new standards would cost $6.5–8.5 billion annually, and although proponents stressed offsetting savings, elected officials and the general public increasingly oppose new federal mandates whose costs are borne by localities and states. In addition, opponents spent $20 million seeking to defeat the standards or, as a dejected spokesperson for the American Petroleum Institute put it, "trying to bring reason to the debate." These forces of reason included nearly 250 members of congress, twenty-seven governors, and more than one thousand mayors. Opponents' idea of what St. Clair and Cockburn describe as the legally mandated "bare minimum" was continuing the status quo, not imposing the most sweeping new restrictions on smog and soot in more than twenty years. Had opponents prevailed and truly bare minimum improvements resulted, environmentalists would have been forced to spend years arguing science in the courts simply for the chance to begin the EPA process anew. Given Browner's experience, it would be very unlikely that a future EPA chief would choose to issue tough standards. The final clean air regulations were stronger than anyone could have anticipated when the battle began and far better than what could have been achieved through the courts.

When conservatives won national political victories on controversial issues such as the balanced budget, tax cuts for the wealthy, welfare, or free trade, their opponents were thrown some crumbs so that they could be seen as having gotten something out of the fight. Such mitigations do not constitute victory. The timetables in the final clean air standards are the type of minor gains that Democratic opponents extracted from Bill Clinton to offset their staggering defeat.

"The Clean Air Campaign Is Just the Beginning"

The success of the national grassroots mobilizing strategy in the Clean Air Act campaign is, as Sierra Club national field director Bob Bingaman puts it, "just the beginning." As the Sierra Club, the PIRGs, and other national groups continue to emphasize the local impacts of national environmental campaigns, fewer congressional districts will elect representatives opposed to enhanced environmental protections. Bingaman believes that the "day is not far away when the House of Representatives has a consistent pro-environment majority."[26] While many elected officials' commitment to the national environmental agenda is entirely dependent on grassroots pressure, the strategy of matching local concerns to national priorities will ensure that citizen activists remain vitally connected to the national arena.

During the period of the clean air campaign the PIRGs turned in thirty-four thousand letters to the EPA in support of the PIRG-drafted federal toxic right-to-know legislation. The PIRGs did not want the measure (H.R. 1636) introduced until its chapters had laid the grassroots groundwork necessary to prevail in a national campaign. When the measure was introduced in May 1997 it had ninety-four congressional cosponsors and nine cosponsors for the companion senate bill (S. 769). Delaying introduction until broad legislative support was demonstrated also ensured that the measure would be taken seriously. Citizen activists and organizations have been fighting toxics locally for years; the federal legislation provides the perfect opportunity to connect these antitoxic activists to the national arena. The political battle around toxic right-to-know legislation involves many of the clean air themes of children's health and environmental safety that overcame industry claims about inadequate science and excessive cost; environmentalists will again have to turn to national grassroots mobilizing to overcome industry's big-moneyed opposition.

Following the clean air victory the Sierra Club immediately returned to its priority issue of federal forest preservation. The Club's campaign has focused on legislation that would eliminate continued federal funding of logging roads used by private timber companies to clear-cut national forests. Taxpayers have already provided 377,000 miles of logging roads to timber companies and spent $245 million building such roads during 1992–94. The house of representatives came within a vote of killing the logging subsidies in both 1996 and 1997, and logging interests are now on the defensive. The Club's leadership in this fight has brought grassroots forest activists into the forefront of a national campaign and shows how forest protection issues have shifted from causing internal Club dissension to providing a unifying national mobilizing force. Chad Hansen, the Club board member who led the effort to reform the Club's forest policies, sees the Club's forest protection campaign as a great sign for the future. Hansen observed in 1997 that he is "extremely positive about the direction of the organization. The Club's reinvigoration of grassroots organizing presents incredible possibilities for future campaigns."[27] The Sierra Club and the PIRGs have shown how to reconnect citizen activists and local organizations to national struggles and provide a readily duplicated model for social-change organizations in all fields.

Chapter 4

The Pentagon

Reclaiming America by Giving Peace a Chance

*Every budget from now on will suck. And each one will
suck worse, from everybody's perspective except the military's. . . . We are either going to cut education, health
care, Superfund, cops on the street or defense. You can't
get to a zero deficit without cutting something, and that
changes the equation—and the opportunity.*

—Congressman Barney Frank
(D-MA), March 1997[1]

During 1996 a delegation of AIDS activists met with California senator Dianne Feinstein to urge increased federal AIDS funding. Feinstein explained to the group that there was simply "no more money"
to be found. She maintained that providing additional funding to combat AIDS would come at the expense of other critical public service
programs and asked the group how they planned to pay for their proposals. As Feinstein was making these remarks Virginia Parks of ACT
UP–Golden Gate noticed several models of bombers on the senator's
bookshelf. She also observed a framed picture of a military bomber
on the senator's wall. The photograph had a salutary message praising
Feinstein for her support. Parks pointed to the photo and told Feinstein that "if we hocked one of these we could have enough AIDS
funding for three years." Feinstein did not appreciate this analysis of
national budget priorities and ordered the group out of her office.[2]

ACT UP's experience is not unique. Activists seeking additional
federal funding for human needs have become accustomed to the
"cupboard is bare" refrain from politicians who consistently find funds
for the military. A clear double standard prevails: whereas politicians
and the media doom new social spending proposals by requiring that
they be revenue-neutral, the Pentagon budget remains immune from

such scrutiny. As many politicians allegedly supportive of human needs programs assert that the balanced budget imperative forces domestic cuts, citizen activists and organizations become almost resigned to such budget realities. AIDS activist Parks believes that "many activists don't think about how much we spend on the military. They don't look at the numbers." As she and her colleagues learned, politicians allegedly sympathetic to funding human needs but whose votes perpetuate what peace activists describe as Pentagon "bloat" do not like having their priorities questioned.

Unfortunately, citizen activists' turning away from national budget struggles has only made it easier for politicians to support an indefensible skewing toward military and away from human needs. The nation's budget priorities are often simply shocking. For example, the White House and congress during the late 1990s chose to fulfill balanced budget targets by ending federal assistance to 150,000 disabled children, cutting billions in food stamps to elderly immigrants and low-income kids, and denying $15,000 a year per person infected with HIV for drugs to prevent their infection from progressing to full-blown AIDS. Meanwhile $193 million in federal spending for military marching bands remained intact, taxpayers paid $31 million to weapons executives for engineering a merger laying off nearly thirty thousand workers, and production of the B-2 bomber—which loses its "stealth characteristics" when wet—proceeded at a cost of $2.2 billion per plane. While even extremely popular domestic programs such as the National Park System fell victim to politicians' "there is no money refrain," the Pentagon continued to receive roughly $265 billion annually, or 53 percent of all federal discretionary spending. America's military budgets during the 1990s exceeded that of 1979 and equaled the Cold War average despite the collapse of the Soviet Union.

In the absence of national activism the once-popular phrase *peace dividend* has been virtually banished from the White House and Capitol Hill. America's military budget equals twenty times the amount spent collectively by the countries that allegedly threaten U.S. security (Cuba, Iraq, Iran, Syria, Libya, and North Korea), and billions of taxpayer dollars continue to be spent defending Europe from a now nonexistent Soviet threat. Politicians who reflexively accused domes-

tic programs of "waste and fraud" apply a different standard to weapons contractors: each of the ten largest defense contractors either
admitted to or was convicted of fraud between 1980 and 1992 but
continued to receive billions in government contracts. Similarly, while
fiscal hawks attacked social programs for creating inefficient bureaucracies, politicians pay scant attention to where military spending actually goes. The U.S. General Accounting Office reported in 1997 that
$43 billion in military spending since 1985 was unaccounted for. The
defense department's comptroller objected, claiming that "only" $18
billion in disbursements could not be linked to items purchased. When
the GAO released its annual government financial audit in 1998 the
Pentagon was deemed the most wasteful department in government.

While politicians approve federal funding for arms contractors to
landscape their facilities, attend Boston Red Sox games, take Hawai-
ian vacations, and purchase thousands of Smokey Robinson tickets,
between eighteen and forty-three billion taxpayer dollars allocated
to the military have simply been lost. This amount greatly exceeds the
annual federal expenditures for subsidized housing, legal aid, AIDS
treatment and prevention, public broadcasting, Head Start, and the
arts and humanities. During the height of the bipartisan balanced budget frenzy during the 1996 presidential election year, six new aircraft
programs were approved with a projected price tag of four hundred
billion dollars for six thousand aircraft and helicopters. The programs'
1997 cost of nine billion dollars was nearly ten times that spent by the
federal government to address rising homelessness nationwide.[3]

In Paddy Chayefsky's 1976 Oscar-winning film *Network*, Peter Finch
plays Howard Beale, a television news anchorman. Beale becomes
a national phenomenon when he uses his show to become "an angry prophet denouncing the hypocrisies of our times." After detailing America's sorry state Beale tells his audience that to change things,
"first you've got to get mad." He convinces thousands of viewers across
America to stop what they are doing, open their windows, and shout,
"I'm as mad as hell and I'm not going to take it anymore!" Advocates
for homeless persons, people with HIV/AIDS, low-income children,
national forests and parks, education, national health care, mass transit, and every other underfunded federal program must echo Howard
Beale and get mad as hell about the military's control over half of

America's available federal tax dollars. Citizen activists and organizations must then vow "not to take it anymore" by joining efforts to redirect Pentagon funds to human needs. Politicians must no longer be allowed to tell housing, health, and environmental groups that "we have no money" while voting to increase the military allocation by $9 billion in the 1999 federal budget. As Barney Frank has noted, activists must either redirect Pentagon bloat or accept further cutbacks and the elimination of domestic programs that national activism created and sustained.

Through much of the 1990s activists and organizations responded to Pentagon bloat's post–Cold War survival with resignation and despair. These feelings have been replaced with a confidence that the battle for new budget priorities can be won. As the impact of federal budget cutbacks on local communities have hit home a new political environment, new constituencies, and new strategies have emerged that provide great promise for a successful national grassroots Pentagon redirection campaign. The campaign's success, however, depends on citizen activists and organizations reconnecting to the national struggle for new budget priorities. Thousands of community-based organizations across America have watched their constituencies and their own budgets suffer from the loss of federal funds. If these groups challenge the Pentagon budget with the zeal they have exhibited against corporate polluters and wealthy developers, their district congressmembers will be forced to redirect Pentagon dollars to human needs. National activism is the only strategy that can make new national budget priorities the status quo of the twenty-first century. Excessive military spending reflects the same misguided policies that have caused child poverty and the gap between the rich and everyone else to grow; activists cannot reclaim America's progressive ideals without redirecting Pentagon funds.

Why Pentagon Bloat Survived the End of the Cold War

The Untimely Decline of the Peace Movement

In 1989 more than one hundred thousand Americans were actively involved in at least one of more than fifteen thousand local, state, and national organizations devoted to advancing peace. Most of this activism was devoted to preventing American military assistance to Central America and to reducing the threat of nuclear war. America's peace movement in the 1980s was likely the most broad-based in the nation's history, with thousands of middle-class, suburban churchgoers dedicating their lives to the cause. The Central American peace movement succeeded particularly in enlisting constituencies previously untouched by antimilitary activism.

Unfortunately, neither the Central American nor antinuclear peace activism of the 1980s provided a springboard for a Pentagon redirection campaign. In fact, only a few years after the height of its power, when the election of Bill Clinton raised expectations of a historic shift from America's wartime economy, the nation's peace movement lay in tatters.

Several reasons explain the movement's sudden and untimely decline. First, many of those who had become involved in national peace activism to prevent American military assistance to antidemocratic forces in Nicaragua and El Salvador left the field after the threat ended. This particularly affected the faith-based organizations that had brought thousands of new volunteers into the Central American campaign. Although the staffs of many of these organizations remained involved in Pentagon redirection efforts, congregants whose sense of moral duty led them to become witnesses for peace or to offer sanctuary to Central American refugees did not feel similarly compelled to join a Pentagon budget fight.

Secular organizations critical to the Central American peace campaign, such as Neighbor to Neighbor, the Nicaragua Network, and the Committee in Solidarity with the People of El Salvador (CISPES), also moved away from military issues following the cessation of American military intervention in the region. Headed by Fred Ross Jr., one of the country's most skilled political organizers, Neighbor to Neighbor had proven extremely effective in building congressional opposition to Reagan's Central American policies. The organization grew to employ more than one hundred field organizers on a budget approaching two million dollars. When the Central America issue faded, Ross and Neighbor to Neighbor moved on to the campaign for universal health care. The Nicaragua Network and CISPES also responded to the end of hostilities by focusing on issues other than military spending. Both groups sought to provide assistance to the region and eventually became active in Central American anti-sweatshop campaigns.

The national grassroots base for a Pentagon redirection struggle further eroded when the exodus of Central American peace activists coincided with the departure of anti–nuclear war activists at the end of the Cold War. Just as the increased risk of nuclear war in the early 1980s brought millions into the streets demanding a nuclear freeze, the end of nuclear tensions with the Soviet Union returned many activists to their homes or to addressing other concerns. Bill Clinton's campaign promise of a peace dividend may also have led many to view a national grassroots pressure campaign regarding Pentagon redirection as unnecessary. Organizations addressing Pentagon spending saw donations drop after Clinton's election, apparently reflecting a lack of urgency about Pentagon issues upon the election of a Democrat to the White House.

As the number of peace activists and organizations declined, many of the foundations that had funded Central American or anti–nuclear war activism shifted resources to other pressing issues. Wayne Jakowitz of the National Security News Service, an organization focusing on investigative reporting for peace and security issues, notes that "foundations walked away" from the Pentagon budget issue by the early 1990s. John Pike, director of the Military Analysis Network at Scientists for Social Responsibility, argues that after the Cold War "the funding community declared victory and went home." Pike was one of the founders of the Military Spending Working Group, a coalition of arms control organizations that tried to get major foundations to support a unified Pentagon redirection effort. According to Martin Calhoun of the Center for Defense Information, "not one foundation" agreed to contribute to such a plan. Elliot Negin, former editor of the *Nuclear Times*, attributes this unwillingness to fund such efforts to the policies of the Clinton administration. Once the administration created a floor on military cuts many liberal foundations "did not want to antagonize the White House" by funding groups that would challenge the president's spending priorities. Negin estimates that foundation funding of peace groups focused on Pentagon spending was reduced from roughly $8 million in 1988 to $700,000 in 1994.

Foundations continued to devote resources to peace and security issues during this period but, as Mary Lord of ACCESS, an organization that monitors peace funding, points out, "the money was mostly spent abroad and on American groups who focused on international issues." Lord notes that many of the activist family foundations that supported peace advocacy through the 1980s may have felt that the grassroots peace movement was "drying up" and shifted resources to address critical domestic issues such as homelessness. She thinks the amount of foundation money remaining for advocacy is even less than Negin's $700,000 estimate.[4]

The refusal of foundations to fund Pentagon redirection efforts during the Clinton years eliminated the prime vehicle for challenging the bipartisan acceptance of Cold War military spending levels. Many of the liberal nonprofit organizations and congressmembers who did not hesitate to condemn Reagan-Bush–era Pentagon spending refused to jeopardize their access to the first Democratic administration in more than a decade by raising similar criticism. Their silence made it even more imperative for foundations to fund peace organizations to wage the peace dividend fight. Unfortunately, the philanthropic community did not provide the resources needed to make up for the loss of volunteers and donations following nearly a decade of successful, nonstop national activism.

Ultimately, national grassroots peace activism to redirect Pentagon spending did not emerge at the end of the Cold War because, unlike Central American and anti–nuclear war struggles, the Pentagon budget did not become a "hot button" political issue. Christian Smith, author of *Resisting Reagan: The U.S. Central American Peace Movement*, argues that such movements emerge "when people's sense of what is right is so violated that they are compelled to not simply criticize, but to mobilize for an end to the violation."[5] During 1993–94 when the Democrats controlled both the White House and congress and there was the best chance for a significant peace dividend in the immediate aftermath of the end of the Cold War, the necessary grassroots movement to redirect Pentagon spending did not develop. As Bob Tiller of the Fund for New Priorities puts it, "the American people no longer feel a sense of urgency" around peace issues. Christopher Hellman of the Center for Defense Information observes that excessive military spending still "is not an issue that the majority of Americans contact their congressman about."[6] Peace groups recognize that politicians will continue to ignore excessive Pentagon spending until, as California Peace Action director Peter Ferenbach puts it, "they are made to feel uncomfortable about the issue when meeting with constituents." Creating this discomfort has become a key strategy of Peace Action and other groups.

Military Spending Maintains the Corporate Sector's Control over America's Economic Life

The Pentagon's Cold War spending levels also survived the Soviet Union's demise because military bloat serves the corporate sector's agenda. This agenda was spelled out as far back as 1949 in *Business Week*:

> There's a tremendous social and economic difference between welfare pump-priming and military pump-priming. Military spending doesn't really alter the structure of the economy. As far as a businessman is concerned, a munitions order from the government is much like an order from a private customer. But the kind of welfare and public works spending that Truman plans does alter the economy. It creates new institutions. It redistributes income. It shifts demand from one industry to another. It changes the whole economic pattern.[7]

The corporate community's assessment that a big military budget is necessary to restrict "elaborate plans for development of natural resources, expansion of public works, and broadening of social welfare programs" is illuminating. It helps explain why the financial markets opposed Bill Clinton's public spending plans set forth in his 1992 campaign while they accepted maintaining Pentagon bloat. Clinton's proposals could have negatively affected an existing power structure that the corporate sector had long used military spending to preserve. This sector continues to favor military spending (as well as prison construction) as the chief government program that does not compete with the private sector or potentially foster social and economic fairness.

The irony of military spending is that, contrary to the arguments of its backers, it produces fewer jobs per dollar than if the same federal funds were spent on mass transit, housing, education, or health care. When hopes were highest for a peace dividend the Economic Policy Institute, the Center for Economic Conversion, and other progressive think tanks had equipped critics of Pentagon bloat with the studies necessary to support economic conversion plans. The Congressional Research Service released a report on February 1, 1993, less than two weeks after President Clinton took office, showing that a shift of only three billion dollars in Pentagon funds to state and local education and public works projects would create a net gain of 18,762 jobs. Community and labor groups had also developed local economic conversion plans such as the Youngstown, Ohio, National Priorities Program. Such plans showed that converting communities' contribution to the military budget to socially productive investments increased local employment. Although congressional districts especially oriented around defense, such as House Speaker Newt Gingrich's Cobb County, Georgia, could lose from such a shift, a majority of congressional districts would gain jobs through redirecting Pentagon spending. The National Commission for Economic Conversion and Disarmament found in 1997 that military spending produces 25,000 jobs per billion dollars spent, while mass transit (30,000), housing (36,000), education (41,000), and health care (47,000) all produce greater employment. Moreover, defense spending will create even fewer jobs in the future because of the Pentagon's shift in the 1990s toward large-scale capital projects rather than personnel expenditures. The Pentagon is steadily employing fewer people per dollar, and another half million defense jobs were projected to disappear from 1995 to 1998 despite stable military budgets. Obviously, the perpetuation of Pentagon bloat fulfills a different agenda than simply job creation.

President Clinton Refused to Reinvent the Pentagon

December 15, 1993, The White House

"Mr. President, I have an idea." "What is it?" "I recommend you spend less money on foreign intelligence and more on the intelligence

*of Americans." "Hmm?" "Take half the CIA's
budget and put it into inner-city schools." The
others around the table are silent. "Let's do
something similar with the defense budget. A
quarter of it into the readiness of Americans
to compete in the global economy. Your advi-
sors talked about this a couple of weeks ago."
For a full five seconds, the Roosevelt Room is
as still as an empty church. B looks at me.
He giggles. I laugh; he laughs. The relief in
the room is palpable. And then it's back to
business.*

—Robert Reich, *Locked in the
Cabinet* [8]

After spending nearly thirty years as chair of the Senate Foreign Relations Committee unsuccessfully trying to restrict Pentagon bloat,
former Arkansas senator William J. Fulbright concluded that "the
power of the president is all that can be used to stop this prodigal
military spending." [9] Unfortunately, Bill Clinton quickly abandoned
his campaign's commitment to redirecting Pentagon funds to human
needs. In *Putting People First: How We Can All Change America* candidates Bill Clinton and Al Gore included an entire chapter on the
"historic opportunity" to shift resources once dedicated to the Cold
War to "fulfilling unmet domestic needs." The future president and
vice president emphasized: "As we cut our defense budget, we must
transfer the savings, dollar for dollar, into investment in the American economy—into roads, bridges, and highways, into advanced communications networks, into research, into schools." The candidates
endorsed proposals for encouraging federal contractors to use or purchase defense facilities, for special conversion loans to small businesses, and for the transfer of defense spending to developing high-
speed rail networks linking major cities. They further endorsed using
defense funds to develop a national information network and environmental technology for cleaner air, water, and energy sources. [10]

The Clinton-Gore campaign's endorsement of Pentagon redirection strategies was not fulfilled. Clinton's first budget did cut Pentagon spending 33 percent from its 1985 peak but his administration's

military budgets have remained at the Cold War average. Clinton re-invented government by slashing HUD, not the Pentagon. Fully 80 percent of Pentagon savings from 1993 to 1997 went to deficit reduc-tion, not social investment.

In his State of the Union speech on January 25, 1994, President Clinton drew bipartisan applause with the following statement: "This year, many people urged us to cut our defense spending further to pay for other government programs. I said no. The budget I sent to congress draws the line against further defense cuts." Clinton raised military spending by $2.8 million in 1994 when the Democratic Party still controlled both houses of congress. By 1996 Clinton had aban-doned even the pretext of supporting the redirection of Pentagon funds to human needs. In *Between Hope and History*, Clinton's book for his 1996 reelection campaign, economic conversion and the peace dividend were not discussed. Instead Clinton repeatedly emphasized that "new threats abound" since the end of the Cold War and argued that Americans were actually "more vulnerable to forces of destruc-tion." Such vulnerability required America's military to be stronger than when he took office. As Michael Closson of the Center for Eco-nomic Conversion put it, "notwithstanding the rhetoric about build-ing bridges to the twenty-first century, evidence that we remain mired in the past [on Pentagon spending] is legion."[11]

The perpetuation of excessive Pentagon spending following the end of the Cold War demoralized activists and deterred organizations from participating in a seemingly unwinnable fight for new national budget priorities. But much was learned from the setbacks of the post–Cold War years and new strategies have emerged that sharply deviate from the failed challenges of the past. The fate of the tobacco industry, which also relied on campaign contributions to maintain congressional support for a destructive agenda, offers hope. An industry that seemed invulnerable at the start of the 1990s quickly saw its financial clout diluted by a popular groundswell of antismoking activists that pre-vented even longtime Big Tobacco political allies from coming to the rescue. Many factors make the start of a new century a particularly propitious moment for national activism to redirect Pentagon bloat to human needs.

Corporate Marketing Challenges
the Promilitary Corporate Agenda:
Business Leaders for Sensible Priorities

During a United Airlines flight in 1997 I was served a lunch that included a bookmark-sized message from the carrier. The message warned of dramatically rising air fares if a proposal then under consideration by congress was not defeated. Phone numbers of key representatives were included so that I could conveniently express my outrage at a new tax on flying. My first reaction upon reading the message was to bemoan the incredible advantage the corporate sector had in mobilizing national support for its agenda. Assuming all United Airline passengers on all flights were receiving this message (and I subsequently learned that American Airlines passengers received similar cards) and that many were business travelers likely to be sympathetic to United's request, the airline would either produce sufficient calls or scare enough representatives to kill the proposed tax (the tax was instead imposed on smaller, short-distance carriers).

My second reaction was to wonder how activists could use a similar tactic to further their goals. Soon afterward I learned that Rhino Records' president, Richard Foos, and Ben Cohen, the cofounder of Ben & Jerry's, were way ahead of me. Foos had seen other record companies include socially responsible messages on CD inserts and came up with the idea of using his and other company's packaging to urge support for redirecting the Pentagon budget to social investment. Foos took the idea to Cohen, who in 1996 had formed a group, Business Leaders for Sensible Priorities (BLSP). BLSP's marketing prowess and business representation has created a new opportunity for mobilizing public and business opposition to the perpetuation of Pentagon bloat.

BLSP can accomplish two key building blocks for a national Pentagon redirection campaign. First, its marketing strategy is designed to dissolve people's alienation and disconnection from the national political arena. This relationship has enabled politicians to maintain Pentagon spending levels that polls repeatedly show their constituents do not support. To awaken and energize potential activists in the fight against Pentagon bloat BLSP members have placed the following slogan on millions of CDs, cassettes, napkins, catalogs, take-out bags, and other materials:

The phone number reaches the famous voice of Lily Tomlin's Ernestine, who then combines humor regarding Pentagon bloat with a message to "press 1" to send a fax to the caller's congressional representative. Tomlin's phone operator character also requests the caller's name, address, and phone number, which are then turned over to 20/20 Vision and Women's Action for New Directions. These groups, described below, will contact callers and recommend actions they can take to help redirect Pentagon spending. BLSP's goal is to have the "Move the Money" message reach the typical consumer at least five times a year, which would mean more than a billion impressions. As the products including the slogan become more widespread the message that one person can do something about wasteful Pentagon spending will add new voices to the grassroots base necessary for a national campaign. The campaign can also be tailored to specific markets as there is no limit to the variety of messages that can accompany the "Move the Money" refrain.

As the corporate sector expands advertising space into such previously untapped zones as fruit labels, consumers will undergo subtle persuasion to pay greater attention to packaging slogans. This will only increase the persuasiveness of BLSP's message. Foos's belief that "a message in a bottle is a pretty inefficient way to convey important information, but a message ON a bottle (or a box or a bag) is a different story" may create an entire new sphere for spreading the message of national grassroots campaigns.

The use of packaging to convey the case against Pentagon bloat fulfills an essential task for ongoing and future national mobilization campaigns: reaching potential supporters and participants outside of traditional media channels. As I argue throughout this book and especially in the chapter on media, a movement seeking progressive change in any field can no longer be fueled by newspaper stories or television news coverage. Although the mainstream media helped build the movements of the 1960s, the whole world is no longer regularly watching national television news or even reading a daily newspaper. Students and other young people who have traditionally played critical roles in national peace campaigns are particularly estranged from daily exposure to mainstream media; this group is as likely to read a message on a Ben & Jerry's Peace Pop as to see a story on the latest weapons boondoggle on the CBS evening news. By extending BLSP's packaging strategy to potentially any material upon which its message can be placed—and Foos's Rhino Records alone distributes ten million products annually—there can be further development of a public consciousness that Pentagon spending can be redirected through national activism.[12]

In addition to creating an effective alternative to traditional media for energizing a new priorities campaign BLSP's persona could finally reshape the business community's long-standing support for military spending as the dominant government enterprise. Soon after its formation BLSP conducted focus groups on the issue of redirecting Pentagon funds to human needs. When asked to select which category of occupation they would find most credible on the issue, the groups overwhelmingly favored military people and businesspeople (college professors, economists, actors, and lawyers all did poorly). The credibility of businesspeople on defense spending renders it imperative that peace organizations reach out to this constituency, which would seem particularly open to cutting various weapons boondoggles on fiscal grounds alone. Expanded economic globalization could also erode business support for Pentagon spending that subsidizes foreign arms sales and weakens overseas purchasing power. Corporate supporters of unrestricted free trade argue that the world is one large market-place; America's massive military budget would seem unnecessary in a world where countries are trading partners. If BLSP can attract enough support from the business community, the long-standing dynamic that has perpetuated military bloat could finally be changed. At the very least having corporate leaders making the economic arguments for new spending priorities is a powerful strategy whose presence through much of the 1990s was sorely missed. The defense industry is geographically distributed through so many states and localities that it has no trouble mobilizing telegrams, faxes, and phone calls from employees/constituents throughout the nation; BLSP creates the prospect of its members' businesses countermobilizing through their own employees—a tactic that may well be unprecedented for the peace movement.

BLSP's corporate representation and the unusual angle of a business group campaigning against Pentagon waste have resulted in heightened media interest in the group's message. BLSP launched its first public announcement on June 23, 1996, with an open letter to President Clinton and Republican nominee Bob Dole published as a full-page ad in the *New York Times*. Titled "It's Time America's Last Sacred Cow Shared the Burden of Budget Cuts," the ad reflected BLSP's strategy of citing business leaders and military experts such as former CIA director William Colby and Reagan defense planner Lawrence Korb to support its call to reduce "Pentagon fat and waste." The ad was followed later in the week by a press conference that introduced the group's membership and goals to the national media. The *Washington Post* account of the press event pictured Ben Cohen spooning out his specially created "Totally Nuts" ice cream, designed to protest America's military budget. After noting that neither Clinton nor Dole supported cutting defense to boost social programs, the *Post* observed that the public had yet to demonstrate interest in such a shift, so BLSP's event "marked a rare instance of public protest." BLSP tried to make such instances less rare by having its members publish editorials in the *Christian Science Monitor* and other newspapers and by placing a full-page ad in the Capitol Hill newspaper,

Roll Call, on May 19, 1997, notifying "U.S. Government Shareholders" that cutting social investments while funding unnecessary military hardware "makes no business or strategic sense."

BLSP's literature and message are punchy and persuasive: exactly what should be expected of a group composed of marketing experts. Ben Cohen is committed to spending one or two days a week working on marketing strategies for BLSP's Pentagon redirection effort. Fortunately, he recognizes that changing federal budget priorities will not take place overnight. In an October 1997 interview Cohen emphasized that he and his colleagues "don't see this as a short-term campaign." He contends that efforts to redirect Pentagon spending have not succeeded in the past "because they come and go with elections and have not been maintained. We need to hammer away day in and day out until we prevail."

Cohen's long-term perspective reflects both the experience of a businessman who successfully waged a David–and–Goliath battle against Haagen-Dazs and the new strategy of Pentagon redirection efforts. Peace activists learned from the 1980s that building organizations around a specific crisis can result in disarray once the cause ends. Rather than attract supporters who will leave if the Pentagon budget is or is not slashed immediately, the message from Cohen, Peace Action executive director Gordon Clark, and others is that the Pentagon redirection campaign is likely to be an ongoing, annual struggle. Otherwise a national grassroots campaign succeeding in redirecting billions in Pentagon funds could quickly be reversed the next budget year. Creating sustainable peace organizations is a critical development that should help institutionalize opposition to Pentagon bloat.

National Peace Organizations

Peace Action

A full-page *New York Times* ad on October 17, 1997, showed photographs of six California congressmembers with the headline: "Are These Politicians 'Strong on Defense' . . . or Are They Just Too Weak to Say No?" The text juxtaposed the representatives' support for some of the worst Pentagon boondoggles with their defense industry campaign contributions. It also showed the link between 89 percent of congressmembers receiving weapons industry funds (more than $11 million in 1996 alone) and broad congressional support for "funding bombers that don't work and submarines we don't need." The ad concluded with a call for taxpayers to reassert control over "our" money by telling congressmembers—"our employees"—to say no to Pentagon bloat. Two of the six targeted by the ads were Democrats, including Vic Fazio, chair of the Democratic Caucus. The other Democrat, Jane Harman, also had thousands of doorhangers hung in her district asking, "Why Does Rep. Jane Harman Keep Wasting Our Tax Dollars?" Similar doorhangers were distributed in swing California congressional districts and in fifteen other states.

This hard-hitting advertisement was paid for by the California chapter of Peace Action. Founded in 1947, Peace Action's sixty thousand members make it the nation's largest peace organization. Its Washington, D.C., headquarters is joined by twenty-seven state and more than one hundred local autonomous chapters. Focusing on redirecting Pentagon bloat is one of the group's three priorities along with nuclear arms reduction and limiting the production and sale of conventional weapons. Peace Action's full-page ads represented a new strategic approach toward focusing public attention on wasteful Pentagon spending. The strategy has three goals: to personalize responsibility for Pentagon bloat, to taint congressional recipients of defense industry campaign funds, and to show that excessive Pentagon spending is produced by an annual budget process that activists working in their own congressional districts can influence. The strategy reframes the Pentagon spending issue by forcing individual politicians to defend probloat votes to their constituents. It finally puts probloat politicians on the defensive, challenging prevailing wisdom that the Pentagon issue can only hurt congressmembers if they are seen as "soft" rather than too hawkish on defense.

Peace Action's new approach also reflects a recognition that previous strategies— such as military experts showing how the Pentagon budget could be slashed by 33 percent without affecting national security—failed to ignite public passion over continued bloat. Pentagon critics could not win public support by prevailing in a battle of experts as to necessary military spending; one leader of a national group involved with peace issues insisted on total anonymity before revealing that he could not mobilize people when cutting the military budget was seen as a matter of conflicting expert opinion over billions of dollars. Linda Stout, founder of the North Carolina–based Piedmont Peace Project (PPP), confirms the difficulty of persuading people through esoteric debates. Stout has observed that peace organizations have long used education materials whose academic language made them difficult for low-income people to use. Stout received a grant for PPP to produce its own materials, which connected community concerns—the need for federal programs to preserve family farms and for job training and education—with wasteful military spending. Although PPP's flyers and booklets were directed toward a target constituency where the adults were at third-grade reading levels, they proved equally persuasive when used across the country in middle-class and affluent communities.[13]

Stout's experience confirms that peace groups must provide a simple-to-understand message to build the national grassroots base necessary for success. As Caleb Rossiter, director of Demilitarization for Democracy, a Washington, D.C.–based peace group, put it, "We need to quit having strategic debates and start explaining that this is a corporate rip-off."[14] Peace Action is accomplishing this by shifting the emphasis from whether $265 or $175 billion is necessary to preserve American security to the more easily conveyed message that weapons industry campaign contributions fuel congressmembers' support for Pentagon bloat. By highlighting that America's budget priorities are effectively purchased by arms manufacturers Peace Action has reframed the debate in a manner necessary to make the public mad as hell and insistent upon reform. Once public pressure for redirecting Pentagon spending is mobilized, congressmembers can use the academic and strategic analyses justifying military cuts to avoid charges that they are "soft" on defense.

Peace Action has expanded two other key vehicles for enhancing grassroots activism toward redirecting Pentagon funds. First, the organization's separate political arm focused on electoral politics has grown greatly in the 1990s. Its Peace Voter '96 campaign handed out millions of voter guides, held candidate forums, distributed thousands of bumper stickers, ran radio ads against promilitary candidates, and placed organizers in some of the thirty-five congressional districts targeted by their campaign. In eighteen of these races, the candidate most willing to speak out against Pentagon waste prevailed. Peace Voter '96 was the largest national electoral effort by any peace organization since the nuclear freeze and Central American anti-intervention campaigns of the 1980s. Based on the success of its 1996 efforts, Peace Action implemented an even more ambitious agenda for the 1998 election cycle. Its October 1997 advertisement was an early salvo, raising the profile of Pentagon bloat prior to the election year so that military spending would become an ongoing campaign topic. By replicating the extremely successful "Dirty Dozen" political targeting initiated by environmental groups in the 1970s Peace Action's political arm can put a spotlight on politicians' probloat votes and increase their discomfort about telling constituents that "there is no money" for human needs.

The second and more critical component of Peace Action's growth is its expansion of its canvassing operations. Prior to 1990 Peace Action had successful canvasses in a dozen states and an infrastructure for expanding this field work to several more. After the organization decentralized that year, individual state chapters had to choose to run canvasses and by 1997 only California and Colorado did. California Peace Action (CAP) has the most effective canvass and its operation has brought steady growth in membership, visibility, and political clout. CAP's executive director, Peter Ferenbach, views canvassing as a "365-day structure for outreach, training, and political education." CAP's canvass, like that of the PIRGs described in chapter 3, brings young people into national activism and offers the financial support necessary to sustain their participation. CAP's experience mirrors that of the PIRGs during the Clean Air Act struggle: those contacted by the canvass became prime resources for the national campaign. During the first eight months of 1997 CAP's canvass produced sixty-four hundred handwritten letters to congressmembers criticizing the military budget. Canvass contacts were also recruited to attend congressmembers' town meetings, where they raise the discomfort level by publicly challenging the politicians' support for Pentagon bloat.

In addition to disseminating information on military spending to local organizations and constituents, CAP's canvass provides critical feedback about the message Pentagon critics must use to make the public mad as hell about national budget priorities. CAP's October 1997 advertisement reflected this feedback and has helped move the entire Peace Action network to focus on "hot button" components of the defense budget such as the $7.6 billion annual subsidy for foreign arm sales and the proposed sale of fighter jets to brutal regimes such as the dictatorship in Indonesia. Peace Action's organizing against the latter led California's Senator Feinstein to speak against the Indonesian sale on the senate floor, and it became a galvanizing issue for student peace activists.

Peace Action's canvass can prove critical for creating the necessary infrastructure for a successful national grassroots Pentagon redirection campaign. The Sierra Club has shown how strong local chapters can create a national mobilizing infrastructure without a canvass but neither Peace Action nor any other peace organization has the organizing staff and resources to replicate the Club's strong local chapter model. Peace Action is closer to the lower-budget PIRGs, whose extensive reliance on canvassing has created a national organizing infrastructure through activists paid for their work. CAP's Peter Ferenbach believes Peace Action chapters should operate a canvass even if it loses money. The canvass's distribution of information about military spending to millions of voters and its harnessing of young activists to the national Pentagon redirection effort are benefits that are not calculated when assessing the strategy in net income accounting terms. CAP's success has led other chapters to consider reviving their canvasses and the vehicle's viability will increase as publicity about Pentagon bloat increases the canvass's potential donor base.

Peace Action's national executive director, Gordon Clark, regularly tours the country in order to energize local chapters and assist in the creation of new ones. Clark recognizes that peace organizations "have not done enough" to arouse public anger over Pentagon bloat and agrees with Ferenbach that Peace Action's adoption of a more confrontational approach will raise the issue's profile and attract more young activists to the cause. Although supportive of congressmembers' efforts to build support among public interest representatives in the nation's capitol, Clark understands that constituencies must be mobilized at the community level to affect Pentagon bloat. Peace Action chapters are working to reengage community-based organizations in the Pentagon redirection fight, and this strategy, along with the group's other new approaches, is building the national grassroots base necessary for new budget priorities to prevail.

20/20 Vision and WAND

The second-largest membership-based group challenging Pentagon bloat is 20/20 Vision. Founded in 1986, 20/20 Vision focuses on generating grassroots pressure regarding peace, campaign finance reform, and the environment. The group draws its name from its members' pledge to give twenty dollars per year and twenty minutes per month toward achieving the group's agenda. Laura Kriv, its legislative and field director, estimates that 65 percent of the group's ten thousand members take some sort of action each month—usually letters or phone calls proposed by national staff. If a twenty-minute monthly commitment seems trivial, recall that congress has been emboldened to perpetuate Pentagon bloat by the lack of correspondence it receives about the issue. This means that the vast majority of people upset about federal spending priorities write no letters and spend zero minutes each month challenging Pentagon waste. A 1981 survey of congressional staff ranked "spontaneous letters from constituents" as the highest-impact source of communication. Political consultant James Carville echoed this point in 1996, stating that "in these days of phony-baloney Astroturf lobbying, real letters from real people count."[15]

Longtime West Virginia senator Robert Byrd stated in 1996 that "the first thing politicians turn to when they open their newspapers is letters to the editor." Activists recognize the positive psychological impact of waking up to a positive letter in the morning's newspaper, yet this cost-free and persuasive method of persuasion is insufficiently used. 20/20 Vision provides the urging necessary to get these letters written, and their impact is often clear. For example, on August 25, 1996, the *Times Union* in Albany, New York, ran four letters from

20/20 Vision–member subscribers questioning their congressmember's votes for excessive military spending while supporting cuts in education and environmental programs. The congressmember then felt obligated to send his own letter to the editor explaining his votes. The 20/20 writers effectively used the letters page to create a news story about national spending priorities rather than simply bemoaning the paper's lack of reportage of the issue. As a phone contact for BLSP's "message on the bottle" campaign 20/20 Vision will have the opportunity to generate the letters to congressmembers and newspapers necessary to make Pentagon bloat a hot political issue.

20/20 Vision is particularly focused on engaging youth in the political process. In 1996 the group created an Education Fund to enhance its outreach and training to those aged eighteen to thirty. The Fund has focused on bringing its message to youth-oriented magazines such as the September 1996 issue of *Mademoiselle*. The group's article, "Write a Letter, Save the World—A Hassle-Free Guide to Unleashing the Political Power in your Pen," generated widespread response from the magazine's young women readers. In 1996 20/20 volunteers also handed out information to attendees at singer Michelle Shocked's more than fifty-city concert tour. Whereas prior peace campaigns regularly used popular rock stars to build student participation, the Pentagon redirection effort has only recently tapped this resource. Ani Difranco did a benefit for Peace Action in 1997, thus exposing thousands of concertgoers to the group and its materials. *Mademoiselle*, Difranco, and Shocked reach audiences that are likely sympathetic to the new priorities message but may not have read about the issue; spreading information through such vehicles is far more effective for building a national base than continually speaking to the already converted. Consistent with this approach, the Education Fund's outreach efforts include a website (www.2020vision.org) that is considered one of the top twenty-five activist sites on the Internet.

Women's Action for New Directions (WAND) is the largest women's peace organization in the 1990s. Originally focused on the nuclear arms race, WAND changed the last two words in its name to "New Directions" to reflect its primary focus on redirecting Pentagon funds to human needs. The group holds monthly informational briefings on the Pentagon spending issue around the country for women officeholders, social service workers, and peace activists. WAND's "Federal Budget Pie Exercise" is an extremely persuasive strategy for educating people about current budget priorities and how the "pie" can be sliced to better serve human needs. WAND compares America's current federal budget priorities to Fred and Martha's family checkbook. Fred controlled the checkbook and after paying monthly charges for the mortgage, utilities, and insurance, he spent more than half of what was left on home security. Martha accepted the need for a home alarm system but became furious when she learned that the reason they could not afford to take vacations or go out to dinner was that Fred had spent thousands to armor the roof, electrify the fence, and install a radar system in the attic. As WAND puts it, "if you think Fred has his priorities out of whack, then say hello to federal spending priorities." The story ends happily, with Martha seizing control of the checkbook and doing such a good job managing the household budget that the president appoints her to be the federal budget director.

WAND's effort to show why "the federal budget is a woman's issue" has been hampered by citizen activists' and organizations' exclusively local focus and disconnection from national budget struggles. In election after election women vote for the candidate that promises to spend more on human needs. Yet their voice is not heard when congress and the White House sacrifice funding for women and children while perpetuating Pentagon bloat. WAND's participation in BLSP's campaign should facilitate its recruitment of women peace activists, who individually and organizationally have played central if not leading roles in prior peace campaigns. As the national grassroots Pentagon redirection campaign builds, its support among women will prove critical to changing politicians' minds about their votes for the military. From the repeal of the federal welfare entitlement to severe cutbacks in federally subsidized family housing, women's interests have been undermined by existing federal budget priorities. Redirecting Pentagon spending to human needs must become a political litmus test both for women's political action committees like Emily's List and for national candidates explicitly seeking women's votes.

Peace Action, 20/20 Vision, WAND, and the venerable War Resisters League, along with smaller local and national groups, constitute the grassroots peace movement of the 1990s. The groups spent less in 1997 than any of the top dozen environmental organizations. This lack of funding has restricted their outreach, mobilizing capacity, and the public impact of their persuasive informational materials, well-researched reports, and detailed economic conversion plans.

But their lack of national profile in the years following the end of the Cold War should not obscure a critical fact: most Americans agree with their message. A November 1995 survey undertaken for the Center for Defense Information found that a majority of Americans want the military budget reduced, with most supporting a 10 percent cut. Seventy-seven percent of respondents opposed the seven billion dollars congress added to the 1995 military budget beyond the Pentagon's request. A July 1996 study by the Program on International Policy and Attitudes at the University of Maryland found that after being informed of the relative size of the military budget compared to other domestic programs, 80 percent of respondents favored dramatically cutting back Pentagon funds. The study concluded that "as Americans get more information about the actual level of defense spending, the majority shifts from wanting modest cuts to wanting deep cuts."[16]

Such polls can be dismissed on the basis that the only polls that count are those on election day, and those elected have supported excessive military spending. But the polls confirm what is apparent from the lack of pro–Pentagon spending letters to the editor and congress and from the lack of editorial support for military excess in the daily press: there is not a popular, grassroots, nationwide constituency supporting Pentagon bloat. Instead military spending levels are sustained by insider lobbying, campaign contributions, the steadily decreasing number of defense industry employees, and the absence of national activism that could force politicians to adopt new budget priorities. The polls show potential majority support for new budget priorities, so creating a national mobilizing base, rather than persuading people to change views, is the key task. National peace groups have adopted new strategies for building this base but other constituencies and organizations must assist their efforts. These include the business sector targeted by BLSP, students, the religious community, and the nationwide network of community-based nonprofit organizations (CBOs). The staffs, boards, and constituencies of CBOs have been so busy addressing the local impacts of federal attacks on the social safety net that they have not actively participated in the battle to redirect Pentagon bloat. CBOs must play a leading role in building and mobilizing the national grassroots base necessary to achieve new budget priorities.

Student Peace Activism

In 1996 the 20/20 Vision Education Fund surveyed Americans between eighteen and thirty years old about federal budget priorities. Only 3 percent of those surveyed said that "maintaining a strong national defense" was the most important problem facing America. Sixty-two percent said that America spent "too much" on defense, with 47 percent feeling that the country spent "a great deal more" on the military than was necessary. Asked to choose between defense and education spending, 77 percent said they would "cut defense and increase education," whereas only 4 percent wanted to increase military spending at education's expense. When the U.S. senate was asked to transfer $1.3 billion (one-half of 1 percent of the entire defense budget) to education and job training programs that year, however, young people's attitudes toward national budget priorities had little impact: the amendment received only forty votes. Whether drawn to support new priorities out of idealism or a desire to revive federal grant programs that would not force them to graduate with a mountain of debt, young people are a natural constituency for Pentagon redirection efforts. The task is mobilizing them.

After receiving scant attention from peace organizations in the years following the end of the Cold War, the groundwork has been laid for students and campus organizations to play central roles in a national Pentagon redirection struggle. Campus peace activism has provided volunteers, resources, and high-profile event venues for past national campaigns, and after graduation student peace activists often become key forces linking campus, community, and national peace organizations. In 1995 Peace Action began rebuilding campus peace activism by creating the Student Peace Action Network (SPAN). SPAN quickly grew to more than seventy-five campus chapters, which have engaged in public protests against American arms sales to Indonesia (at Illinois State University and several others), the launching of plutonium to fuel the Cassini mission to Saturn (at Wesleyan), the continued operation of the U.S. Army's "torture training" School of the Americas at Fort Benning, Georgia (Goshen College students protested at the site), and both Pentagon bloat and a university's multimillion-dollar Department of Defense contracts (Syracuse University). SPAN established an official organizing department in February 1997 and hired a field organizer to build campus chapters and membership. The organizer particularly focuses on increasing the group's racial and ethnic diversity. Such outreach is essential because communities of color have been most harmed by the perpetuation of Pentagon bloat at the expense of funding human needs. By enlisting young, racially diverse peace activists, SPAN can help mobilize participation in the Pentagon redirection campaign among communities already receptive to its message.

On March 15, 1997, SPAN convened its first national campus summit in Washington, D.C. Fifty student activists from around the country joined the parent organization's "Spring Cleaning Congressional Education Days" directed toward 135 house and senate members. SPAN's summit agenda focused on a range of military-related issues and included civil disobedience at the Indonesian embassy on March 17, 1997, to protest Clinton administration plans to sell F16 fighter jets to that country's brutal dictatorship. Opposing the sale and supporting a code of conduct prohibiting American military sales to undemocratic regimes that violate human rights were the year's galvanizing issues. California Peace Action conducted a training at the summit in its popular street theater, the "Incredible Feats of Stupidity." One skit includes asking people to insert their tax dollars into a five-sided black box. A sign says, "Ask the General where the money goes," but the General's only response is, "That's classified. Please move along." The "Budgetary Keno Wheel" demonstrates the nation's skewed budget priorities by using a wheel whose spaces are marked for education, health care, and the environment. The wheel is spun by a Peace Action volunteer dressed as a weapons industry lobbyist and every spin results in more money for the military. Another skit uses three volunteers dressed in suits, who wear placards reading "Senator," "Weapons Contractor," and "Weapons Industry Lobbyist." The trio dramatizes their message by simply handing huge wads of tax dollars back and forth to one another. Street theater is far more likely to reach students than a literature table. By contrasting Pentagon bloat with the far lesser spending for environmental protection—likely the most popular student cause—the skits seek to broaden student interest in changing national budget priorities.

SPAN chapters have found that students were best mobilized against specific, hot-button aspects of the Pentagon budget, such as the seven billion dollars in annual subsidies for foreign sales of arms that benefit dictators seeking to repress popular opposition or, in the case of Somalia, that were targeted against American troops. The struggles to defeat arms sales to Indonesia and for a broader code of conduct governing foreign arms sales also evoked students' sense of moral duty and human rights. Students like Peace Action volunteers Cheryl Wisniewski and Tonia Secor of Illinois State University saw such arms sales as fostering "genocide" and as so "morally wrong and dangerous" that protesting to stop the sales was essential. National student activism helped build the public support necessary to make the White House and congress sufficiently uncomfortable about the proposed Indonesian arms sales that the deal was withdrawn. The campus experience confirms Peace Action's analysis that focusing on taxpayer subsidies to the weapons industry, defense contractors' support of undemocratic regimes, and egregious pork-barrel spending projects is a surer strategy for making people mad as hell and eager to cut bloat than providing detailed alternative military budgets.[17]

Not every component of the military budget can arouse such passion but the Pentagon contains billions of dollars in programs that would be attractive targets for student activists. But students cannot help when their potential contributions are not recognized. For example, during the period of SPAN's March 1997 summit congressmembers Ronald Dellums (D-CA) and Barney Frank (D-MA) introduced an alternative military budget for 1997 that provided for 10 percent annual Pentagon cuts for five years. SPAN chapters were not involved in the proposal's development. Nor was SPAN given any assistance in mobilizing campuses behind the measure, whose introduction came too late in the school year for students to become informed about the proposal. Without extensive background discussions regarding political strategy, students could justifiably ask why they should feel outraged enough to actively work to cut the Pentagon budget only 10 percent rather than 25 percent or 50 percent. There was no serious effort to harness student (or any other grassroots) activism behind the Dellums-Frank measure, so the campuses were not involved in the fight for passage.

Building campus activism around cutting Pentagon spending requires the assistance of off-campus leaders and organizations. In the anti-sweatshop campaigns discussed in chapters 1 and 2, Global Exchange, AIWA, UNITE, and other groups bolstered campus activism by providing student groups with information, literature, and the training needed for them to assist national efforts. UNITE's outreach and training of students created the student-led "Stop Sweatshops Campaign" that proved so effective in the Guess campaign. Peace Action created SPAN, but other groups must also help harness student activism. The East Timor Action Network and other human rights groups have continually worked to build student opposition to foreign arms sales and subsidies to dictators and the campuses responded. The Syracuse University event that focused on Pentagon bloat was boosted by the cosponsorship of the War Resisters League and other off-campus peace groups. National and local peace activists, as well as community-based organizations participating in the struggle for new national budget priorities, must consciously work to connect campuses to the Pentagon redirection fight. Federal politicians critical of Pentagon bloat can also rally campus activism and help build the vehicles necessary to enlist students in the cause.

Progressive Politicians:
Voting against Bloat Is Not Sufficient

When House Ways and Means chair Bill Archer (R-TX) wanted to build grassroots support for a total rehauling of the federal tax structure in 1997, he did not simply hold a Capitol Hill press conference. Nor did he rely on meetings with Beltway lobbyists whose clients support lower federal taxes. Instead, Archer and fellow conservative congressmember W. J. Tauzin (R-LA) embarked on a three city "Scrap the Code" tour. Their trip not only energized and expanded their base but also brought widespread media attention to their issue, including two lengthy stories in the *New York Times*. It is significant that a powerful congressmember such as Archer, whose agenda is strongly backed by the corporate and moneyed sectors, found it necessary to build grassroots support for his cause rather than simply hand the issue to Washington insiders and the vaunted conservative media machine. Even more significant is how seldom progressive politicians, who need grassroots support far more than Archer does, take to the road to build a national mobilizing base for their proposals. The willingness of progressive politicians to cross the nation galvanizing opposition to specific Pentagon programs and for redirecting military spending to human needs would greatly enhance the cause.[18]

Consider the Dellums-Frank proposal for an alternative military budget that would have transferred $217 billion from the military to domestic programs over five years. The measure was supported by virtually all of the Washington D.C.–based peace and public interest groups and the Congressional Progressive Caucus. Its premise was that there are three "national security accounts": the military, domestic programs, and foreign aid. By redefining "national security" to include nonmilitary spending and providing a detailed critique showing that America's security would not be hurt by defense cuts, the Dellums-Frank strategy offered a thoughtful alternative to the status quo. Although this approach inherently lacked the emotional power to make Americans mad enough to mobilize for its passage, its congressional supporters could at least have used the measure to tour the country stirring support for future Pentagon redirection efforts. But this did not occur. In fact, probably very few Americans ever learned about the Dellums-Frank measure prior to, or even after, its defeat. Meanwhile, progressive congressmembers' reliance on a sober, expert-based approach led them to refrain from the type of high-profile and confrontational attacks on weapons industry campaign contributions and specifically egregious projects that build public interest in and support for new budget priorities.

Congressmembers have star quality. Ron Dellums apparently did not like speaking at his district's University of California at Berkeley campus even though he attracted huge crowds. Dellums did not see his role as a campus mobilizer, yet as a dynamic speaker and the highest-ranking Democrat on the House Armed Services Committee, he could have fostered student activism around defense issues on any campus where he appeared. Neither he nor most of his colleagues have lent their staffs and ample resources to building the campus infrastructures that are so critical to creating a national grassroots mobilizing base for new priorities. Nor have most congressmembers used their celebrity status to raise the national and local profile of the Pentagon redirection issue. The potential of such congressional activism is clear. For example, when California congressmember Maxine Waters held public meetings in her South Central Los Angeles district to discuss allegations that the CIA was involved in the area's crack cocaine epidemic, thousands attended. Waters's local involvement sent a message that the national government was listening; a far less empowering signal would have emerged had Waters confined her concern to a Capitol Hill press conference or simply urged people to contact their representatives to demand an official investigation. Similarly, when Michigan congressmember and Democratic leader David Bonior crossed America on a "Fair Trade, not Free Trade" bus tour, he and other representatives galvanized the grassroots support necessary to defeat President Clinton's request for expanded "fast-track" trade authority.

Amy Quinn, a full-time SPAN organizer and Freeman Fellow during 1996–97, found few congressmembers encouraging campus organizing against Pentagon bloat. Quinn got the impression that congressmembers "don't emphasize college campuses. They feel that students are only their constituents for a short time and keep going in and out." A vocal congressional critic of Pentagon bloat during the Clinton years confirmed Quinn's perspective when he spoke at SPAN's March 1997 summit. Quinn reported that the congressmember told the attendees that campus organizing was essentially a waste of time and that all that counted was for students to send letters and lobby inside the Beltway. While the representative may have been giving his own insider sense of what motivates his colleagues, his comments certainly did not bolster campus recruitment efforts. His assessment also reflects a strategic misperception that afflicts even progressive politicians. Instead of helping supporters build a grassroots mobilizing capacity at the district or state level that can successfully pressure congress-members or senators, such officials continually push their allies to target their efforts to Capitol Hill—the opposition's strongest turf—where the financial clout of Washington lobbyists most often prevails.[19] Political activist and author Barbara Ehrenreich, a speaker at a January 9, 1997, Capitol Hill "Progressive Challenge" forum designed to launch ongoing collaboration between the Congressional Progressive Caucus and national public interest groups, noted that she geared her remarks to "taking the Progressive Caucus people by the shoulders, shaking them and saying get out there." But when the Progressive Challenge subsequently held a series of issue symposiums in the fall of 1997, including one on demilitarization, they were held on Capitol Hill.[20]

Such distant events are inadequate for building activist support for two reasons. First, politicians can best motivate people while in their presence. This is why candidates for everything from school board to the presidency spend so much time in the field. If they felt they could persuade most people without meeting them or speaking to their groups, they would. Congressional opponents of Pentagon bloat must take their cause to campuses, union halls, environmental groups, and other forums. If members of congress directly urged their supporters to wage war against bloat, new resources for a Pentagon redirection campaign would emerge. When such a campaign is not raised at small meetings or fund-raisers but instead only through Washington, D.C., forums, the message is that the issue is not really a top priority.

The second problem with Capitol Hill forums as a mobilizing strategy is that it erroneously assumes a close connection between national public interest groups and the thousands of CBOs throughout the country working exclusively on local issues. As discussed in chapter 5, such connections primarily consist of shared informational materials rather than any ongoing personal contacts or common strategizing. The national groups have not claimed to have a direct pipeline to local organizations and probably few CBOs even know that congress-members met with national public interest groups in Washington,

D.C., in 1997 to build the human-service sector support for Pentagon redirection efforts. The Progressive Caucus had the right idea in seeking to mobilize groups whose federal funding is jeopardized by Pentagon bloat, but this effort must occur through meeting directly with the targeted groups in the communities where they work. Capitol Hill meetings simply reaffirm the erroneous view that national activism only occurs in Washington, D.C. They also suggest that the thousands of grassroots and community-based organizations unable to attend are not important to the national political arena. Rather than heed Ehrenreich's message that congressmembers need to "get out there," these well-meaning politicians are furthering the alienation from national political life that facilitates Pentagon bloat.

Some have argued that activists should not rely on progressive politicians to organize or mobilize either because that is not their orientation or because they have too many conflicting agendas to be effective. But these factors have not stopped Bill Archer, Newt Gingrich, and other "movement conservatives" from organizing constituencies and identifying themselves as political mobilizers. Nor have they stopped Maxine Waters, David Bonior, and former representatives such as Bella Abzug from using their positions as congressmembers to mobilize progressive constituencies. It appears that while conservatives elect mobilizers, progressive constituencies are supposed to be grateful if their congressmembers merely vote correctly during an era of rightward drift. Many progressives have become timid, fearful of asking what benefit is obtained from a representative whose only contribution to Pentagon redirection efforts is to be on the losing end of a one-sided military appropriations vote. Those who dare to ask for more are called unrealistic, unappreciative, or simply cranks. Congressmembers have access to media, free mail, and staff that can all be legally used to educate, not lobby, the public about the need for new budget priorities. Opponents of excessive Pentagon spending have a right to expect their representatives to use these resources to help build a national redirection campaign. If progressive politicians care more about not stirring up an internal Democratic Party fight over military spending than with changing priorities, then citizen activists and organizations should act nationally by working to replace them.

Bloat as a Partisan Issue

One reason that progressive politicians must be willing to challenge fellow Democrats' support for excessive military spending is the strategic value of bloat becoming a partisan issue. Former Neighbor to Neighbor leader and current congressional staffer Fred Ross Jr. believes that winning in congress is extremely difficult on a nonpartisan issue. Ross sees the Democratic congressional leadership's strong opposition to military aid to the Nicaraguan contras in the 1980s as causing many Democratic representatives to follow suit on partisan grounds. This enabled activists to focus on the small number of swing Democratic representatives whose votes would prove conclusive and to ultimately defeat various contra aid measures. In contrast, congressional support for aid to El Salvador was not framed by the Democratic leadership as a partisan issue. This not only spread activist resources thin by putting a sizable number of votes up for grabs but also sent a message to Democratic representatives that they were free to vote in favor of such assistance. Ross sees the lack of political partisanship toward El Salvador aid as critical to the movement's failure to defeat such measures.[21]

Peace Action recognizes that Democrats supporting Pentagon bloat are those most likely to be influenced by constituents supporting new budget priorities. The group's targeting of a powerful Democratic leader, California's Vic Fazio (who announced his retirement soon after Peace Action's criticism of his record began), reflects this strategy. While Republican Party fiscal conservatives can help defeat certain weapons systems, there are few if any congressional Republicans calling for redirecting military spending toward programs serving social and human needs. This means that the leadership of the Democratic Party must be pushed to redirect Pentagon bloat.

The antislavery, civil rights, and anti–Vietnam war movements all grew as the leadership of a national political party increasingly aligned itself with opposition forces. Once political partisanship confines the battle for new budget priorities to several swing districts, activists' person-to-person contacts can overcome the weapons industry's campaign contributions, Beltway lobbyists, and vast financial superiority.

Religious Groups:
New Challenges, Fewer Funds

Jesuit Fr. Robert F. Drinan was a leading Pentagon critic while serving as a Massachusetts congressmember during the 1970s. Since leaving office Drinan, now a professor at Georgetown University Law Center in Washington, D.C., has frequently commented on peace issues as a columnist for the *National Catholic Reporter*. After attending a reception in 1994 commemorating the twenty-fifth anniversary of the anti–Vietnam war moratorium, Drinan observed that those celebrating this achievement urgently needed a "unifying, coherent call to action" to demilitarize America and the world. He hoped and prayed that America's religious communities, particularly Catholics, would issue this "rallying cry" but saw no movement in this direction from the mainline religious community. Drinan attributed this inaction to the lack of someone to "demonize" and to the sense that "there are few causes related to peace that make a march on Washington a mandate of conscience." By 1997 Drinan's pessimism had been replaced by a belief that a "new moment is here" for a reenergized peace movement. Stating that the cause of world peace "should top the list of issues calling for our attention," Drinan concluded that only a "genuine people's movement can change the thinking or attitudes of officials who spend about one billion dollars every working day on improving the capacity of the U.S. government to purchase weapons we neither need nor can afford."[22]

Drinan's perspective is representative of longtime peace activists replacing their sense of disappointment with a renewed commitment to mounting a national struggle for new budget priorities. Faith-based peace activism was such a powerful force from the 1960s to the 1980s that its sharp decline in the early 1990s was particularly disappointing. Despite this decline religious organizations such as the Friends Committee on National Legislation, American Baptist Churches USA, the Presbyterian Church, the Union of American Hebrew Congregations, the Jesuit Ministries, and the National Council of Catholic Bishops continue to actively support redirecting Pentagon spending to human needs. The staff and leadership of these groups recognize the importance of the battle. The challenge is arousing interest in the Pentagon redirection issue among local congregations.

One problem is that the non-fundamentalist, non-evangelical Protestant denominations that traditionally provided leadership and resources to national peace activism lost members and financial resources through the 1990s. Two recent major studies of church finances found widespread cuts in local and national church budgets and serious fiscal woes. Many of these denominations have also been forced to redirect their available resources from national social-change campaigns to providing daily food and shelter to congregants and others now ignored by federal government policies. Calls by the corporate and political elite for increased volunteerism and private responsibility for the poor have further increased pressure on congregations to focus on immediate, local needs. Although the demands on churches have risen as their funding has declined, many still expect the faith community to provide key resources for social-change struggles. I recall hearing a minister of an African-American congregation recount how the most frequent question asked him was "Why isn't your church doing something about this particular problem?" The minister noted that he already had his hands full working seven days a week, sixteen hours a day simply trying to serve the needs of his congregants. His situation is all too typical yet the impression lingers that churches have sufficient resources to devote to broader causes.[23]

National groups are building congregant support for new budget priorities through vehicles like the Citizens Budget Campaign. The CBC is a coalition primarily composed of religious organizations, which also includes peace and human needs groups. The Coalition's faith-based peace groups send monthly action alerts to congregants in an effort to foster greater concern over Pentagon excess. For example, the National Ministries of the American Baptist Church USA sends out a "Faith in Action Alert" that discusses the military budget and encourages congregants to contact their congressional representatives about the issue. The alert also refers readers to free CBC materials about how military spending could be reduced. The Friends Committee on National Legislation distributes a monthly "Washington Newsletter" that provides extensive analysis of excessive Pentagon spending and makes the case in plain "dollars and cents language" for new budget priorities. The newsletter also offers free CBC materials.

The faith-based groups' distribution of alerts and CBC materials provide congregants with far more information about the need for new national budget priorities than can be found in other media. This explains why Drinan and others continue to see the religious community as representing a key potential base for a national Pentagon redirection campaign.

Kathie Guthrie, the Campaign's field program director, sees the CBC's effort as "getting people to look at the Pentagon spending issue in regards to how it affects local communities." This approach governed environmentalists' national grassroots mobilizing for tougher clean air standards and may be the best way to convince congregants upset about homeless persons sleeping in doorways and families begging for food to join the fight for a federal budget that would seriously reduce hunger and homelessness. Many religious leaders regularly make the connection between rising homelessness and hunger and misguided federal budget priorities, and the congregations and denominations long active in peace issues are likely ahead of the general public in recognizing excessive Pentagon spending's harmful effects.[24]

Faith-based institutions maintain staff, office space, mailing lists, technical support, and access to grassroots volunteers. Religious organizations supporting new budget priorities must continue to build congregant support for committing such resources to a national campaign. Robert Drinan has observed that the faith-based peace activists of a previous generation "are just as dedicated to peace and world justice as they ever were" but they await a "new or old movement." As congregants recognize that federal budget priorities have assigned religious institutions the responsibility—but not the resources—for maintaining America's safety net, and as the specific abuses of the Pentagon budget become more notorious, their wait will soon end.

Community-Based Nonprofits: Key Partners in a National New Priorities Campaign

As I discuss more fully in the next chapter, community-based nonprofit corporations must become active participants in national struggles to reclaim America's progressive ideals. In no area is CBOs' involvement more crucial than in the campaign to redirect military spending to human needs. Unlike students, women's groups, and religious institutions, CBOs do not have a history of significant participation in peace activism. But CBOs may have the greatest incentive of any sector to actively mobilize for new national budget priorities. Many CBOs actively opposed Reagan administration's attacks on federal human needs programs, and their capacity to combine local-oriented work with participation in national budget fights in the 1980s enabled these programs to survive, albeit often in reduced form. When CBOs failed to mount a similar national response to the revival of these attacks in the mid 1990s both their constituencies and their own budgets suffered. Unleashing this powerful resource requires CBOs to recognize that their successes at the community level will continue to be undermined by the withdrawal of federal funds and that engaging in local and national activism is not an either/or choice.

As the executive director of the community-based nonprofit Tenderloin Housing Clinic in San Francisco for nearly twenty years, I have repeatedly seen city officials respond to policy proposals with the refrain: "That sounds great, but of course we do not have the money." In some cities this is simply a cover for not wanting to take action but in many others local officials genuinely share activists' frustration at the lack of resources necessary to improve people's lives. Nonprofit groups serving the urban poor have become particularly familiar with the "sorry, we have no money" refrain as federal funding for low-income communities has steadily declined over the past two decades.

Community-based nonprofit organizations are the chief implementers of what remains of the federal government's urban agenda. CBOs receive federal funds to build affordable housing, assist in community economic development, and provide a wide range of services including health care, education, and job placement. Although the source of the funds is federal, the allocations for programs such as the Community Development Block Grants (CDBG) and urban empowerment and enterprise zones are made by local political leaders. In San Francisco, where my organization has received CDBG funds since 1983, the overall federal CDBG allocation has greatly declined since 1981. This downward funding trend slowed but continued through the Clinton years. Considering that pre-Reagan CDBG funding levels preceded the onset of AIDS and that sharp reductions in other federal programs have negatively affected CDBG-eligible clients, the target population's needs have significantly increased while funding has been reduced. As a result an increasing number of constituencies and non-profit organizations annually compete for shares of the shrinking CDBG pie. Competition among CDBG applicants has come to re-semble the 1950s-era *Queen for a Day* television show as the low-income beneficiaries of nonprofits testify at public needs hearings about the desperate void that will be left should the particular group not receive CDBG funds. This sad and depressing display proceeds in communities across America while the annual Pentagon appropri-ation is approved in near-empty hearing rooms where no defense con-tractor is required to plead—or hold bake sales—for funds.

It does not take a trained political organizer to recognize the pos-sibilities created by the above scenario. Rather than compete among themselves for steadily declining federal allocations, community-based nonprofits should follow bank robber Willie Sutton's lead and go where the money is: the Pentagon budget. To assess interest in this idea I did a survey in 1997 of seventy community-based nonprofits that re-ceive funds under San Francisco's CDBG program. One question asked which of four statements best described the respondent's view of na-tional politics. Of the twenty-nine executive directors who responded, most selected the statement "Community-based organizations should spend greater resources seeking to influence national policies since lo-calities are greatly impacted by national decisions." None chose the opposing alternative, which stated, "Local activists and CBOs lack the capacity to influence national policies." These responses appear to show community-based nonprofits' recognition that federal budget decisions greatly affect their programs and constituencies. Another survey ques-tion sought to measure whether executive directors would assign or-ganizational staff to work on a national campaign to redirect Penta-gon funds to human needs. A majority of respondents said no, and those agreeing would commit only four to ten hours of weekly staff time to such an effort.

The survey confirms that nonprofit recipients of federal funds are particularly conscious that national political decisions greatly affect local community life. Although most respondents would not devote staff to a Pentagon redirection campaign, another response revealed that a near-majority would provide such assistance to national campaigns seeking to fund human needs by increasing taxes on the wealthy and/or corporations. Significantly, the executive directors' willingness to commit staff to work on either issue exceeded their organization's prior level of involvement in such campaigns. The vast majority of respondents run organizations whose budgets exceed one million dollars and employ staffs of more than twenty-five people. This means that organizations concerned about Pentagon spending but currently unwilling to provide staff for a national redirection campaign might instead provide office space, mailing lists, and other necessary assistance. The groups already committed to providing staff would be even more likely to provide such additional resources.

Community-based nonprofits' employees, board members, members, clients, and their core constituencies, as well as vendors providing goods or services to such organizations, represent a new potential grassroots base for a national Pentagon redirection campaign. The prospects for CBOs becoming partners in a national struggle for new priorities have never been greater. Although CBOs largely returned to exclusively local struggles after turning back the assaults on domestic programs in the 1980s, this increased localism may have reflected the expectation that the war had been won and that Democratic congressional allies and the Clinton administration would forestall future attacks. When Republicans seized congress in 1995 and Democrat Bill Clinton accepted the severe reduction or dismantling of key federal programs, CBOs' mistaken reliance on national politicians rather than national activism became clear. If CBOs once felt that they could safely avoid national struggles and that a Democratic Party congress or president made national activism unnecessary, this attitude has been dispelled. CBOs' commitment to enhancing neighborhoods and local community life now makes it imperative that they join the national struggle for new budget priorities.

Foundations: The Time Has Come to Help

Activists and organizations seeking to redirect Pentagon funds to human needs overwhelmingly believe that additional foundation support is essential for the struggle's success. While the expected peace dividend in the early 1990s led some foundations to assume funding for a new priorities campaign was unnecessary, the error in this assumption has long been evident. The philanthropic community's withholding of funds for challenging the perpetuation of Pentagon bloat at the expense of human needs has become nothing short of morally inexcusable. Far fewer foundation dollars are needed to capitalize upon the Pentagon redirection struggle's existing infrastructure and new strategies than many might assume. A good model is the former Central American peace group Neighbor to Neighbor's ability to field one hundred organizers in the late 1980s on a total organizational budget of two million dollars. A single foundation or consortium of foundations could readily match today's equivalent of this amount (four million dollars) to create the coordinated field operation necessary for seriously influencing politicians' support for Pentagon bloat. This initial obtainable amount would be leveraged by the resources of national and local peace organizations, student activists and campus organizations, BLSP's "Move the Money" marketing campaign, religious institutions, and community-based organizations driven by ideology and financial self-interest to act nationally for new budget priorities. In addition, millions of dollars in free publicity for the campaign could be generated if the one hundred foundation-funded organizers are joined in active mobilizing by supportive congressmembers and confrontational, media-generating tactics are used. I am not suggesting that the philanthropic world limit its contribution to four million dollars or that significantly more funds would not help greatly. The goal is immediately securing the four million dollars sufficient for taking the struggle for new priorities to a new level. To avoid disputes over control of the funds a new national Pentagon redirection consortium could be created that would employ the organizers and implement the agreed-upon plan. Since many peace and human needs organizations are already aligned through coalitions like the Citizens Budget Campaign and there is wide agreement on the Pentagon programs to be targeted, the consortium could hit the ground running.

National activism can overcome big-money opposition but mobilizing "people power" requires a minimum threshold of resources. Global Exchange's entry into the anti-Nike campaign in the spring of 1996 (chapter 1) brought previously unavailable funds, public relations staff, and a confrontational activist consciousness to the struggle; pervasive mainstream media coverage of Nike's labor abuses and grassroots protests against the company soon swept the nation. Asian Immigrant Workers Advocates began its national campaign against Jessica McClintock, Inc. (chapter 2) with only four full-time staff and an organizational budget of $200,000. But these modest resources were sufficient for AIWA to conduct campus outreach, media-generating protests, and to enlist workers' rights groups nationwide in the ultimately successful struggle. The Sierra Club, the PIRGs, and other environmental groups were dramatically outspent by industry opponents of tougher clean air standards (chapter 3). But environmentalists had the organizing staff, media budget, and grassroots base sufficient for success. What is the precise amount of funds necessary for a campaign for new priorities to make weapons contractors and their political allies nervous? The truly national scope of the campaign requires at least the hundred organizers whose field presence on the eve of key congressional votes proved pivotal during the Central American peace campaign. Foundations claiming to support human needs should do no less than assure that such organizers receive the necessary financial support.

A final question about the national struggle against Pentagon bloat involves leadership. Signaling that even sympathetic politicians still doubt the issue's grassroots potency, no nationally recognized political figure has staked out the Pentagon redirection issue as his or her route to higher office or the national spotlight. When those opposed to excessive Pentagon spending see no political benefit in harnessing their future to the cause, a message is unintentionally sent to their less passionate colleagues that perpetuating the status quo is acceptable. Activist leadership for a national Pentagon redirection campaign must also emerge. Peace activists who can inspire others, catalyze action, and participate in high-profile, confrontational direct action activities greatly boost national struggles. Judi Bari played this role in the Headwaters Forest issue and succeeded in transforming a dispute in a remote area of northern California into a passionate national campaign. Medea Benjamin of Global Exchange not only crafted and personally participated in direct action at Nike's Beavertown, Oregon, headquarters but had the media respect and credibility to almost single-handedly undermine President Clinton's diversionary Sweatshop Task Force strategy. Bari and Benjamin brought a cutting-edge sensibility to their campaigns that enhanced mobilizing efforts. The activist leaders of a national grassroots Pentagon redirection campaign already exist; they simply need the money necessary to broaden the struggle. These leaders are working with peace groups, campuses, religious groups, and in the thousands of local-focused community-based organizations that have recognized that national activism is essential for reclaiming America's progressive ideals and enhancing community life.

New Budget Priorities for the Post-Bloat Era

In an era when a Democratic president announces that "big government is dead" and Republican leaders stumble over each other to claim that they will increase the size of the federal government only "over my dead body," eliminating Pentagon bloat is just the beginning. New budget priorities also require convincing the public to shift military spending to domestic programs rather than earmarking it for budget reduction or politically popular tax cuts. When Republican House Budget Committee chair John Kasich denounces the B-2 bomber as corporate welfare but then demands that domestic spending be cut by $46 billion over five years, it is clear that opponents of bloat have widely divergent agendas.[25]

Unfortunately, it is not only balanced budget hawks who will strongly oppose using Pentagon savings to restore the New Deal and Great Society programs severely curtailed in recent years. The general public's mistrust of federal programs will hamper efforts to revive and strengthen them. Many seasoned activists organizing for universal health care in the early 1990s, such as Fred Ross Jr. of Neighbor to Neighbor, were themselves surprised at the level of government mistrust among constituencies, such as seniors, that had long supported expanding federal programs. Even accounting for the strategic incompetence that plagued Clinton's universal health care campaign, Ross and others concluded that "in the end, the public did not trust the government solution."[26]

Restoring public faith in the federal government is a long-term project. In the meantime, Pentagon redirection efforts should emphasize the benefits of increasing funding in two categories of federal programs. The first are those that have maintained a stronger level of political support, such as education, children's health care, AIDS and breast cancer research, expanded mass transit, national park maintenance, and environmental protection. These programs have opponents, but their expansion will be difficult to characterize as a return to the allegedly failed approach of our "Big Government" past. The second category of federal programs includes housing, the arts and humanities, legal services, and a broad array of social welfare programs whose proposed return to pre-Reagan funding levels will bring calls of denunciation from Christian Coalition pulpits and fiscally conservative Democrats alike. Rather than pursue a doomed strategy of seeking to redirect Pentagon spending to enhance recently curtailed programs, activists can redesign their approach to achieve the same goal. For example, efforts to dramatically expand new subsidized housing programs will, by political necessity, have to rely on increased tax credits for developers of low-income housing. The specter of aging baby boomers could fuel significant new funding for affordable senior housing, while refundable renter's tax credits could replicate once flourishing federal programs that enabled low-income tenants to obtain housing by providing government rent subsidies to their landlords. Similarly, commuter tax credits may have to compensate for decreased federal mass transit subsidies and legal tax credits can provide middle- and lower-income people with access to the legal system. Since refundable tax credits, unlike deductions, benefit those who pay no taxes, they can be used to create new budget priorities without raising alarm bells that "Big Government" is back.

Reinventing government does not have to be synonymous with downsizing. By escaping the baggage of past programs whose success has been obscured by antigovernment rhetoric, citizen activists and organizations can rebuild the political support necessary for new federal budget priorities that reflect America's progressive ideals.

Part Three

Resources for National Activism

Community-Based Organizations, the Media, and the Internet

Chapter 5

Community-Based
Nonprofit Organizations

From Demobilizers to Agents of Change

When I was in school in the late 1970s my goal upon graduation was to work for a community-based nonprofit organization (CBO). Nonprofits seemed the best employment opportunity for activists, as their staffs appeared to provide the organizing prowess and technical expertise often needed for low-income people to successfully assert their rights. In San Francisco's Tenderloin district, where I was observing nonprofits in action, many staff members were recent college graduates whose jobs gave them immediate entry into the activist world.

I joined with other law students in starting a nonprofit organization, the Tenderloin Housing Clinic, in February 1980. I have been the Clinic's executive director for my entire professional life. As a result of my experience and from talking to and reading about others long involved with CBOs, I have concluded that my initial view of nonprofits as agents of social change was off the mark. To my dismay I have found that community-based nonprofit organizations are reluctant to engage in local struggles and are largely absent from the national battles that significantly affect their constituencies. Most CBOs are funded to address strictly local concerns, and their proliferation has funneled activist resources away from the national arena and toward individual client service. This exclusive focus on individual and neighborhood needs has persisted even when the CBOs' target constituency is under siege from national policy decisions. Because such national decisions undermine the CBO's ability to significantly help those it is paid to help, the CBO becomes much like the characters in Kobo Abé's *The Woman in the Dunes*: it spends its days digging out sand only to have the surrounding winds refill the area by morning. Instead of mobilizing their constituencies around policy fights or using their unrestricted funds to influence such struggles CBOs often act as innocent bystanders.

As I discussed in the preceding chapter on efforts to redirect Pentagon spending to human needs, CBOs must reconnect to national grassroots mobilizing campaigns. With thousands of potential activists siphoned off into working for organizations with an exclusively local, neighborhood, or individual client focus, the proliferation of CBOs since the late 1970s has greatly contributed to the corresponding decline in national activism. For all the great work many CBOs do every day, year in and year out, national decisions—ranging from the repeal of the federal welfare entitlement to the ending of new federal housing subsidies to the grossly inadequate funding targeted to the urban areas where most CBOs operate—have become increasingly determinative and will continue to fundamentally hurt the CBOs' constituencies. If CBOs could once ignore the national arena, they can do so no longer. CBOs committed to fulfilling the goals set forth in their mission statements must do everything in their power to fight nationally for their constituencies' interests.

This chapter discusses why and how CBOs not presently engaged in national debates can become involved in national activism. Because my analysis is targeted to those CBOs that are the best prospects to foster grassroots mobilizing capacity for progressive national campaigns, I focus exclusively on the segment of the nonprofit world that claims to be "community-based," that engages in "advocacy," and that receives public funds. I use the term *community-based* to describe CBOs primarily focused on self-identified communities based on such unifying features as geography, economic status, ethnicity, gender, nationality, sexual preference, disability, or health impairment. The CBOs I am discussing have representatives from the communities they serve on their boards, are locally controlled, and typically use the term *community-based* to define themselves.[1]

CBOs that make no claim to engage in "advocacy" are not likely to provide resources for national activism. My analysis thus excludes strictly service organizations, technical consultants, and nonprofit construction companies. Such organizations, unlike community-based nonprofits claiming to do advocacy, do not attract and potentially demobilize budding young social-change activists. Finally, I focus on CBOs receiving public funds for two reasons. First, these CBOs typically have larger budgets and more resources to devote to assisting national campaigns. Second, it is this segment of CBOs that has the largest untapped potential. These are the groups whose advocacy efforts have often been eclipsed by their service provision and whose client- rather than constituency-centered focus must be expanded to embrace national campaigns.

My discussion begins with a story that illustrates how even CBOs begun as social-change vehicles can be quickly transformed into service bureaucracies posing no threat to the status quo. Recognizing the widespread skepticism that surrounds CBOs' potential involvement in national grassroots campaigns, I then discuss the most commonly viewed obstacles to CBOs assuming this role. The chapter concludes with a discussion of a survey I conducted regarding CBOs and national activism, and specific ways that CBOs can act nationally without sacrificing their local focus or funding.

The CBO Story:
How Activists Became Bureaucrats

In a common story in which only the names and location change, a single mother and her two children have become homeless. Forced to live in a shelter, the mother rallies with others to publicly demand that the city provide homes for low-income families. She joins a squatters' group planning a housing takeover of an abandoned, city-owned ten-unit apartment building. Calling on strategic and organizing skills she did not know she had, the mother becomes the group's leader and spokesperson. As the media becomes interested in this fiery speaker for the disenfranchised, pressure is put on the city's political leadership to address the group's demand to be given ownership of the building. The city cannot simply give money to private individuals so officials tell the woman and her group that they must form a nonprofit corporation to receive the property. The group follows this course and soon the once homeless woman is executive director of Empowerment Housing Development Inc., a 501(c)(3) nonprofit corporation.

As executive director the woman finds that much of her time is initially spent with architects and construction crews who are renovating the building to meet local codes. Once the renovation is complete the executive director learns about all of the federal, state, and local tax forms that must be submitted for the organization each month. In addition the purchase of the building with a combination of local, state, and federal funding sources requires the executive director to prepare monthly activity reports. These reports must be approved before the public entities can reimburse the nonprofit for its salaries and expenses for the preceding month. Frustrated at all the hassles involved with public money, the executive director begins meeting with foundations. The foundations are excited to see an executive director who has formerly been homeless and they urge the woman to submit grant proposals to increase the group's funding. The woman is a dynamic speaker and leader but her formal writing skills are weak and she lacks computer expertise. She is advised to hire a development director to handle fund-raising.

The development director turns out to be terrific. She has not only raised foundation funds to provide child care and other services for the corporation's tenants but she has arranged a fund-raising dinner to put the group on even firmer footing. In order to bring in the big money the dinner will honor the CEO of a major downtown corporation for his concern about homeless families. The CEO is part of a local business group that has opposed increases in county welfare benefits, supported a decrease in business taxes, and pushed for new city services to be contracted out to nonprofits rather than adding to the city's unionized work force. His company can be counted upon to buy a five-thousand-dollar table at the event, and this will facilitate other corporate table purchases. The mayor has agreed to moderate the dinner, which will cause many of his corporate political backers and lobbyists to attend the event to show that they are loyal to his allies. The event nets forty thousand dollars, astonishing for a first-year dinner. The future looks so bright that there is talk about buying another building. Of course, obtaining the needed funds requires staying on good terms with the mayor, and some corporate representatives are placed on the group's board to increase credibility with lenders and foundations. The executive director still identifies herself as an advocate for disenfranchised people, however, and is not worried about the new influences on the organization.

At this point the story can go in various directions. Sometimes the executive director irrevocably puts her stamp on the group and it continues to focus on outspoken advocacy for its constituency. More often, the executive director moves comfortably from advocate to administrator and when she leaves, the job announcement for her successor requires prior administrative, fund-raising, and computer experience but says little or nothing at all about advocacy or organizing. Over time the group founded through the confrontational activism of outsiders fits cozily into the corporate and political world. The organization's mission becomes narrowed to providing for its current clients. It is their needs, not the needs of those similarly situated in the community or across the nation, that become the exclusive focus of organizational work programs. The funds from dinners and other events, as well as individual donations, have no restrictions on their use but are spent to enhance client services rather than to influence the national or even local policies negatively affecting the vast numbers not fortunate enough to receive agency assistance.

The above story illustrates many of the factors that have transformed CBOs from their origins in activist struggles into bureaucracies advocating only for their clients' needs rather than for entire constituencies. The story highlights the factors that have led many to doubt CBOs' potential to assist national grassroots campaigns. These factors include the inherently bureaucratic nature of CBOs, the swallowing of advocacy by a service emphasis, funding sources targeting local service rather than advocacy, the unwillingness of CBOs to oppose funders' political agenda, and CBOs' lack of incentive to mobilize their constituency bases other than for the groups' own funding. Each of these factors is discussed below.

CBOs Are Necessarily Bureaucratic

CBOs are unavoidably bureaucratic. Nonprofit organizations are small businesses responsible for payrolls, accounting, personnel policies, and state and federal tax filings. Recipients of public funds must also submit monthly expense statements, narratives, and reports comparing goals/accomplishments for every separate program or contract. Many federal programs, including those addressing homelessness, require separate audits. These requirements compel staff to spend considerable time keeping records, filling out forms, and using basic office skills. In employee selection, applicants with computer or grant-writing skills that can satisfy the CBO's administrative needs often gain priority over those who can relate better to clients. Mary Beth Pudup, a professor in the community studies department at the University of California at Santa Cruz since 1989, has observed that her students spending a semester interning with CBOs increasingly spend more time on internal office assignments than directly working with the agencies' constituencies. Pudup has also found that students now see grant-writing, rather than organizing or advocacy experience, as the key skill necessary for obtaining nonprofit employment.[2]

The time-consuming process of complying with mandated administrative requirements is not matched by similar monitoring of program performance. CBOs learn that it is rare to lose public funding for mediocre performance, whereas failure to comply with administrative requirements can readily cause the nonrenewal of their contracts. Program managers are reluctant to terminate funding for substandard performance because their assessment can be challenged for its subjectivity; but failing to turn in reports on time provides an objective measure of the CBO's failure. As CBOs' survival depends on complying with government forms, executive directors are chosen who can administrate, not agitate. When the leader of a CBO has a bureaucratic mindset, he or she is less likely to create an organizational culture conducive to effective advocacy.

CBO Services Overwhelm Advocacy

Second, the CBO's service component can readily overwhelm its advocacy function. Tim Sampson, a professor of social welfare who has been active in CBOs and sat on their boards for thirty years, provides a classic example of this. During the 1960s a grassroots movement of

Latinos, labor activists, and neighborhood progressives in San Francisco's Mission District forced city officials to target federal Model Cities funds for housing, job training, youth programs, and other community services. The CBOs receiving the funds were deeply committed to neighborhood advocacy. These groups, however, soon used their new political clout to develop the growth of their own programs rather than continuing the process of building a broad-based people's organization. For someone with a job providing a badly needed service to a disenfranchised community, it is easy to equate advocacy for the continuation or expansion of this service with community advocacy. The CBO's chief goal becomes advocating for itself rather than helping people at the grassroots advocate for community needs or building the broad-based organization essential for achieving significant social change.[3]

When I was on the board of the San Francisco Gray Panthers in the early 1980s the traditionally exclusively advocacy-oriented group faced a decision on whether to continue operating a health insurance counseling program that it had launched. Because ongoing funding had unexpectedly been obtained, I supported using the service to help fund the group's advocacy. My board colleagues disagreed, maintaining that the Gray Panthers was not a service organization. I long lamented the board's vote since the chapter's finances soon declined, hampering its effectiveness. But I came to understand the board's decision. The Gray Panthers' ambitious goal of reforming the nation's health system would not be directly advanced by counseling seniors on their health insurance options. Providing the service created opportunities to educate those served about the need for reform, but I know from twenty years of tenant counseling that those seeking personal advice are often not interested in broader policy discussions. Most of my fellow board members were longtime activists prior to the proliferation of CBOs in the late 1960s. They had never expected to be paid for their advocacy work so the idea of needing to provide a service to fund advocacy was not persuasive to them. Nor did they confuse solving an individual problem with social-change advocacy. By contrast, CBOs' service work has created the false sense among staff that they are "advocating" for a constituency when they are in fact providing a "service" to their clients. The CBOs' confusion of service and advocacy may explain how groups funded to perform advocacy only affect those they serve.

Funders Support Individual Services, Not Advocacy

A major factor in CBOs' retreat from national advocacy is that there is no money in it. Most foundation and nearly all government funding related to domestic needs is for the local provision of services and in some cases for community advocacy. There is scant public or foundation funding for CBOs to engage in national advocacy. In a July 1997 report written for the National Committee for Responsive Philanthropy, researcher Sally Covington found that whereas conservative foundations focus their funds on influencing national public policy, grantees of liberal foundations like Ford and Rockefeller are not "rewarded or encouraged for their public policy activism and are often required to downplay their policy commitments." Liberal foundations ask grantees to focus on a short-term quantifiable result rather than providing support for general operations, constituency development, or mobilization strategies. Thus "while conservative funders see themselves as part of a larger movement to defeat 'big government liberalism,' and fund accordingly," mainstream foundations have adopted a "problem-oriented, field specific approach that ignores the reality that the national impact on state, local, and neighborhood issues is so big that the federal framework cannot be overlooked." Foundations' focus on funding specific projects explains why so many CBOs comprise staffers working on unrelated programs, thus weakening the organization's capacity to focus all of its resources on any one campaign. The propensity for progressive funders to support single-issue, specific projects through one-year grants, rather than providing the multiyear support necessary for winning national struggles, also explains why CBOs must devote more staff time to fund-raising and less to getting programmatic work done.[4]

Whereas the Sierra Club and the PIRGs (discussed in chapter 3) use their national budget and staff to assist local chapter mobilizing, the national public interest research and advocacy groups working on housing, welfare, employment, and other urban issues lack the resources to facilitate CBOs' national advocacy. A 1996 study by the Applied Research Center found that few if any Washington D.C.–based public interest groups had the capacity to mobilize CBOs for national campaigns.[5] The only resource the vast majority provided to CBOs was informational materials. Unlike the environmental movement, in which foundations have favored the funding of national organizations that in turn could mobilize locally, the funding stream for addressing urban issues has been directed locally. This means that CBOs often have far greater resources than their national public interest counterparts and thus local resources will have to be used for national mobilizing. As long as CBOs are economically dependent on providing local services, their programs will be focused accordingly.

CBOs' Advocacy Is Curtailed by Public, Foundation, and Private Funds

The steady depoliticization of CBOs is most widely attributed to their increasing reliance on public funds. Prior to 1960 80 percent of nonprofits received no public funds. By the 1990s about 50 percent of total nonprofit revenues came from the government. Many see CBOs' receipt of government funds as compromising their capacity to zealously advocate for the disenfranchised, whose plight is often a direct result of official neglect. For example, Teresa Funicello's *Tyranny of Kindness: Dismantling the Welfare System to End Poverty in America* details how politicians use CBOs to build and maintain their political base.[6] Noting the symbiotic relationship between "politicians and the social welfare agencies who pimp for them," Funicello views most CBOs as "patronage bases who help maintain the status quo at all levels of government." Funicello describes how the War on Poverty programs of the 1960s were designed to rebuild local Democratic Party political machines whose control of patronage was limited by urban reform movements. Since big-city Democratic mayors could no longer simply add their friends and political supporters to city payrolls, they could channel federal poverty funds to selected CBOs to achieve the same result.

The original policy architects for Lyndon Johnson's antipoverty programs were quite aware of the programs' patronage potential. Their strategy was to fund CBOs directly, thus bypassing the local officials whose policies fostered and reaffirmed inner city poverty and despair. Unfortunately, some of the CBOs that initially received funding were disorganized and misspent money while others were so organized that urban mayors saw them using federal money to create independent political bases that challenged mayoral power. Faced with a political revolt by Democratic mayors just as the war on poverty began, the Johnson administration redrew the programs so that local officials would control the distribution of funds. This scenario explains why Chicago's original Mayor Richard Daley, who cared little about ameliorating poverty or racism but who foresaw how federal antipoverty funds could build a nonprofit patronage machine, arranged to get himself appointed the head of the Conference of Mayors Task Force on the War on Poverty.

Funicello's depiction of New York City's nonprofit patronage operation mirrors what I have witnessed in San Francisco under a succession of mayors. CBOs dependent on mayoral funding decisions rarely publicly challenge mayoral policies, even when such actions harm the CBOs' constituencies. Since CBO leaders are perceived as representing neighborhoods or constituencies, their reaction to mayoral actions shapes public attitudes. When they do not openly oppose mayoral policies that hurt low-income people, dissent by activists deemed less representative is marginalized. This pattern has been particularly manifested around the related problems of homelessness and urban gentrification. Since widespread visible homelessness emerged in urban America in 1982, San Francisco's CBOs have rarely publicly criticized mayoral policies on homelessness. Nor have these CBOs challenged mayoral opposition to strong rent controls or other land use measures that prevent the displacement of the CBOs' own constituencies from the city. Politicians' patronage power allows them to count upon the silence of CBO leaders, thus facilitating policies that ignore or worsen the life situations for CBOs' low-income clientele.

Receipt of public funds is not the only factor that deters CBOs' advocacy. Foundations and private donors may play an even greater role in stifling CBO dissent. In San Francisco and other cities, staff from foundations such as the United Way have long been part of neighborhood and homeless policy planning groups. The foundation's involvement seems innocent enough; the United Way ostensibly enters low-income communities in order to help build local community decision making structures. Yet as I witnessed firsthand in San Francisco's South of Market community, a community planning process consisting largely of United Way–funded nonprofit organizations means that foundation staff has tremendous influence over what is decided. The staff does not have to act in an authoritarian or high-handed manner; the groups funded understand that attacking the proposals of foundation staff jeopardizes the renewal of their own grants. The foundation-funded CBOs also understand that the foundations and local governments see each other as partners, not adversaries; such groups will not challenge mayors on whom the foundation is counting to provide ongoing funding for its neighborhood-planning processes or other projects. Similarly, when the United Way and other foundations sit on a mayor's homelessness planning council, that body is not going to publicly criticize the mayor's failure to commit adequate resources to reduce homelessness. A CBO that criticizes mayoral homelessness policies, approved by such councils, is unlikely to receive a favorable response to its next grant application.

Similarly, all the focus on CBOs' receipt of public funds obscures the far greater deterrent impact of wealthy and corporate donors. These donors' importance to CBOs has magnified as Americans' overall charitable giving to the poor has declined. CBOs severely harmed by precipitous reductions in United Way allocations along with government cuts feel they have no choice but to seek funds from the economic elite. The CBOs' most common vehicle for obtaining such contributions is through an annual dinner. These dinners seek to tap corporate and affluent donors whose political agenda has often harmed the CBO's constituency. Buying a five-thousand-dollar table at a CBO fundraising dinner is great corporate public relations and can lead the CBO to make the corporation's CEO a future dinner honoree. With CBOs turning to the corporate sector for funds, it is no surprise that CBOs will not touch local legislation to raise business taxes. Nor will CBOs support other measures that require downtown areas to pay their fair share for neighborhood services. If public funding were the main obstacle to advocacy, CBOs would support mayoral revenue-raising proposals opposed by the corporate sector. But many CBOs are far more fearful of losing corporate and individual support, which can be ongoing, than of alienating a mayor who will one day be replaced and whose favor can be regained by walking precincts at election time.

CBOs' reliance on funding sources that deter local advocacy, however, should not restrict their participation in national campaigns. Most mayors deciding local funding allocations would be thrilled if CBOs fought for increased federal funding for cities and for federal programs whose positive local impact will inevitably be credited to mayoral leadership. Foundations certainly would not oppose CBOs' acting nationally to increase funding for neighborhood improvements and human services; such funding would reduce pressure on foundations to spend a larger percentage of their assets to meet the rising needs caused by federal cutbacks. Although the CBOs' corporate and affluent supporters could deter CBO national advocacy on some issues (such as raising corporate taxes), such figures played no visible role in the successful national efforts to reduce federal spending to cities, legal services, the arts, and other domestic programs. CBOs' wealthy donors would be unlikely to deter the groups' participation in national campaigns seeking to increase federal funding for such programs.

Do CBOs Have Any Incentive to Mobilize Their Bases?

Finally, many doubt CBOs' motivation for assisting national campaigns. If most CBOs are run by administrators rather than social-change activists and are not funded to provide national advocacy, what is their incentive to mobilize? The answer is both financial and ideological.

First, as noted in the previous chapter, national campaigns' success at shifting federal spending toward human needs will increase CBOs' funding. Meanwhile, failing to challenge Pentagon bloat and other misguided national priorities virtually ensures future federal cuts for human services—and CBOs. New federal money will limit local officials from having to choose between funding CBOs providing housing and CBOs providing child care services; enough funds would be available for both. As CBOs recognize that their long-term survival depends on assisting national struggles for new priorities, they will be motivated to focus on national activism with the same energy that they direct toward annual dinners and other fund-raising activities.

In addition to CBOs' financial incentive, their staffs philosophically support government programs for low-income people. Unlike much of the American public, there is little talk around CBOs of the alleged evils of "Big Government." CBO staffers are also far more likely than most Americans to see social and economic rather than individual factors as determining people's life situations. CBO salaries do not match comparable government work (which is why many conservatives support CBOs as a cheaper private alternative to city services), so their employees have often chosen to earn less for the opportunity to work at the community level. Many young people join CBOs as a vehicle for engaging in social-change advocacy and soon are disappointed by the lack of emphasis on this activity; such staffers would be strongly motivated to help reconnect CBOs to national struggles. Ultimately CBOs have great potential to bolster national social and economic justice campaigns because most of their thousands of employees are already supportive of progressive social change; they do not need to be convinced, only mobilized. CBOs have an economic and ideological incentive to act nationally to reclaim America's progressive ideals; they need a road map showing them how they can reconnect to national struggles without sacrificing their local work.

Survey: CBOs and National Activism

In order to help assess CBOs' potential for increased national activism I conducted a survey in 1997 of San Francisco CBOs that received federal Community Development Block Grants (CDBGs). I mailed surveys to seventy organizations, only excluding those that clearly had no advocacy function or plainly had no capacity to assist national campaigns. I received twenty-nine responses, all from executive directors and all anonymous. I learned from the responses that the vast majority had annual budgets of more than one million dollars and staffs of more than twenty-five people. The size of these organizations affirms the importance of enlisting their resources in national campaigns.

The survey responses establish that executive directors of CBOs want their agencies to spend greater resources on national campaigns but have not figured out how to proceed. When given four statements to assess their view of national politics, the respondents chose the following by a two-to-one margin: "Community-based organizations should spend greater resources seeking to influence national policies since localities are greatly impacted by national decisions." None selected the statement: "Local activists and CBOs lack the capacity to influence national politics." Other responses revealed that the vast majority of respondents discuss national policy issues with staff and that these discussions usually take place through staff meetings. Newsletters and mailings/action alerts were also used to discuss national issues.

Responses to questions regarding past or potential involvement in national campaigns largely confirmed CBOs' tangible disconnection from the national arena. A majority would not commit staff time for a national Pentagon redirection campaign, though half would assist efforts to increase taxes on the wealthy and corporations. But when asked how much weekly staff time they would commit to such causes, none would devote more than ten hours and most would limit the staff's commitment to four hours a week. Although twenty-two responded that their CBOs had "taken action to defeat welfare reform," there was in fact very little evidence of such action by CBOs in the months preceding the measure's enactment. The nearly unanimous claim to have taken such action was likely based on letters to federal officials, action alerts, and newsletter discussions. Since most of the CBOs reported that their newsletters devoted less than 10 percent of their space to national issues, CBOs' "action" was apparently not geared toward mobilizing. The only aspect of welfare reform that aroused public CBO action was the provision discontinuing disability payments to elderly immigrants. CBOs in San Francisco's Chinatown community, as well as the city's many immigrants' rights groups, engaged in protests and demonstrations on this issue; this may further explain the survey response.

My overall assessment from the survey that many if not most CBOs would increase participation in national activism if they knew how is bolstered by a response indicating that one-third of respondents felt their organizations' 501(c)(3) status prevented them from lobbying on issues. I am continually surprised at the number of nonprofit staffers, board members, and journalists who erroneously believe that nonprofit 501(c)(3) corporations cannot lobby. One CBO executive director with a Washington, D.C., office told me that Washington lobbying and advocacy by the nonprofit sector has been reduced since the introduction of the Istook Amendment in 1995. The measure, sponsored by Representative Ernest Istook (R-OK), would have prevented advocacy by groups receiving federal funds. Groups cannot use federal funds to lobby, but the Istook legislation sought to deny federal funding to recipients that lobbied with nonfederal funds. Although defeated, the so-called gag rule has apparently had a chilling effect on nonprofit advocacy; some executive directors responding to the survey may believe that it passed.

CBOs can lobby both "directly," which means influencing legislation through directly communicating with legislators, and through the "grassroots." Grassroots lobbying seeks to influence legislation by mobilizing the public in what are commonly described as grassroots tactics such as rallies, demonstrations, and phone campaigns. The chief difference between the two forms of lobbying is that the Internal Revenue Service imposes greater financial limits on grassroots lobbying expenditures by 501(c)(3) CBOs. Most survey respondents could legally spend more than one hundred thousand dollars annually on direct lobbying and at least forty-three thousand dollars on grassroots lobbying; few CBOs come anywhere close to these limits, so federal lobbying expenditure ceilings have not been an obstacle to CBOs' national activism.[7]

Finally, the survey responses and CBOs' overall stance toward national activism are undoubtedly affected by the absence of national organizations that can enlist and direct CBO resources in national campaigns. There is no equivalent to the Sierra Club or the PIRGs for mobilizing local organizations around federal housing, social welfare, and economic development programs. The AFL-CIO nationally advocates for such programs but cannot be expected to mobilize predominantly nonunion CBOs around increased funding for urban America. The absence of a national organization that can harness local activists and organizations helps explain the relative lack of public opposition to welfare reform. It even better explains why the Clinton administration's agreement to eliminate new affordable housing opportunities was enacted in virtual silence. It is not that nonprofit housing corporations were not paying attention; rather there was no national organization coordinating the groups to make a major public fight over the issue. When Representative Barney Frank warned CBOs and human services groups in early 1997 that the Pentagon budget, if left unchecked, would soon require steep cuts in their own programs, he used a Capitol Hill meeting with the national public interest sector to make his case. But this sector has little face-to-face connection with CBOs nationally and lacks the resources to mobilize such organizations in response to Frank's assessment.

Why are there national organizations focused on environmental, labor, and human rights that can mobilize grassroots activists and organizations and yet nothing comparable for the issues covered by CBO work programs? One answer is foundation funding patterns. After national environmental groups suffered a string of defeats early in Bill Clinton's first term and further setbacks were projected after the November 1994 elections, foundations intervened to create the National Environmental Trust (NET). NET was given the resources to bolster national environmental campaigns and its strategizing and technical expertise has complemented environmentalists' new national grassroots mobilizing strategy (detailed in chapter 3). By contrast, foundations did not similarly intervene when CBOs' constituencies and programs were under attack. Whereas a well-funded national group like the NET could have built and coordinated CBO and popular opposition to the federal funding cutbacks of the 1990s, foundations remained fixated on addressing community needs locally. Foundations ignored the need for national activism to protect federal funding for local communities; their insistence that community people make the decisions affecting their lives should have compelled their funding of a national group to coordinate opposition to federal efforts to eliminate community resources.

But foundations cannot be blamed for CBOs' own failure to financially support national mobilizing organizations. In the early 1980s Reagan administration officials raised the prospect that HUD's CDBG program would be severely reduced. This threat was met with action alerts to all CDBG-funded agencies, public demonstrations, local congressional hearings attesting to the need for the program, and a lobbying blitz by the National League of Cities. No equivalent mobilizing challenged congressional and White House–accepted plans since 1993 to quietly but steadily decrease the total CDBG allocation. Despite widespread evidence that CBOs' low-income beneficiaries are suffering even greater need, CBOs have not followed the Sierra Club and other environmental groups in changing their approach to national politics. CBOs' ability to mobilize nationally on their constituencies' and their own behalf was no greater at the start of 1999 than in previous years. CBOs cannot afford to wait for a foundation to fund a national coordinating and mobilizing vehicle; they must use their unrestricted funds to create this entity.

How CBOs Can Act Nationally

Use Newsletters to Assist National Campaigns

The first and easiest step for CBOs to reengage with the national arena is to use their newsletters to help national campaigns. The Sierra Club's *The Planet* (described in chapter 3) shows the newsletter's effectiveness as an organizing and mobilizing tool. Newsletters are an increasingly critical information vehicle for two reasons. First, as mainstream media coverage of both local and national activism declines, newsletters become the chief vehicle for expanding campaigns and notifying activists that their individual activities are part of a broader movement. Articles about people attending rallies, leafleting, or engaging in direct action around a particular campaign or issue encourage readers to become similarly involved. People are more motivated to table at a shopping center for a national campaign if they know that their action is not isolated but part of a nationwide effort that will have a powerful cumulative impact.

The newsletter stories do not have to focus only on events the CBO has organized or led; one way CBOs with limited available resources can assist national efforts is to publicize events and campaigns that might attract participation from the CBOs' constituencies or donor bases. Also effective is newsletters' highlighting of national campaigns involving issues not directly related to the CBOs' own work. For example, a local environmental publication in the San Francisco Bay Area included a full page on the anti-Nike campaign. Such cross-fertilization broadens knowledge about other struggles and increases the likelihood that newsletter readers will write a letter, make a phone call, or take other action to help other causes. Using one column on one newsletter page for action alerts for the Nike, Guess, Disney, or other campaigns is a simple, cost-effective strategy. CBOs working with children or on health issues could similarly use their newsletters to support national campaigns for clean air, toxic right-to-know legislation, and other environmental health issues. CBOs could also devote newsletter space to their local Peace Action chapters so readers could better connect the CBOs' underfunded programs with ongoing Pentagon bloat.

CBOs' devotion of at least 25 percent of their newsletter space to national campaigns, including a column of national action alerts, would help compensate for the lack of media coverage of such struggles. This strategy would also reconnect, both practically and psychologically, CBOs and their constituencies to the national arena that so greatly affects them. CBOs could use their newsletters as the first step toward becoming organizations whose local focus has not obscured their obligation to assist national campaigns.

The second reason newsletters are important is that people read them. As I discuss in the next chapter on the media's mobilizing role, it is increasingly difficult for social-change campaigns to ensure that their message has been received by their target audience. Since newsletters are the chief means by which donors and supporters follow organizations, they attract a particularly responsive readership. This gives CBOs the perfect opportunity to take advantage of their audience's rapt attention by using newsletters to mobilize.

Unfortunately, a mobilizing emphasis was not reflected in my review of dozens of CBO newsletters. Most appear to follow an almost standard format. They include a message from the executive director, a staff profile, articles on recent activities, photos from the latest fund-raising event, and from one to as many as four pages listing donors. The newsletter articles are long rather than punchy. Only a few urged readers to take action and none could possibly be construed as primarily designed to mobilize reader activism. On the contrary, the newsletters appeared designed to avoid inciting action or offending anyone. Rather than focusing on the major challenges faced by their low-income constituencies and calling for necessary social action, the newsletters emphasized the CBO's contribution to improving specific individuals' lives. This reliance on individual success stories is problematic if not accompanied by analysis of the broader and systemic challenges facing America's low-income population. Such analysis was typically absent. CBOs can show donors that their money is effectively spent without creating a Ronald Reagan–like "Morning in America" commercial that defies social reality. Newsletters should inspire readers to tackle larger social concerns, not convince them that an annual contribution to the CBO fulfills their social obligations.

CBO newsletters represent a tremendous opportunity to enhance social-change activism. For no additional cost or time CBOs could use newsletters to bolster national campaigns seeking to benefit both themselves and their constituencies. Using CBOs' newsletters to foster national activism is a small but important step in reconnecting activists and organizations to national policy struggles.

Use Unrestricted Funds for National Advocacy

The CBOs in my survey are typical of most in that their budgets are primarily composed of funds that must be spent for a specific purpose. This purpose is almost always local. Money collected from CBOs' fund-raisers, however, can be spent for any legally permitted purpose. These unrestricted funds, like individual donations made for general support, should be used to bolster national campaigns. In my experience, CBOs use their unrestricted funds to provide special services to their clients rather than to advocate for the needs of the broader constituency. It is unusual for CBOs to use these funds to engage in high-profile advocacy or mobilizing on their constituencies' behalf. If every CBO devoted at least twenty-five thousand dollars of its unrestricted funds to support national advocacy, the total resources for national campaigns would increase overnight. Considering that many CBO dinners include five-thousand-dollar tables and even higher corporate sponsorships, this amount should be viewed as a reasonable allocation for building support for national struggles whose support will benefit CBOs and their constituencies.

Establish a National Mobilizing Vehicle

What many find most frustrating about CBOs is that groups created out of grassroots pressure have often lost their organizing mentality. The message that the 1990s brought home to national environmentalists—that "people power," not insider lobbying, is essential for national success—has gone unheard or at least unacted upon by the CBO sector. This may be because the contracting out of city services has enabled many nonprofits' budgets to grow despite federal funding cuts. Nonprofits also remain extremely popular with even politically conservative big city mayors, both for their patronage function and as alternatives to municipal public employee unions. But I know from my experience in San Francisco that CBOs' executive directors and staffs are greatly distressed by the lack of federal assistance for their constituencies. The challenge is for CBOs to reinvent themselves and their mission to include influencing the national arena.

Creating a national CBO mobilizing capacity is not as expensive as it may sound. The anti-Nike campaign (profiled in chapter 1) was operated by existing organizations that decided to focus resources on the issue. AIWA launched and carried out its national campaign against Jessica McClintock, Inc. (discussed in chapter 2) with a two-hundred-thousand-dollar annual budget. CBOs could not match the budgets of the national environmental groups described in chapter 3, but environmentalists need more resources because their opponents could afford to spend twenty million dollars on the Clean Air Act campaign alone. CBO efforts to direct more federal funds to local neighborhoods and communities and to stop federal attacks on the poor would not face such powerful, economics-driven opposition. I noted in the preceding chapter on redirecting Pentagon bloat that Neighbor to Neighbor employed one hundred field organizers on a two-million-dollar budget at the height of the Central American anti-intervention campaign. Based on this precedent from the late 1980s I assumed that a four-million-dollar budget could create a similar operation today. If every CBO that responded to my survey contributed only ten thousand dollars for national organizing supporting its agenda, San Francisco alone could raise $290,000. Similar commitments throughout the country would raise at least two million dollars, enabling the hiring of about forty organizers. These organizers would at the very minimum mobilize sufficient public outrage over future CDBG cuts to maintain the current inadequate levels. Each CBO's ten-thousand-dollar investment would thus not only pay financial dividends but, unlike resources devoted to dinners and events wooing wealthy donors, such funds would be working to build national support for policies enhancing social and economic fairness.

CBOs in the Twenty-first Century: Who Will Call the Shots?

If CBOs had begun fostering national activism as late as the early 1990s America would likely have maintained its longtime affordable housing program. Many of the federal actions contributing to growing social and economic inequality might still have occurred, but they would not have been enacted quietly. This book shows what national grassroots mobilizing by a trained organizing staff can accomplish and how students, progressive public relations firms (chapter 6), and other underutilized resources can create momentum and publicity for national campaigns that can overcome powerful, well-funded adversaries. We also know what happens when such mobilizing does not occur: the results are visible in low-income communities and in the political decisions that shaped the century's final decade.

CBOs' commitment to national activism has importance beyond their capacity to assist national campaigns seeking to reclaim America's progressive ideals. CBOs' increased dependence on wealthy and corporate donors has been an outgrowth of federal funding cutbacks, and this dependence restricts and could eventually curtail CBOs' capacity to mobilize for progressive change. Balanced budget imperatives require sharp domestic spending cuts in the early twenty-first century absent national action for new priorities. If CBOs do not join this struggle and cuts in their federal funding proceed, many CBOs could become so financially dependent on elite donors as to become corporate- or affluent- rather than community-directed. CBOs that speak of forging private-public partnerships to replace lost public funds may have forgotten that private money expects to call the shots. There is a difference between wealthy and corporate donors providing a small fraction of a CBO's budget and their providing a percentage so meaningful that they expect a major say in setting policy. CBOs' national activism is necessary to avoid this potential shift in control. By joining together to create new federal budget priorities CBOs can also forestall the turning away of important institutions created by past social movements from the people they were founded to serve.

Chapter 6

The Media

Mobilizing through the Echo Effect

The obstacles to using the media to mobilize national activism can be seen in the following stories.

Thuyen Nguyen's Vietnam Labor Watch report in February 1997 on Nike's abusive labor practices brought the banker-turned-activist widespread publicity. Nguyen's photo appeared in newspapers and he was interviewed on camera by CNN and other national and local television stations. Nguyen was prominently featured in the *New York Times* news section and in Bob Herbert's *Times* columns. His report was even the subject of a week of Gary Trudeau's *Doonesbury* comic strip. When I asked Nguyen how it felt to be a major news celebrity, he laughed and told me that his own sister, who lived in New York, had never heard of him. She was not aware of his report and had been surprised to learn of his media attention.

In April 1997 I met with diverse groups of campus activists at Clark University in Worcester, Massachusetts. Most of these concerned and dedicated young activists did not read a daily newspaper. Nor did most, with the exception of the foreign students, daily monitor other news sources such as television or radio. The students relied on picking up information "here and there" and would peruse weekly news magazines when they got the chance.

Jeff Cohen, executive director of the media watchdog group Fairness and Accuracy in Reporting (FAIR), was speaking on the radio about journalism's "echo effect." This phrase refers to a story appearing in one news outlet that then reaches a far broader audience as it is discussed, featured, and "echoed" through other media sources.

Cohen noted that news stories of interest to conservatives readily enter the national public debate by echoing through such sources as radio talk shows, televised discussions by Beltway pundits, and the writings of syndicated columnists. By contrast, a front-page exposé or newspaper series on corporate wrongdoing or a similar story that advances a progressive agenda is unlikely to be echoed; such stories then quickly pass from public consciousness.

The above stories underline this chapter's main themes: national campaigns for social and economic justice grow through ongoing coverage that mainstream news reporters and most of the "alternative" media only rarely provide. Today's activists cannot accurately chant that "the whole world is watching" because fewer people closely follow national news; those who do are not watching, reading, or listening to the same source. Since the media retain the capacity to mobilize activists and build national campaigns it is imperative for citizen activists and organizations working on national campaigns to use innovative strategies to create an echo effect. It is also critical for activists to use creative approaches to mobilize people, particularly students and those under thirty, who are increasingly unreachable through traditional media.

This chapter first discusses how alternative weeklies and progressive periodicals largely fail to build support for national grassroots campaigns. This has left Pacifica radio as the chief progressive media resource committed to the ongoing coverage of national struggles that is essential for mobilizing national activism. I then discuss how organizations must use progressive public relations firms to create an echo effect through the alternative and mainstream media that would otherwise not occur.

Do the Alternative Media Mobilize?

Tom Rosenstiel, director of the Project for Excellence in Journalism, sponsored by the Pew Charitable Trusts, has found that "There is more of a team mentality on the conservative side. There is, for instance, a great deal more intellectual collaboration between the *Wall Street Journal* editorial pages and Republican policy makers than there is with any liberal editorial page and any Democratic policy maker. There is no sense of loyalty to party among liberal commentators and editorial pages." Supporting this view is William Kristol, who went from advising Vice President Dan Quayle to founding and editing the *Weekly Standard*. Kristol observed that whereas "conservative editorial writers often think of themselves as 'shaping the agenda for a movement,' liberals have 'the tone of preaching eternal truths to an unenlightened citizenry.'"[1]

The reluctance of mainstream media to mobilize support for the liberal causes they favor is not surprising. Media dependent on advertising dollars cannot afford to use their news and editorial bureaus to build campaigns in favor of policies that their advertisers likely oppose. Nor have the mainstream media sought to identify themselves as aligned with national campaigns seeking to seriously challenge the status quo. But although Rosenstiel and Kristol were discussing the mainstream media, their comments also apply to the weeklies and progressive periodicals. Their editorial support for progressive causes is rarely matched by ongoing coverage of national campaigns or any other approach for mobilizing national activism. Mainstream media editors do a better job of maintaining support for the status quo than the weeklies and progressive periodicals do for building the national grassroots campaigns necessary for changing it.

The Decline of the Weeklies

Activists in the national struggles of the 1960s circumvented the mainstream media's inadequate coverage of their campaigns by creating their own "alternative" media. This primarily took the form of weekly newspapers. Unfortunately, as David Armstrong described in *A Trumpet to Arms: Alternative Media in America*, the period of weekly newspapers written by activists who saw themselves as the voices of a movement was short-lived.[2] By the early 1970s the alternative media were less and less the voice of a political movement and more and more a vehicle for linking corporate advertisers to hip, young consumers. This trend has continued. Most of today's weeklies do not offer a political alternative to the status quo and largely ignore national issues. The political content in what has become the weeklies' cookie-cutter format is found among the half-dozen "in short" news items or in the single lengthy feature article on a local issue or personality. But the impact of even the best of these stories, focusing on such topics as local development fights or official malfeasance, is diluted by the surrounding materials that comprise the overwhelming bulk of the publication. As weeklies refrain from making political endorsements and retrench from offering a specific social or economic agenda, the value of their political content is easily lost amidst pages and pages of advertising, entertainment reviews, and consumer tips on wine or futon purchases. Many weeklies draw important revenue from advertisements for phone sex or escort services. More people may pick up these papers for their extensive personal ads than for their handful of pages addressing political themes.

As fewer weeklies seek to build activism around even local issues, their lack of coverage of national grassroots campaigns and issues represents a lost opportunity for fostering national activism. Even worse, many weeklies are either "postpolitical" or openly opposed to progressive campaigns. This is particularly troubling since the circulation of the nation's alternative weeklies more than doubled during the 1990s and the weeklies attract young readers who often do not read daily newspapers. In some cases a medium created to provide a viewpoint at odds with the political and corporate elite now seeks to reaffirm the status quo. For example, on successive trips to New York City I noticed that the "alternative" weekly most commonly stacked in cafes was the *New York Press*. One issue featured an attack on welfare. Another contained four separate articles attacking rent control. The New Times Corporation, which owns nine weeklies, routinely attacks progressive organizations for either causing social problems or profiting from them. For example, the company's *San Francisco Weekly* blamed the nationally acclaimed Center for Juvenile and Criminal Justice for inhumane jail conditions. The reason? The Center supports and operates alternatives to incarceration and has publicly opposed the costly prison building boom that New Times endorses. Similarly, the chief political writer for the paper's Los Angeles outlet criticized "the homeless lobby" for attributing widespread visible homelessness to the lack of low-cost housing rather than to willful alcohol and drug abuse by poor persons. New Times not only advances a political agenda hostile to progressive interests but also has purchased and then closed weeklies whose editorial policies challenged corporate power. The company's papers have a hip design, provide detailed arts and entertainment listings, and represent a media product solely designed to attract advertisers. Once a New Times paper enters a city, its resources make it difficult for less established but more political weekly papers to compete.[3]

Fortunately, some weeklies still offer a political alternative and can foster national mobilizing. The *Valley Advocate* in Northampton, Massachusetts, helped build the anti–nuclear power movement and regularly addresses national issues. The *Sacramento News & Review* is trying to build weeklies' national capacity by coordinating issues around specific subjects. *SN&R*'s editor, Melinda Welch, had the idea of having other weeklies use their first May 1997 issue to discuss rising local and national poverty. Sixty-five papers participated. Welch thinks weeklies would similarly join to mobilize support for specific national legislation "if it was the right issue at the right time." Such an opportunity may be hard to find, however, since publishers and editors of the weeklies "are not activists and do not have an activist mentality." Welch sees future coordination as most likely on issues affecting the media and regretted that the weeklies had not come together to help defeat the Telecommunications Act of 1996, which facilitated media conglomeration. Welch also senses an increased willingness among the independent weeklies to take on national issues that have local impacts. Since stories demonstrating the local impact of national struggles facilitate national activism, these weeklies could easily profile local problems and explain how national action is part of the solution. Because Welch has an activist mentality, her paper regularly makes the local/national connection; activists in most cities will have to push hard for their local weeklies to help mobilize support for national campaigns.

Progressive Periodicals: Critics, Not Mobilizers

With the weeklies' capacity to build national campaigns limited, it is even more imperative for progressive periodicals to assist national mobilizing. Unfortunately, few appear interested in the task. These publications editorially support progressive causes but do little more than the neutral or unsympathetic mainstream media to mobilize or build support for national campaigns. While the editor of the *Wall Street Journal* can brag about the paper's becoming a "billboard" for mobilizing around conservative proposals, progressive editors either feel that mobilizing is not their responsibility or that readers already know how to get involved with national struggles. Rather than provide the ongoing story lines that are necessary to grab readers' attention and build national campaigns, these periodicals appear to emphasize writing about new or previously unreported topics. Since national campaigns represent the leading vehicles for implementing the periodicals' professed ideals, such lack of coverage reflects a lack of activist consciousness that is as injurious to national mobilizing as the mainstream media's lack of coverage.

When progressive periodicals do cover national struggles, it is invariably after a major campaign event has occurred. The goal is to report on what happened, not to create in advance a level of urgency and excitement among readers that would persuade them to participate. The periodicals do not even make a special effort to mobilize readers to attend important national campaign events scheduled long in advance. For example, the long-planned October 18, 1997, International Day of Protest against Nike arrived without articles urging readers to attend their local protest. Do weeklies like *The Nation* simply assume that other media will alert people to such events or that progressives have such a tight national network that everyone knew about the Nike protests? Considering that greater participation in national campaigns would bring new readers to the periodicals covering them, the publication's failure to bolster them is a missed economic as well as political opportunity. Similarly, such publications could build campaigns and readership by reaching a more racially and gender-diverse audience; yet as *The Nation* columnist Katha Pollitt pointed out, with some exceptions the "left liberal media is a club of white male journalists."[4] Noting that periodicals such as *Mother Jones* and the *Utne Reader* have "moved both rightward and lite-ward over the past decade," Pollitt has frequently had cause to criticize the overwhelmingly white male writers of *The Nation*. Because racial minorities and women comprise the largest progressive constituencies, periodicals seeking to mobilize potential activists would logically rely on writers and subjects capable of attracting such groups.

When I was speaking to audiences at bookstores and other venues while promoting *The Activist's Handbook*, I was surprised to learn how few activists read progressive periodicals, and particularly how few young people. It seems that those working for social change on a daily basis are less likely to read such publications than are the academics, journalists, and think tank scholars who write for them. By not adequately covering national activism, progressive periodicals have become disconnected from the participants in national social and economic justice campaigns. As periodicals realize they are not reaching an activist audience, they become even less geared to building volunteer participation in national campaigns. This unfortunate cycle is among the problems created when progressive periodicals lose connection to activists and national grassroots campaigns. Three other problems also have emerged. First, such periodicals are failing to help "legitimize" activist leaders so that other media will solicit them as spokespersons. Katha Pollitt has observed that the left liberal journalist seeks validation from the mainstream media; such writers should instead elevate the standing of activist leaders so that the mainstream media become more comfortable quoting their voices and favorably covering their campaigns. Second, the periodicals' isolation from activists has let scholars' "blueprints" for progressive campaigns go unread by those who could benefit from and would be the implementers of such ideas. Third, periodicals isolated from activist leaders and organizations are more likely to get the story wrong and actually undermine national mobilizing efforts.

The most obvious example of this demobilizing impact is seen in progressive periodicals' coverage of national environmental issues. Their dominant perspective, as reflected in chapter 3's discussion of Alexander Cockburn and Jeffrey St. Clair's criticism of the Clean Air Act campaign, is that most national environmental groups compromise on the brink of victory. Such compromises are never described as a function of a problematic political situation but only of their leadership's strategic ineptitude. When the national grassroots mobilizing campaigns of the Sierra Club and the PIRGs do not fit this neat picture, the campaigns go unreported or are redrawn to fit the prevailing frame. The net impact is to convince readers not to support, join, or become active in national organizations focused on environmental issues.

If progressive periodicals saw themselves as connected to a movement their news stories on national environmental groups would quote all sides. The authors could still conclude that the national groups completely failed but readers would hear from those criticized, so they could make their own assessment. Instead, what readers get are journalists rejecting the successful national grassroots struggle for cleaner air as green groups simply "blowing smoke." Jeffrey St. Clair and Alexander Cockburn's nationally syndicated clean air story avoided quoting officials from the Sierra Club or the PIRGs on the issue; the views of activists who spent countless hours tabling, phoning, walking the streets, and doing the unpublicized and unglamorous tasks essential for success were also ignored. Instead, the only account of the clean air resolution that appeared in most progressive periodicals was St. Clair and Cockburn's assessment that the struggle represented yet another example of the national groups' "smoke, mirrors, and collapse" in the face of industry and Democratic Party opposition.[5] It would be hard to create a more perfect strategy for demobilization. The message is that national environmental groups are incompetent, destructive, and "largely irrelevant," that their only remaining political function is as "full-time fund-raising machines and reflexive cheerleaders for compromised and flawed policies, such as the new clean air rules."[6] Since "the larger a group gets, the less effective it becomes," these critics reason that activists should work exclusively with local environmental groups even if this means giving industry and anti-enviro forces free rein in the national arena.[7]

It would have been very easy for progressive periodicals to give the Sierra Club, the PIRGs, or other national groups involved in the clean air campaign the opportunity to respond to the harsh charges leveled against them. If their critics' analysis was correct the groups' presumably weak rebuttals would render attacks on their strategies and tactics even more convincing. The only reason not to follow an approach that protects against demobilization is if the journalist is more concerned with asserting his or her own power than with the health of a movement. Unfortunately, as progressive periodicals have lost their connection to participants in activist campaigns, journalists' accountability to social-change struggles has diminished.

Progressive periodicals can demobilize national activism even when avoiding criticism of activist groups. *The Nation* ran a cover story on the Clean Air Act struggle during the campaign that failed to even mention the Sierra Club or the PIRGs. The "other side" of the standards battle was identified as simply "dozens of non-corporate-backed scientists and health professionals," along with the American Lung Association. The article's theme was that industry's big-moneyed opposition was likely to prevail and readers were given no indication that the Sierra Club and the PIRGs were leading a massive, nationwide grassroots mobilizing effort to overcome this spending imbalance. A lengthy cover story that could have been used to mobilize readers to participate in a national struggle instead ignored grassroots environmental activism and left readers resigned to yet another triumph by the corporate sector.[8]

Progressive periodicals primarily preach to the already converted. Imploring readers to believe what they already know to be true or filling in additional facts to an already established framework is less important than helping to build support for the national campaigns that represent the best hope for reclaiming America's progressive ideals. Such publications devote ample space to criticizing mainstream media; this has apparently obscured their own limitations in fulfilling their stated political mission.

Pacifica Radio:
Still Mobilizing after All These Years

As weeklies and progressive periodicals have largely abandoned ongoing coverage of national campaigns, the Pacifica radio network has become the last remaining progressive media institution that serves to mobilize national activism. Pacifica's five stations, located in New York (WBAI), Washington, D.C.(WPFW), Houston (KPFT), Los Angeles (KPFK), and Berkeley (KPFA), reach more than seven hundred thousand listeners each week on an annual budget of only nine million dollars. Pacifica covers 22 percent of all American households, with some of its shows reaching additional listeners through the two hundred college and community stations affiliated with the National Federation of Community Broadcasters (NFCB).[9] Pacifica shows have a demonstrated capacity to push campaigns into the national media spotlight. Two recent cases in point: Mumia Abu-Jamal and the Head-waters Forest struggles.

In 1995 a previously little known male African-American activist became a pervasive presence in liberal communities and college towns. He was not a movie or sports star, he did not have a publicity budget, and he could make no personal or televised appearances. What Pennsylvania death-row inmate Mumia Abu-Jamal had going for him was the media savvy of Prison Radio Project director Noelle Hanrahan and the Pacifica radio shows that repeatedly publicized the material she provided them. As Pacifica's national and local shows covered every angle of Abu-Jamal's plight his core of supporters grew steadily. The mobilizing for the campaign to prevent his execution became so insistent that local and national mainstream media outlets began explaining what all the fuss was about. Pacifica's coverage came to "echo" throughout the mainstream and alternative media, dramatically increasing public awareness about the case.

Pacifica's importance to Abu-Jamal's campaign subsequently became even more clear. After Abu-Jamal's original execution date was stayed, Hanrahan recorded his words for public exposure. Pacifica's Amy Goodman, host of its national *Democracy Now!* show, premiered the thirteen newly recorded essays in March 1997. While more than one million people heard Abu-Jamal's words, residents of his own state did not. Temple University's radio station and its affiliates not only canceled the broadcasts just prior to airing, but canceled all Pacifica programming.[10] Hanrahan deserves credit for continually bringing new material to Pacifica's attention, but without Goodman and other Pacifica hosts willing to regularly cover the story, her efforts might have produced little. The Abu-Jamal example shows how ongoing coverage in the progressive media can percolate stories into the mainstream.

Pacifica also mobilized national support for the campaign to save Headwaters Forest. In addition to ongoing coverage Pacifica had as many as four different daily shows discuss the campaign during critical junctures. The shows gave forest activists forums for mobilizing support for the campaign and reflected Pacifica's individual hosts' and producers' recognition that the story was of sufficient importance to justify having it discussed throughout the day. Pacifica's KPFA outlet even provided live coverage of an Oakland, California, hearing about Headwaters. In September 1996, when Pacific Lumber's clear-cutting was about to begin, some KPFA shows, like that hosted by former California governor Jerry Brown, exhorted listeners to assist the fight. Brown's national Pacifica audience was urged to contact the White House and California's senators and to engage in local protests to save Headwaters. Since Pacifica's Houston affiliate is based in the home-town of Pacific Lumber owner Charles Hurwitz, live reports of pro-tests outside Hurwitz's office were broadcast across the Pacifica net-work. Pacifica's coverage built a sense of urgency that compelled people to drop whatever else they were doing and plan to go up to Headwa-ters for the massive rally and blockade designed to save the redwoods. The public pressure forced California's Governor Wilson, Senator Fein-stein, and the White House to reach a last-minute deal with Hurwitz to save part of the Headwaters grove. The national grassroots activism of forest activists elevated the Headwaters story but, as with the fight to save Mumia Abu-Jamal's life, the campaign's activities might have remained largely unknown and unreported without Pacifica's coverage.

Aileen Alfandary, KPFA's longtime news director, saw a parallel between the Abu-Jamal and Headwaters campaigns. In both cases activists continually urged radio hosts to provide coverage of their fights. Alfandary observed that "we were always hearing from people in these campaigns, and they always had speakers available and the latest information to move the story." Alfandary and her Pacifica col-leagues are all too unusual among progressive journalists in recogniz-ing the newsworthiness of grassroots struggles. Pacifica's providing ongoing coverage of national campaigns facilitates grassroots activism and the mobilizing necessary for their expansion and success. This applies even when campaigns lack the urgency of a pending human or ecological execution. Moreover, as Amy Goodman and other Paci-fica hosts give priority to coverage of national grassroots campaigns, they also give national activist leaders like the late Judi Bari, Medea Benjamin, and Noelle Hanrahan the stature necessary for expanded mainstream media exposure. Pacifica's role in percolating and legit-imizing stories for the broader media has become so critical that it is dif-ficult to imagine a new national activism emerging without Pacifica's support.

Enhancing Pacifica's Mobilizing Capacity

National activism would greatly benefit from a Pacifica network that matched conservative radio's national mobilizing capacity. Three factors have restrained this development. First, Pacifica lacks the resources to regularly cover all national grassroots campaigns. Federal cutbacks in funding for the Corporation for Public Broadcasting have forced Pacifica to return with ever-increasing frequency to its listeners to make up the difference. Funds that could have gone to expand Pacifica's influence are instead maintaining existing operations. Second, Pacifica shows are not heard nationally. Their absence is particularly felt in key population centers such as Chicago and Boston. Pacifica's influence extends beyond its stations in Los Angeles, New York City, Washington, D.C., Houston, and the San Francisco Bay Area through independent radio stations carrying its shows. Where its voice is not heard and there is no other daily progressive media vehicle, a critical resource for mobilizing activists in these communities is lost.

Finally, Pacifica's mobilizing potential depends on its attracting more listeners, particularly young people. Only 1 percent of Pacifica's potential audience listens to the network each week and its shows are particularly missed by those eighteen to thirty years old. When I attended a KPFA listeners' forum in Berkeley in 1997 most of those present were over sixty and nobody appeared to be under thirty years of age. Pacifica has great strength among veteran movement activists but many members of the upcoming generation are not even familiar with its stations. This requires a media outlet dedicated to peace and social justice to implement strategies to attract young activists. One approach is to include younger hosts. Marcos Frommer, host of Pacifica's KPFK morning drive-time show *Up for Air* in Los Angeles, obtained his current position in 1996 at the age of twenty-eight. Although KPFK's primary audience is thirty-four to forty-five, Frommer's show is listened to most by those aged thirty to forty, and then those twenty to thirty. Frommer believes that Pacifica should look at how commercial stations attract young listeners through youth-friendly formats. In Pacifica's case this would include snappier music, shorter interviews, and a focus on stories that do not continually leave young listeners "feeling defeated." Frommer feels that "you can't understand tragedy without comedy" and that a steady focus on depressing stories demobilizes listeners by convincing them that progressive struggles are hopeless. Frommer tries to mobilize listeners by focusing on about six stories and then using ongoing coverage to show how grassroots campaigns can prevail.

Implementing Frommer's ideas at Pacifica sounds easy. A priority could be placed on filling newly available time slots with young hosts speaking to their generation's concerns. These hosts would connect young activists to Pacifica as their baby boomer colleagues did for the movement activists of the 1960s and 1970s. Pacifica could strive to become the voice of a new activist generation. This effort would serve the station's historic mission of supporting peace and justice campaigns and lay the groundwork for a future listener funding base. In addition the station's public affairs and cultural programming could emphasize attracting younger listeners, much as Pacifica has sought to increase its African-American and Latino base. Format changes, including shortening segments and providing more up-tempo musical introductions and a greater mix of positive stories, would also help. Some Pacifica stations have moved to attract young people through offering hip-hop and youth call-in shows. Listening to such shows is a revelation, since younger voices are rarely heard on Pacifica. Such programming is a good start to fully integrating young people's concerns into Pacifica's primary public affairs format. It also shows that there are forces inside Pacifica that do not want the institution to repeat the peace movement's experience (chapter 4) of declining through a failure to recruit new generations of potential supporters.

Despite the obvious benefits of following Frommer's suggestions and becoming the voice of a new activist generation, changing Pacifica to enhance its current and future mobilizing capacity will not be easy. Like many institutions committed to social change in the broader society, Pacifica has great difficulty making internal reforms. The biggest obstacle to change is structural: there is a lack of consensus over who should decide programming and other format changes. Pacifica management has been attacked for not providing listener input into programming decisions, and it remains unclear how Pacifica could proceed to adopt these proposals. Listeners distrustful of management could view Frommer's idea of looking at how commercial radio attracts young listeners as Pacifica abandoning progressive politics for a corporate agenda. Creating young-person-friendly formats could renew charges of growing commercialization at the station. Some Pacifica critics equate efforts to expand listenership with moderating the stations' politics. Many also view their local Pacifica station as a community resource rather than a national mobilizing vehicle; their call is for greater local control over Pacifica stations and less national Pacifica programming or decision making. Having seen progressives repeatedly lose in the national arena in the 1990s, Pacifica critics see local control as essential to preserving the stations' mission.

Unfortunately, failing to expand the audience for the progressive media institution most committed to local and national mobilizing only deprives national campaigns of a key resource necessary to help them prevail. Pacifica can become more democratic without abandoning its national mission under the rubric of "local control." As its demographic audience continues to age, the institution's long-term survival depends on attracting new generations of activists. Pacifica supporters should all agree on this need. With the decline in the mobilizing focus of alternative weeklies and progressive periodicals, Pacifica's ability to attract and mobilize young listeners is more critical than ever.

How Public Relations Firms
Create a Mainstream Media Echo Effect

Despite their limitations the progressive media have increasingly become the chief focus for national activists resigned to a lack of ongoing mainstream media coverage for their campaigns. Some assume there is little point working with media that are editorial cheerleaders for the economic and social status quo. National campaigns, however, make a big mistake if they do not seek to garner ongoing mainstream publicity. The anti-Nike, Jessica McClintock, and clean air campaigns previously discussed show how this publicity can be achieved. What has not been discussed is how it comes about. Absent extraordinary circumstances, stories about progressive national campaigns only echo through the mainstream media when a public relations firm accomplishes this goal. Many are unaware of activists' reliance on communications experts. I had not used public relations firms through 1996 and did not discuss using such firms in *The Activist's Handbook* published that year. I now believe that the days when activists on their own could generate ongoing national publicity in diverse mainstream media outlets are gone. As the national media have acknowledged their sharply reduced coverage of direct-action protests and other events that once generated publicity, activists must retain progressive communications experts to create a mainstream media echo effect.

Communication Works: P.R. for Progressives

In the anti-Nike campaign discussed in chapter 1, I observed that magazine, newspaper, and television news stories had failed to ignite broad media inquiry into Nike's labor and human rights abuses. When Global Exchange entered the campaign in the spring of 1996 it brought Tony Newman of its in-house public relations staff and Newman's affiliated firm, Communication Works, into the struggle. When Newman and Communications Works entered the anti-Nike campaign, media coverage galvanized. This was not a coincidence. For example, the most echoed story of the Nike struggle has been the widespread labor abuses among the company's Vietnamese work force. There had been little publicity about such abuses until Thuyen Nguyen visited the Vietnam plants and wrote a shocking report for his group, Vietnam Labor Watch. Thuyen sent a press release about his report throughout the national media but received no response. He then contacted Global Exchange, which put Newman and Communication Works to work. Communication Works took Nguyen's previously ignored report of Nike's Vietnam labor abuses and created a packed New York City press conference that brought widespread national media coverage. The Vietnam Labor Watch findings subsequently echoed through editorial columns, sports pages, and a series of strips in *Doonesbury*. Media stories about the anti-Nike campaign invariably cite Nguyen's report and the story is likely to echo for years after its release. Yet without the intervention of Communication Works Nguyen's pathbreaking report would likely have remained unknown.

Public relations firms not only create mainstream media stories but also work to ensure the ongoing coverage necessary to keep the story alive. When news editors failed to assign ongoing coverage of the Nike campaign, Newman and Communication Works worked with Bob Herbert of the *New York Times* and other editorial and sports columnists to keep the story echoing. A story by one columnist gives others a similar idea, and Communication Works optimized the likelihood of other columnists following Herbert's lead by faxing his and other columns to major media outlets. The firm has also enabled the anti-Nike campaign to preempt Nike's own public relations offensives. For example, Global Exchange received a leaked copy of Andrew Young's Nike-commissioned report on the company's overseas labor practices on the day before its release. Communication Works and Global Exchange activist Medea Benjamin spent all night preparing a detailed critique and rebuttal. The firm's professional-looking analysis was then faxed to all media prior to Young's morning press conference. This not only enabled reporters to target the weaknesses of Young's review but also helped create a negative spin on Young's report that will likely continue to echo through the mainstream media for the duration of the campaign. The firm's chief critique—that Young failed to examine workers' wages—became the dominant media response even in such corporate-oriented publications as *Business Week* and the *Wall Street Journal*. By cultivating reporters and not prejudging editorially conservative news sources, Newman and Communication Works created ongoing mainstream media coverage of the anti-Nike campaign that would likely not otherwise have developed. Such coverage broadened public concern about Nike's labor abuses and expanded the national campaign.

Michael Shellenberger, who joined with Newman in founding Communication Works, says the firm's unofficial motto is "It's the follow-up phone call, stupid." While activists are busy organizing, strategizing, and protesting, firms like Communication Works can spend the hours on the phone often necessary to place stories. The placement of one story leads the firm to send copies of it to other reporters, columnists, and editors who are then more likely to cover the campaign also. When a media gatekeeper like the *New York Times* includes the story the firm saturates other media, realizing that editors want their papers to follow the *Times*'s lead. Communication Works has days when it calls a hundred reporters; this is often what it takes to reverberate a national campaign story through the mainstream media.

Communication Works and other public relations firms have advantages unavailable to most activists in obtaining mainstream media. Public relations staffers develop relationships with editorial page editors, columnists, and reporters that give them the opportunity to at least pitch the story. They not only have more time than activists to make phone calls, but editors and mainstream columnists are accustomed to being called by public relations companies pitching stories. Unlike activists, such firms are viewed by editors as an integral part of the news business; their relationship can approach a sense of collegiality. Further, the media have an interest in cultivating relations with people who have access to breaking news and potentially juicy material. This means that media decision makers will at least listen to Communication Works and on close calls may run its story in the expectation of receiving news tips in the future. Activists can create such symbiotic relationships with local reporters and possibly a few national figures but lack the ongoing relationships, inside contacts, and reciprocity opportunities that public relations firms use to win the widespread mainstream coverage necessary for national campaigns.

In a media world where reporters and interview show hosts regularly make last-minute demands for information or guests, public relations firms are essential. While activists are in the field or at meetings, firms like Communication Works can always be reached and can immediately respond by fax, e-mail, or Federal Express to media inquiries. In the highly publicized October 1997 videotape of Humboldt County sheriff's deputies using pepper spray to torture Headwaters Forest activists, the protesters' attorney lacked the media contacts or communication vehicles necessary to manage the news cycle. The attorney turned the tapes over to Shellenberger of Communication Works, who then negotiated with national media outlets for the best placement of the story. The firm Federal Expressed the video to the *New York Times*, national television network news departments, and, after receiving a call from the White House expressing high-level interest in the story, to the White House. Communication Works spent nearly a week lining up media coverage, scheduling interviews with the protesters, and providing information to the more than three hundred outlets that contacted them about the story. Few if any social-change organizations have the expertise and resources to similarly maximize a story's impact. In fact, the contrast between media coverage of the pepper spray incident and the earlier car bomb explosion targeted at Headwaters Forest activists Judi Bari and Darryl Cherney is striking. The bombing incident led to nearly a week of media stories blaming the victims for the attack, while the activists were in no position to respond. Had Communication Works been involved in the Headwaters struggle at that time they would have launched a mainstream media counteroffensive that would quickly have cut off the FBI's own public relations campaign.

Public relations staff is so critical to national campaigns that organizations like Global Exchange maintain such expertise in-house. When this is not financially feasible, using progressive public relations firms remains an extremely cost-effective strategy. For example, many campaigns use full-page *New York Times* ads to raise their national profile. With donated design services, a national ad costs at least $22,000. When a campaign is seeking to make a powerful visual statement or to win quickly through a knockout blow, such ads make sense. In most national campaigns, using just half as much money to hire a public relations firm has a far greater public impact. This is particularly true when, as I noted at the outset, people's sources of information are increasingly fragmented. In the Clean Air Act campaign discussed in chapter 3, the National Environmental Trust provided both advertising and public relations assistance. The Trust's use of radio and newspaper ads and its placement of national news stories bolstered the campaign's grassroots activism in the field. National campaigns face difficult choices regarding funding priorities but public relations firms garner so much free media publicity that they have become a cost-effective and essential national mobilizing tool.

Is Anybody Paying Attention?
Reaching beyond Conventional Media

Communication Works and other public relations firms increase the chances that people who rely on at least one news source will assist a national campaign. But campaigns still must reach the growing num-ber of potential activists who do not regularly track the news. This problem only recently emerged. In 1965 a Gallup poll of twenty-one- to thirty-five-year-olds found that 67 percent of those surveyed had read a daily newspaper the day before. In 1990 a similar study by Pew showed the number declining to 38 percent, and to 31 percent by 1998. This trend may be difficult to understand for the many long-time activists who read daily newspapers and the free weeklies, listen to Pacifica, National Public Radio, or an independent local station, watch local and/or national television news shows, and subscribe to news-oriented periodicals. I have had enough experience that I am no longer surprised to learn that many people who care deeply about issues do not follow the news. Larry Bensky, Pacifica's national af-fairs correspondent and the host of its daily *Living Room* call-in show, teaches a course in mass communications at a state university. Bensky surveys his students at the start of each term and has found that even most students in a media-centered course do not regularly read daily newspapers.[11]

National campaigns must recognize the traditional media's limited exposure and use other means to reach their activist base. Advertisers have already developed alternative means of attracting consumers, particularly young people. Movie videos are now marketed on fruit labels and new films at fast-food restaurants. Computers, sportswear, and other products are marketed on moving vehicles such as coffee carts, billboards mounted on trucks, the backs of messengers' bicycles, and the increasingly pervasive commuter buses wrapped bumper to bumper with advertising. When the nation's largest airlines were seek-ing to mobilize public opposition to federal destination taxes in 1997 they did not depend on newspaper ads; instead they served up cam-paign messages, complete with congressmembers' phone numbers, with passengers' meals. Nike's advertising is less visible in newspapers and magazines than in its sponsorship of golf tours, soccer leagues, and college athletic programs, and on the clothes worn by its en-dorsers. In order to mobilize national activism when potential partic-ipants are not following the news, unconventional informational vehi-cles must also be used.[12]

Several of these vehicles have been used by the national campaigns described in earlier chapters. The most effective mobilizers, as shown by the Sierra Club's *The Planet*, are organizational newsletters. Also effective is the inclusion of mobilizing messages on everyday materials. The placement of a "redirect Pentagon bloat" message on CDs, yogurt containers, and other products associated with Business Leaders for Sensible Priorities will help enlist new activists in its cause. The phone bills for Working Assets Long Distance (WALD) include two national policy messages each month. WALD gives its customers the option of making free phone calls about the issue or paying to have a "CitizenLetter" sent to the target. In 1997 alone WALD's mobilizing strategy generated an average of 32,000 calls and letters for each of the twenty-four struggles it highlighted. These included demands that the Presidential Sweatshop Task Force endorse a living wage and that Nike CEO Phil Knight pay his company's workers a living wage and ensure them safe working conditions. WALD even uses the outside of its envelopes to communicate its views: its December 1997 payment envelope noted that "Nike earned $798 million in profits, yet they only pay their Asian workers $1.60 a day to make their shoes. Make a free phone call to Nike CEO Phil Knight and tell him to pay a living wage to factory workers."

In an age when people increasingly focus on communicating through new technologies, the value of traditional ways of spreading information is often overlooked. Cesar Chavez's United Farm Workers movement never expected to get fair media coverage and relied on tabling at locations such as supermarkets and campuses to bring its message directly to people and to recruit young activists. The Sierra Club and the PIRGs used this strategy to mobilize support for stronger clean air standards; they proved that tabling remains a viable strategy for national grassroots campaigns. Supporters of Mumia Abu-Jamal made up for the early media blackout about his case by putting up enough posters to make his face easily recognizable in many urban areas and college towns. The Student Peace Action Network used street theater to get students to listen to its message about cutting Pentagon bloat. The Clean Clothes project of the Resource Center of the Americas and other anti-sweatshop activists have brought their campaign message directly to classrooms, and one enterprising fourth-grade teacher even took her class play about sweatshops to Broadway. When the hit television series *Beverly Hills 90210* included criticism of sweatshops in a fall 1997 episode, this message likely reached more people than any news story. All of these methods can substitute for and potentially even exceed the mobilizing benefits of conventional media coverage.

A particularly effective but underutilized way for national campaigns to grow without relying on the media is the leafleting and door-to-door literature distribution usually only seen during election campaigns. The PIRGs' canvassing operation is a version of this strategy and enables the groups to get their message directly to people without relying on the media. Unlike a canvass, which involves paid, full-time staff, a literature-distribution operation depends on the willingness of a large number of volunteers to walk the equivalent of an electoral precinct. In urban or otherwise densely populated areas, one volunteer can drop literature to about four hundred households in two hours. This means that instead of organizing one hundred people for another protest, national campaigns can use these volunteer resources to directly reach forty thousand people. When the numbers of volunteers involved in the national synchronized protests for anti-sweatshop campaigns are added up, it is clear that the resources exist for distributing literature to millions of households in a single day. Prior to elections, so many campaigns distribute materials that people stop reading; issue campaigns, between elections, rarely use this approach to mobilize potential supporters. This strategy should be used, since receiving social-change campaign literature on one's doorstep is unusual enough that even those living outside the media world are likely to read it.

National campaigns are clearly boosted when they receive widespread alternative and mainstream media coverage. Since our quick-media-turnover world makes ongoing coverage of multiyear struggles difficult to maintain under the best of circumstances, building national campaigns without long-term dependence on the media provides the strongest foundation for success. The decline of what was formerly the alternative press has hampered national activism and has led many to conclude that today's activists must follow the lessons of the 1960s movements and create their own media. Since it has become too expensive to replicate the alternative weeklies of an earlier era, many activists see the Internet as the alternative medium for national campaigns of the new century. The mobilizing capacity of the information superhighway is discussed in the next chapter.

Chapter 7

The Internet

Mobilizing in Cyberspace

Does the Internet facilitate social change? Can the information super-highway become the medium and voice for national grassroots campaigns? I have sought answers to these questions through books, articles, conversations with activists, and my own experience using e-mail and operating a website (igc.org/activist). I reached the following conclusions, discussed in this chapter, about the Net's potential as a mobilizing resource for national campaigns. First, any discussion about Net activism should distinguish between e-mail and the Web. The former has proved helpful to national activism in many ways; websites' role as mobilizing agents is less clear. Second, Silicon Valley executives have used their wealth generated by the information superhighway to shift the Democratic Party's national economic policies rightward. These high-tech Democrats have co-opted the traditional Republican procorporate agenda and have actively opposed government efforts to reverse America's growing social and economic inequality. Third, few social-change campaigns or organizations owe their existence to the Internet. The most commonly cited are campaigns focused on Internet privacy or first amendment issues but these Web-centered efforts merely advance the Net's libertarian culture. The best case for the Net as a national mobilizing tool that I have found is represented by Bastard Nation, an adoptees' rights organization formed through the Internet in 1996. Bastard Nation's campaign for open records would not have emerged at the time but for the Internet, and the group's development shows the potential for both transforming Net denizens into activists and for using the

Internet as a national mobilizing vehicle. Finally, I conclude by briefly assessing whether the Internet can assist the national campaigns of the twenty-first century as the formerly alternative weeklies did for 1960s-era social movements.

E-Mail: A Boost for National Activism

People love e-mail. It is fun to get messages from friends, family, or complete strangers day or night from anywhere in the world at apparently no cost. A system developed for intra-corporate communication has become the lifeblood for many among the estimated 20 percent of Americans using e-mail. E-mail has many obvious benefits for activists. It is used for discussions, information sharing, news updates, and for reaching group decisions without time-consuming and often impractical face-to-face meetings. Once an e-mail message is typed it can be instantaneously sent to thousands and even millions of recipients. This enables social-change groups to bypass the time-consuming and more expensive copying, labeling, and mailing process. The broader mobilizing shortcomings of e-mail are also well known. E-mail use is concentrated in the prosperous classes and among the college-educated. Many people have access to e-mail through their employers and are reluctant to receive political material; this is particularly true for those working in government jobs. An even greater shortcoming is that e-mail cannot be used for mobilizing low-income people because the system is seldom used by the disenfranchised. The vast majority of low-income tenants with whom I work cannot afford monthly telephone service, let alone e-mail. Proposals for providing e-mail access to low-income and homeless persons through community centers, public housing projects, or shelters are well intentioned, but such individuals desperately need money for food and rent. Many supporters of committing resources to "democratizing" the Internet have no idea how many of those they seek to help are fully preoccupied with daily survival. Further, if low-income people have to go somewhere to pick up their e-mail, then voice-mail, which my own organization and many others offer to welfare recipients and which can be accessed from anywhere, is a far less costly alternative.

Although the Internet is not an effective vehicle for mobilizing most low-income people, its national mobilizing potential has been exhibited in many of the campaigns previously discussed. The Campaign for Labor Rights (CLR), a project of the Central American support group the Nicaragua Network, produces a Labor Alerts/News Service providing comprehensive information and updates about the anti-Nike struggle and other national anti-sweatshop campaigns. CLR's reports enable activists working on the campaign to learn about events in other cities, to read the latest reports from on-site observers of Nike's Indonesian, Chinese, and Vietnamese factories, and to clearly feel that they are part of a national campaign. In a fight where there is not one large national membership organization producing and distributing materials, the groups and organizations involved in the campaign would not be as close-knit without e-mail.

CLR started in 1996 with a total budget of ten thousand dollars. Faxes or regular mail would have quickly depleted this amount and forced CLR to limit its communications, so it turned to e-mail instead. As CLR's budget rose to eighty-four thousand dollars in 1997 it was able to bolster its capacity to connect individual activists interested in the anti-Nike campaign. For example, among the four hundred e-mail requests for information that CLR receives weekly were five from Chapel Hill, North Carolina. Chapel Hill had no organized group working on the Nike issue, so CLR coordinator Trim Bissell put the five interested activists together and urged them to mobilize around the October 18, 1997, International Day of Protest against Nike. Bissell acknowledges e-mail's ability to connect grassroots activists with each other and to national campaigns. He also feels it played a crucial role in expanding and accelerating the Nike campaign. But Bissell agrees with CLR's decision to use its growing resources to hire a grassroots anti-sweatshop organizer rather than to expand its Internet efforts in 1998. Recognizing that e-mail is no substitute for direct personal contact and organizing (compare showing a slide show about sweatshops to high school students with distributing the same information by e-mail), Bissell emphasizes that CLR is "an activist organization that uses the Internet to enhance grassroots organizing." CLR demonstrates that groups with an organizing mentality are likely to best understand how e-mail should be used for national mobilizing.

E-mail also plays a critical role when strategic decisions must be immediately communicated to people throughout the country, and particularly where some are in transit. Because the PIRGs (discussed in chapter 3) are state organizations that jointly work on national campaigns through their Washington, D.C., office, e-mail rapidly and inexpensively communicates up-to-the-minute information and strategies through an otherwise far-flung network. PIRG field staff can access e-mail from anywhere. Groups heavily involved in field outreach and organizing could use cellular phones instead of e-mail but the cost would be astronomical, it would be far more time consuming and labor intensive, and sending lengthy messages or documents would be impossible. Reviewing the PIRGs' e-mail communications from the height of the clean air campaign, I was struck first by the timeliness: events occurring all over the country on a Thursday were fully reported the following day. Second, the PIRGs' urgent conveying of up-to-the-minute information was inherently mobilizing. A PIRG canvass director receiving an action alert from the Washington office a few minutes after it was composed has to feel greater pressure to immediately act than if the communication was received by fax several hours or a day later. I am not a fan of creating artificial crises and time deadlines to improve productivity, but in the clean air and other national campaigns time often was of the essence. E-mail enables progressive national campaigns to at least approach the expensive instantaneous communication networks of their adversaries.

What about e-mail as a cost-effective means of circumventing the expense of political campaigns? Seattle's Nick Licata, a former leader of WASHPIRG, ran a successful race for city council in 1997 after providing weekly updates and analysis of the city's political affairs via e-mail to three hundred subscribers. Licata's "Urban Politics" column (NickELT@aol.com) was transformed into "Campaign Notes," sent to an e-mail list of four hundred subscribers plus media contacts. Licata turned to his subscribers for campaign funds and even held an event for which publicity was limited to an e-mailing to about six hundred people. Unfortunately, only fifteen people attended the event and Licata's attempts to raise funds through e-mail were equally unsuccessful. Licata found that e-mail was best used for communicating with specific reporters and attracting volunteers but the system reached too few households to have an impact in the campaign. His victory was attributable to his two decades of activism, not his creative use of e-mail. Since Licata's lack of Internet success occurred in the home city of Microsoft, where an unusually high percentage of the electorate likely had e-mail access, it will likely be some time before political candidates can begin relying on the Net.[1]

Finally, e-mail's vaunted capacity for the dissemination of information may deter as much as foster the initiation of social-change activism. Many believe that e-mail subscriptions give activists incomparable access to critical information that enhances the prospects for their campaign's success. E-mail's providing of information about national mobilizations, grassroots activities, or national campaign issues for those activists involved is also beneficial. But reading interesting information can easily be confused with activism. People who are well informed may feel more comfortable expressing their views or better capable of winning an office or dinner table debate, but the sheer volume of e-mail information distributed can potentially deter activism. Someone who is occupied keeping up with their e-mail may not have time to make phone reminders for a protest or even to attend the event. The disparaging phrase *e-mail activist* has been coined to describe those unwilling to engage in the many noncomputer tasks essential to social-change campaigns. E-mail, like television and other new technologies, inevitably but stealthily shapes its users' lives. Let us hope that e-mail does not lead people to limit their activism to engaging in spirited debate only at their computer terminals.

The Web: Worth the Trouble for Activists?

Websites have become as de rigueur for social-change organizations as butcher paper and fax machines. Groups lacking websites risk being perceived as out of touch, living in the past, or fearful of the future. To go without a website, or to fail to update one's site at least weekly, risks turning off Net-surfing younger activists. There are also many activists who are convinced that websites provide a critical method for social-change organizations to broaden their exposure.

One can reach one's own conclusion regarding websites' potential as a national mobilizing vehicle by examining the sites of the Institute for Global Communications (IGC). IGC is exploring every possible avenue for using the Web to foster social change. Through its operation of PeaceNet, EcoNet, LaborNet, and WomensNet computer networks, IGC is a nonprofit, progressive alternative to American Online and other commercial providers. As outlined by its former acting executive director and longtime Net activist Scott Weikart, IGC's chief goal "is helping people use the Internet effectively to do their political work."[2] IGC deserves tremendous credit for trying to provide activists with Internet tools that can facilitate social-change campaigns. In collaboration with Z magazine, IGC offers a series of "Learning On-line" courses that include instruction in organizing, electronic activism, and a variety of political themes. Such courses, which are also available through the excellent "COMM-ORG" site on community organizing edited by Randy Stoecker of the University of Toledo (randy @uac.Rdp.utoledo.edu), might enhance people's mobilizing skills. IGC's newsgroup and COMM-ORG's listserv may also inspire activism among those not already involved. But the sites included in the above networks are primarily informational. Organizations should not feel compelled to divert potential organizing resources toward building and maintaining a website to provide information that is unlikely to mobilize most browsers.

The Politics of the Web

In *What Will Be: How the New World of Information Will Change Our Lives* author Michael Dertouzos states that "left to its own devices, the Information Marketplace will increase the gap between rich and poor countries and between rich and poor people." Questioning the contention that information technology can improve education and health and free poor people from poverty, Dertouzos observes that "the hardware and software needed to achieve these lofty aims cost a great deal of money. Poor nations and poor people acting alone will not find the money needed to begin leveraging the Information Marketplace." Fearing that "violent protests could well emerge" from information's widening of class gaps, Dertouzos provides no road map for ensuring that the Information Marketplace is not "left to its own devices," but urges attention to this problem.[3]

Dertouzos's prediction of violent class struggle emerging from the information technology gap might be dismissed as the ravings of a neo-Luddite Marxist. But far from being a radical, Dertouzos headed MIT's Laboratory for Computer Science for more than two decades, he advises leaders of Fortune 500 companies, and his book includes a foreword by Bill Gates. Dertouzos's announcement that the information superhighway leads to greater social and economic inequality and his caveat—that social upheaval will occur if the technological gap is left to its own devices—are reason for alarm. During the dramatic growth of the Net during the 1990s the American political environment has hardly been hospitable toward providing greater resources to the disenfranchised sectors that also lack access to information technology. Efforts to address the information gap by wiring public elementary schools or providing Net access in libraries and community centers will have little impact on those whose educational development is hampered by poverty, hunger, racism, and the steady withdrawal of resources from low-income communities. For example, the installation of a computer room in San Francisco's Valencia Gardens housing project received widespread publicity. The effort allegedly ensured that poor people would not be left behind on the information superhighway. Predictably for the beleaguered housing project, the computers were soon left unused for months awaiting repair. Although computer installations in other public housing sites across the nation have met a better fate, such access cannot begin to overcome the larger negative forces affecting children growing up in desperate poverty and rundown housing in San Francisco and throughout America.

David Shenk observed in his book *Data Smog* that "cyberspace is not politically neutral. It favors the political ideals of libertarian, free-market Republicans: a highly decentralized, deregulated society with little common discourse and minimal public infrastructure."[4] Unfortunately, the dominant national political impact of cyberspace has been to help transform the Democratic Party into a proponent for these traditionally Republican ideals. President Clinton's frequent trips to California during his first term were not to raise money from Hollywood movie stars but to maintain close personal relationships with Silicon Valley's wealthy high-tech leaders. Al Gore visited the area at least sixteen times in the first five years of his vice presidency. In 1996 Silicon Valley CEOs contributed millions shortly before the November election to defeat a California initiative preventing a tax cut for the state's wealthiest residents. Few Democratic Party politicians supported the initiative, even though it would have brought millions in desperately needed funds to local governments and schools. The measure was ignored by representatives and mayors from the state's urban centers such as Los Angeles and San Francisco and by the liberal Democrat serving as the state superintendent of public instruction. Democrats were clearly reluctant to alienate their wealthy Silicon Valley benefactors by supporting the initiative, which lost by less than 1 percent after leading in polls for months. The last-minute contribution of millions of dollars by high-tech leaders to the opposition campaign made the difference.

In July 1997 Silicon Valley's millionaire CEOs formed TechNet, a lobbying group pushing the industry's political agenda. According to a *San Francisco Examiner* story about the group, in TechNet "there's no difference between Republicans and Democrats. Silicon Valley Democrats have co-opted the traditional Republican pro-business agenda, essentially eliminating the ideological gap between the two parties." What is this common agenda? According to the *Examiner*, it comes down to "don't raise taxes, keep your hands off the Internet, promise to overhaul public education but be vague about the costs, and don't talk too much about social programs except maybe for a little quiet support for abortion rights."[5] Considering that unions, free trade restrictions, and government regulation are all anathema to these affluent Silicon Valley Democrats, is it any wonder that the national economic policies of the two parties have converged as the information superhighway has grown?

Silicon Valley executives have implemented their social and economic vision for America in their own backyard. While the average yearly compensation for the hundred highest-paid Silicon Valley chieftains nearly quadrupled from 1990 to 1996, wages fell 18 percent for the bottom quarter of earners in the surrounding San Jose area. One reason for this disparity is that the Bay Area's African-American and Latino populations have been denied access to the Silicon Valley boom.

Employment records for thirty-three leading high-tech firms in 1998 showed that their Bay Area staffs were 4 percent black and 7 percent Latino; this is only half of each group's percentage of the surrounding labor force. Rather than address this "digital divide" by recruiting blacks and Latinos for high-tech careers, the Silicon Valley firms successfully pressured Congress to ease restrictions on the importation of skilled foreign workers. These high-tech Democrats are using the information superhighway to widen rather than restrict social, racial, and economic inequality throughout the land.[6]

To paraphrase Michael Moore, those seeking a window into the dominant character of the Internet must read *Wired* rather than *The Nation*. Cartoonist Tom Tomorrow has observed that *Wired*'s great success lies in its ability to celebrate free markets and corporate leaders as "hip and cutting edge."[7] Activists scorn *Wired,* yet one cannot separate the cultural implications of the Net from its most widely subscribed to and heavily advertised publication. Those viewing the Internet as opening up new frontiers for progressive change have reason to detest a publication that reminds us that the information superhighway exists for corporations to make money. Media critic Norman Solomon has pointed out that the Internet's control by a handful of major corporations is rarely discussed in the press; *Wired* not only reflects this corporate dominance but exults in it.

The classic *Wired* story is "The Long Boom" by Peter Schwartz and Peter Leyden. This widely praised cover story argues that "we're facing twenty-five years of prosperity, freedom, and a better environment. We are riding the early waves of a twenty-five-year run of a greatly expanding economy that will do much to solve seemingly intractable problems like poverty and to ease tensions throughout the world." Although the authors do not explain why the current boom has actually worsened the life circumstances for America's poorest 20 percent and much of the world, they insist that economic growth after 2005 will mean that "unlike the last time, almost every region of the planet, even in the undeveloped world, participates in the bonanza." Even better is that starting around 2000 "a spirit of generosity returns and the vast majority of Americans are genuinely sympathetic to the plight of those left behind." The authors' cheery scenario is dependent on following their formula for success: Open, good; closed, bad. Restrictions on free trade or economic globalization, seen by the authors as "the closed route," will create a vicious downward spiral. In fact, in the authors' dream world "no one talks about reverting to big government," since there will be "innovative approaches" that will cut people's taxes while benefiting the public at large. Ronald Reagan's failed economic policies appear to have found a new life in cyberspace.[8]

The views expressed in *Wired* reaffirm rather than challenge the corporate-driven economic policies that have caused America's growing social and economic inequality. As ridiculous as many may find "The Long Boom," the article perfectly served the bipartisan free-market agenda and won wide praise. Its supporters were not confined to the world of the Net; soon after the article's publication Christine Miller, executive vice president of the Magazine Publishers of America, relied on the "superb" Long Boom thesis in an article charting the future of magazines.[9] The problem for national activism is not simply that the information superhighway has created a new class of elites supporting regressive policies; rather, it is that some activists willingly ignore the obvious danger signs and have become boosters of technology-centered approaches that empower their political opponents.

I have a very simple suggestion for those who enjoy the Internet, find it useful to their activism, and yet recognize that the information superhighway is worsening social and economic inequality: do not encourage technological solutions to non-technological problems. Neil Postman, an educator whose special insights infuse every subject he touches, has emphasized that most of the nation's serious problems have very little to do with information. Nor are they amenable to technological solutions. Information is "no substitute for human values," and what is lacking in America is a broader commitment to social and economic fairness, not data. Many activists understand Postman's point but the hype surrounding the Net is so pervasive that raising skepticism can be seen as reflecting one's failure to recognize that the hype is deserved.

Every national struggle profiled in this book had to overcome its opponents' hype. Nobody did hype better than Nike, yet it was surmounted. Oil and timber companies have proved less effective in deceiving the public, and environmentalists' power has grown accordingly. The information superhighway is here to stay, but activists should not remain silent as schools without books are wired and scarce resources are directed toward technology rather than the food, housing, clothing, and other basic human needs that many Americans lack.

Bastard Nation:
How the Net Created a Movement

Most people's experience online involves exchanging ideas with people through newsgroups, bulletin boards, or similar vehicles. The organization of these tens of thousands of discussion groups into subject areas creates the possibility for participants to learn from each other and potentially join in collective action. In 1994 the Internet Usenet news group alt.adoption was formed. This newsgroup quickly became the largest adoption-related discussion group on the Web, with thousands of subscribers. At the time the established adoption groups did not have a position on many adoptees' rights issues. Some people felt that when they tried to raise issues about open records and adoptees' civil rights at meetings of the American Adoption Congress, their concerns were ignored and/or marginalized. They came to see the alt.adoption newsgroup as their only venue for seriously discussing their issues.

As these online discussions about adoptees' rights grew, Marley Greiner began signing her postings under the name "Bastard Nation." Several others followed suit, eventually giving themselves humorous titles in the then-mythical Bastard Nation organization. As serious discussion about adoptees' rights ensued and the postings showed that many individuals were angry about the denial of the civil rights of adoptees, Damsel Plum conceived the idea of creating a Bastard Nation website. The self-proclaimed "Sub-Commandante for Public Relations" for the emerging group, Plum collected material from people on alt.adoption and on June 19, 1996, announced the Bastard Nation website to the Internet world. The site immediately began receiving more than a thousand hits per month and in September moved to a custom domain: http://www.bastards.org.

Bastard Nation has one overarching goal: open records for adult adoptees. Adoptees' birth records are sealed in all but two states: Kansas and Alaska. Bastard Nation sees this sealing as reflecting society's "unspoken, unacknowledged attitude of SHAME toward adoption." The group's name explodes the myth of shame by reclaiming the word "bastard" and all of society's myths and fears regarding adoption. Plum maintains that adoptees often suffer from a psychology of self-defeatism that inhibits their public opposition to society's restrictions on their birth records. The anonymity of the Internet enabled people to speak publicly about their feelings for the first time and to learn how many other adoptees felt similarly. Once this connection was made Bastard Nationalists did not hesitate to implement the "by all means necessary" approach used by disability rights activists, gay and lesbians, and other long-stigmatized constituencies fighting for civil rights.

After the Bastard Nation website confirmed the national interest in building an open records advocacy organization, a volunteer executive committee was created. The committee was formed and drafted a mission statement and bylaws, entirely through the Net. As what began as an "insider Usenet joke" transformed into a well-organized national membership organization, Plum ensured that the group's website continued to set a different tone from other adoption-related sites. Whereas such sites focused on happy reunion stories, Bastard Nation's site included information on how to search for birth parents and where to send protest letters or to picket, and a collection of personal testimonies from adoptees describing their burdens under prevailing closed-record policies. The site's message attracted those like Shea Grimm, who became the group's legislative director. Grimm had been frustrated by her experience working on adoption reform, and sought to join a group "less about nurturing support and more about political action." Bastard Nation's website was designed to recruit those primarily seeking a vehicle for civil rights activism rather than simply information.

The group took the opportunity to shift from the Net to the streets with the widespread release of British director Mike Leigh's Oscar-nominated film *Secrets and Lies*. The film focuses on the reunion of a young woman with her biological mother. The woman had received her birth mother's name from a government office (in England, as well as Norway, Israel, Mexico, and many other countries, such records are open). Bastard Nation activists in New York, California, and Washington held "positive pickets" in front of theaters showing the film to educate people that adults in America were denied such access to their past. The group distributed fliers calling for "No More Secrets and Lies" and won media coverage for their efforts from newspapers in New Jersey, Ohio, and throughout California. When *Secrets and Lies* was nominated for an Oscar for best picture, Bastard Nationalists held a black-tie rally at the Academy Awards on March 24, 1997. Since the media expends great resources in covering every aspect of the glamorous Oscar event, Bastard Nation's capitalizing on this interest resulted in a live interview of member Ron Morgan on CNN and many local features on other members of the group. Director Leigh and Brenda Blethyn, the film's Oscar-nominated star, offering support for Bastard Nation's cause, appeared at an open-records rally on March 10 outside a theater showing the film in Beverly Hills. Their public support, coupled with the unusual frame of holding a protest in favor of a movie's message, fostered media interest.

For many, particularly those not online, the publicity Bastard Nation received around *Secrets and Lies* was their first exposure to the group. The film and the passage of a partial open-records bill in Tennessee in the summer of 1996 spawned a nationwide debate about adoptees' rights and open records. Bastard Nation seized upon this momentum to increase its Internet and public activism. In Oregon, Bastard Nationalist Helen Hill led a massive grassroots campaign to qualify an initiative for the November 1998 ballot that would require the issuance of Oregon birth certificates to adult adoptees upon request. Voters approved the open-records initiative, building support for similar campaigns across the country. Bastard Nation's reliance on mobilizing through e-mail alerts and more traditional methods is creating a sea change in American attitudes toward adoption.[10]

Future Prospects for
Net-Spawned Activist Groups

With hundreds of thousands and soon to be millions conversing in Internet chat rooms and newsgroups organized by common interest, should we expect these discussions to create new national political activist organizations? A major reason Bastard Nation formed through the Internet was the absence of an organization that was already pursuing an uncompromising, open-records agenda. The anonymity of the Internet and its capacity to help adoptees identify and locate birth parents also fostered online participation by potential adoption-rights activists. There is no shortage of causes lacking a focus by existing groups. There are also other constituencies whose members have reason to prefer the Internet's anonymous expressions of dissent to public activism. For example, nonunion employees of large corporations risk discharge or subtle harassment for complaining publicly about company practices. The Internet could spawn an organization of such workers to pressure for just-cause termination, enhanced workplace safety, or other workers' rights legislation. Even if the organization's activism was limited to the Internet it would provide a vehicle for increasing workers' influence and forging common bonds. An Internet organization for corporate whistle-blowers could emerge for similar reasons. Bastard Nationals were able to break out of the pattern in which most of the Net's political chatter remains unconnected to specific or concrete action. This pattern can create online friendships and give people a sense of community but it should not be confused with activism.

Can the Internet Become
the New Alternative Medium?

I stated in the media chapter that aside from some of the weeklies and Pacifica radio there is little left of the truly alternative political media that were the voice of the movements of the 1960s. With the costs of newspaper or periodical production having forestalled the emergence of a new alternative press, some see the Internet as a potential substitute. The idea of a national weekly or even daily Internet newspaper that provided ongoing coverage of national and local grass-roots campaigns is so good that one is forced to ask why it has not emerged. A major reason could be the difficulty even highly capital-ized online ventures have faced in obtaining an audience. Wired Ven-tures, apostle of the Long Boom and the Digital Revolution, initi-ated major layoffs at its online division, Wired Digital, only six months after its old-fashioned paper product declared that we were living in the best of all possible worlds. Wired Ventures made its profits from its print division while its online sector lost money.[11]

It is also possible that a sufficient audience for a politically alterna-tive Internet newspaper does not yet exist. A nationwide survey in 1998 found that only 7 percent of Internet users had made contact with an elected official online or expressed an opinion on a political issue. Although this was twice the percentage that did so in 1996, the survey results, along with others showing that the Internet is primar-ily used by politically mainstream white males, have likely deterred those considering the launching of an Internet vehicle focused on covering progressive national struggles. Younger activists who do not regularly read newspapers may be equally disinclined to follow news online, while others may have time to read news only while commut-ing or drinking coffee in a cafe. Perhaps nobody has the time to main-tain such an ongoing project or is interested in launching a venture that would need a large promotional budget to attract readers. Such a vehicle could be launched by unpaid staff but there is likely an insuf-ficient number of high-quality writers willing to volunteer their time to produce stories on an ongoing basis. Whatever the reasons, the prospect of the Internet becoming the voice of new broad-based na-tional movements for the next century remains to be realized.[12]

Conclusion

In Frank Capra's 1939 film, *Mr. Smith Goes to Washington*, James Stewart plays Jefferson Smith, the idealistic young head of the Boy Rangers who is unexpectedly appointed to fill a vacant U.S. senate seat. Smith arrives in Washington, D.C., reciting the ideals of Lincoln and Jefferson. His belief that the national government should actually live up to principles of democracy and equal justice amuses and then irks his aide, fellow senators, and the cynical capitol press corps. When Smith introduces a bill to create a national boys' camp in his state so that "boys of all nationalities and creeds can work together and learn American ideals," havoc results. Smith has proposed the camp for a site that is secretly owned by James Taylor, his state's largest newspaper publisher. Taylor's political machine controls the state's politicians and the magnate has arranged for the state's other senator to pass legislation for the federal government to purchase Taylor's land for a completely unnecessary dam. When Smith learns of the corrupt deal, the tall, lanky patriot from the land of tall grass and the prairies refuses to "play ball." He is shocked to learn that his colleagues are taking orders from a powerful elite and goes to the senate floor to denounce the graft and corruption that is tarnishing American ideals. In response the entire U.S. senate moves to expel Smith from office and Taylor orchestrates a "tailor-made" media smear campaign against Smith. As "all of official Washington comes to be in on the kill," Smith packs his bags and prepares to return home. But as he departs, he stops by the Lincoln Memorial and reads its words. He decides that he cannot go home and "tell those boys that this isn't your country, it belongs to the James Taylors." He returns to the senate and launches an all-night filibuster that ultimately results in victory as his fellow state senator is finally moved to concede the truth of Smith's charges.

Capra's film provides a harsher indictment of the national political arena than anything produced by Oliver Stone; considering the criticism targeted at Stone for hinting at official corruption, Capra's depiction of a corrupt and totally corporate-controlled U.S. senate would not likely find major studio financing or theater space today. When official Washington saw a gala premiere of the film prior to its release, pandemonium ensued and it was attacked as useful for Nazi propaganda. But as much as national politicians and Beltway insiders despised the film, the public loved it. Jefferson Smith's ultimate refusal to be driven back home by official Washington corruption struck a chord, as did his unwillingness to accept Washington's perversion of constitutional ideals into "fancy words that only suckers believed."

The last quarter of this century has seen citizen activists and organizations increasingly accepting Jefferson Smith's initial impulse to "get away from the whole rotten [Washington] show." The control of the national government by the interests of corporations and the wealthy may be more subtle than Capra depicts, but the public perception that these special interests are thwarting democratic ideals—through renting the White House's Lincoln Bedroom or spending millions on electoral campaigns—has grown further since the film was released. The persistence of Capra's Washington world for the past sixty years has led many to doubt the chances of grassroots activists being able to shape the national agenda. As a result many of America's most dedicated activists and organizations have left the battle to reclaim the country's progressive ideals; they instead work to impose such values in the communities and neighborhoods where they live or work. This work must continue, but addressing the growing social and economic inequality and environmental harm that undermine community life requires a new commitment to national activism.

National activism means building a grassroots mobilizing base for national struggles in one's own backyard, not walking the corridors of congress. Contrary to popular wisdom, organizations do not need full-time Washington lobbyists in order to shape national politics. The campaigns described in this book demonstrate this. National anti-sweatshop campaigns have fundamentally altered America's policies governing workers' wages and working conditions while operating outside of the Beltway political scene. National environmentalism's success often depends on winning votes on Capitol Hill, but the Clean Air Act campaign showed that federal politicians are best targeted by grassroots mobilizing in the communities they represent.

The new national activism enlists citizen activists and organizations in campaigns that solve national and local problems. Community-based organizations, local-oriented environmental groups, and local political clubs must join the national struggles shaping America's future.

When Jeff Ballinger in 1992 raised the first concerns about Nike's overseas labor practices, who could have anticipated that five years later Nike's self-touted role as a "model of corporate behavior in the global economy" would subject the company to widespread media attack? The Nike swoosh has yet to experience the fate of the fallen statues of the Soviet empire, but companies abusing workers have quickly gone from popular models of conduct to emblems of scorn. Organized labor in the early 1990s was considered entirely irrelevant to shaping America's future; by 1997 conservative commentators and free trade advocates were setting off alarm bells that labor was now controlling the global economy debate. Similarly, critics declared the national environmental movement all but dead by 1995 and activists were told to work exclusively on local preservation battles. The shift toward a national grassroots mobilizing strategy and a "fear and loathing" relationship to politicians brought the national groups a victory on new clean air standards that few considered possible.

The new national activism does not guarantee success but it means that a national grassroots campaign to redirect Pentagon spending to human needs should not be dismissed because Beltway-centered efforts to achieve this goal failed. It also means that prior difficulties organizing around economic justice issues should not deter the launching of a national living wage movement. The harnessing of citizen activists and organizations to national campaigns changes the prevailing rules and provides a road map for the reclaiming of America's progressive ideals at the dawn of a new century.

Notes

Chapter 1: Just Don't Buy It:
Challenging Nike and the Rules of the Global Economy

1. Interview with Jeff Ballinger, June 2, 1997. Ballinger's quotations throughout are from this and subsequent conversations with the author.

2. Jeffrey Ballinger, "The New Free-Trade Heel," *Harper's*, August 1992, p. 46.

3. James Bennet, "In Denver for Economic Talks, Clinton Calls for Freer Trade," *New York Times*, June 20, 1997.

4. Donald Katz, *Just Do It: The Nike Spirit in the Corporate World* (New York: Random House, 1994), pp. 145, 146.

5. Ibid., p. 236; Calhoun's comments were made on WBUR radio in December 1995, cited in *Nike in Indonesia*, the newsletter of Press for Change, February 1996.

6. Donald Katz, "Triumph of the Swoosh," *Sports Illustrated*, August 16, 1993.

7. Katz, *Just Do It*, p. ix.

8. Ibid, pp. xii, 190–91.

9. Ibid, p. 192.

10. Cynthia Enloe, "The Globetrotting Sneaker," *Ms.*, March/April 1995, p. 36.

11. Max White, "Just Doing in Third World Workers," *The Portland Alliance*, Progressive Community News, June/July 1996, p. 1.

12. Interview with Max White, June 1, 1997. White is a founder of the Portland, Oregon–based Justice! Do It Nike, (503) 292-8168, whose compilation of articles proved enormously helpful to this chapter.

13. White, "Just Doing in Third World Workers," p. 6.

14. Edward Gargan, "An Indonesian Asset Is Also a Liability," *New York Times*, March 16, 1996, p. 17; Sean Nelson, "Nike Refutes Criticism of Asian Labor Practices," *The Asian Reporter*, June 1996. In addition to attacking Gargan, Gibbs claimed that the photos of child labor in Sydney Schanberg's June 1996 *Life* magazine story about Nike's soccer factories in Pakistan were "deliberately staged."

15. Martin Lee and Norman Solomon, *Unreliable Sources: A Guide To Detecting Bias In News Media* (New York: Lyle Stuart, 1990), pp. 19–20.

16. Interfaith Center on Corporate Responsibility, 475 Riverside Drive, Room 566, New York, NY 10115.

17. General Board of Pension and Health Benefits of the United Methodist Church, 1261 Davis Street, Evanston, IL 60201.

18. White interview; Jeff Manning, "Nike Battles Back, but Activists Hold the High Ground," *Portland Oregonian*, November 10, 1997, p. 1.

19. John McClain, "Sweatshops Become Issue for the Pulpit," Associated Press, *Portland Oregonian*, October 23, 1996, p. D1.

20. Nancy Gibbs, "Cause Celeb," *Time*, June 17, 1996, p. 29. For a similar Jordan response, see *Nike in Indonesia*, July 1997, p. 3.

21. Gibbs, "Cause Celeb," p. 29.

22. Bob Herbert, "From Sweatshops to Aerobics," *New York Times*, June 24, 1996; Bob Herbert, "Nike's Pyramid Scheme," *New York Times*, June 17, 1996.

23. Sydney Schanberg, "Six Cents An Hour," *Life*, June 1996, p. 40; Ballinger interviews.

24. Global Exchange, 2017 Mission St., Rm. 803, San Francisco, CA 94110.

25. Bob Herbert, "Trampled Dreams," *New York Times*, July 12, 1996.

26. *Portland Business Journal*, July 26, 1996.

27. Interview with Medea Benjamin, June 18, 1997.

28. Letter from Phil Knight to Global Exchange, July 19, 1996.

29. White and Benjamin interviews.

30. Jeff Manning, "Nike Joins Ranks of Sweatshop Opponents," *Portland Oregonian*, August 3, 1996; Julie Whipple, "Nike Vows to Improve Monitoring in Asia," *Business Journal*, July 26, 1996, p. 1.

31. Benjamin interview.

32. Ibid.

33. Rachel Zimmerman, "Nike Laces Up Vietnam Factories," *Portland Business Journal*, May 5, 1996.

34. "'48 HOURS' Uncovers Nike 'Sweatshops,'" CBS News press release, October 16, 1996.

35. See Howard Kurtz, "CBS Reporter Creates Internal Furor over Nike," *Washington Post*, February 11, 1998.

36. Interview with Thuyen Nguyen, July 8, 1997.

37. Bob Herbert, "Brutality in Vietnam," *New York Times*, March 28, 1997, p. A19.

38. Nguyen interview; e-mail message from Nguyen to Justice! Do It Nike, March 24, 1997.

39. Mitch Albom, "Mind Your Money because Nike Wants Both," *Detroit Free Press*, April 5, 1997.

40. Ron Curran, "Spiked by Nike," *San Francisco Bay Guardian*, March 26, 1997, p. 26.

41. Stephanie Salter, "Up against the Swoosh," appeared in the *San Francisco Bay Guardian*, March 26, 1997, p. 9.

42. Bob Herbert, "Nike's Boot Camps," *New York Times*, March 31, 1997, p. A11.

43. "Nike and Its Critics," *Portland Oregonian*, July 7, 1996; "Nike's Vietnam Offensive," *Portland Oregonian*, April 1, 1997.

44. Conversation with Jeff Ballinger.

45. "Vietnam Makers of Nike Shoes Deny Charges of Labor Mistreatment," Hanoi, AFP, March 28, 1997; "Nike Tells Vietnamese to Toe the Line: Report," Hanoi, AFP, April 6, 1997.

46. "Andrew Young to Assess Nike," Associated Press, February 25, 1997.

47. Herbert, "Brutality in Vietnam," p. A19.

48. Ian Stewart, "Vietnam's Fed-Up Workers Striking for Rights," Associated Press, *San Francisco Chronicle*, June 23, 1997, p. A10.

49. Ibid.; "Working Conditions Remain Harsh at Nike Factories," Associated Press, *San Francisco Chronicle*, June 23, 1997, p. A10.

50. Dan Levy, "Not Sold on Nike," *San Francisco Chronicle*, February 21, 1997; Wendy Tanaka, "Protesters Lace Nike Labor Practices," *San Francisco Examiner*, February 21, 1997, p. B1.

51. Levy, "Not Sold on Nike," p. A21.

52. Jeff Manning, "Nike Plants Balk at $2.36 a Day," *Portland Oregonian*, April 3, 1997; Jeff Manning, "Nike Factories in Indonesia Will Pay $2.36 Minimum Wage," *Portland Oregonian*, April 4, 1997.

53. "Dispute Settled at Nike Factory Near Jakarta," Associated Press, *Wall Street Journal*, April 28, 1997, p. B8.

54. Richard Read, "New Report Puts Nike in Labor Spotlight," *Portland Oregonian*, September 21, 1997, p. B6.

55. Jeff Manning, "Nike Cuts Four Factories from Team," *Portland Oregonian*, September 23, 1997, pp. A1, A10; Josh Felt, "Seeing Reds," *Willamette Week*.

56. "Andrew Young to Assess Nike," Associated Press, February 25, 1997.

57. Dana Canedy, "Nike's Asian Factories Pass Young's Muster," *New York Times*, June 25, 1997, p. C2.

58. *New York Times*, June 25, 1997, p. A7.

59. Linda Himelstein, "Nike Hasn't Scrubbed Its Image Yet," *Business Week*, July 7, 1997, p. 44.

60. Bob Herbert, "Mr. Young Gets It Wrong," *New York Times*, June 27, 1997, p. A29.

61. Stephen Glass, "The Young and the Feckless," *New Republic*, September 8 and 15, 1997, p. 20. Although Glass was subsequently fired for fabricating key elements of at least three stories, his critique of Young's report paralleled those of others and was not publicly challenged by Nike.

62. Steven Greenhouse, "Nike Shoe Plant in Vietnam Is Called Unsafe for Workers," *New York Times*, November 8, 1997, p. A1.

63. Interview with Tony Newman, November 8, 1997.

64. Conversation on May 27, 1997 with a Smith College representative who insisted on anonymity.

65. John Diconsiglio, "Who Is Making Your Sneakers?" *Scholastic Update*, March 7, 1997, p. 9.

66. Rethinking Schools, 1001 East Keefe Ave., Milwaukee, WI 53212.

67. Evelyn Nieves, "Pupils' Script on Workers Is Ruled Out," *New York Times*, June 26, 1997. Nike's sponsoring of programs in ten cities whereby elementary school classes learn about environmentally friendly products by building Nike shoes also galvanized anti-Nike sentiments as organizations such as the National Education Association denounced this "despicable" use of classroom time. See Josh Felt, "Nike in the Classroom," *Willamette Week*, April 15, 1998.

68. Manning, "Nike Battles Back, but Activists Hold the High Ground," p. 1; Nat Hentoff, "The Trouble with Role Models," *Washington Post*, October 25, 1997; Nat Hentoff, "The Just War against Nike," *Village Voice*, December 23, 1997.

69. Steven Greenhouse, "Nike Supports Women in Its Ads but Not Its Factories, Groups Say," *New York Times*, October 26, 1997, p. 15.

70. Dottie Enrico, "Women's Groups Pressure Nike on Labor Practices," *USA Today*, October 27, 1997; also see Robin Pogrebin, "Adding Sweat and Muscle to a Familiar Formula," *New York Times*, September 21, 1997, p. 3.

71. Steven Greenhouse, "Apparel Industry Group Moves to End Sweatshops," *New York Times*, April 9, 1997, p. A11.

72. Medea Benjamin, "No Sweat for Companies to Agree," *Los Angeles Times*, April 17, 1997.

73. "A Modest Start on Sweatshops," *New York Times*, April 16, 1997, p. A18.

74. Glenn Burkins, "Clinton Plan to Eliminate Sweatshops in Apparel Industry Called Too Weak," *Wall Street Journal*, April 15, 1997, p. A2.

75. Interview on Pacifica Radio's *Democracy Now*, hosted by Amy Goodman.

76. "Nike: Rpts from Local Committee," e-mail message from Campaign for Labor Rights, October 23, 1997.

77. "Nike Update" and "Duke Anti-Sweatshop Policy," e-mail messages from Campaign for Labor Rights, November 3 and 5, 1997.

78. Allan Wolper, "Nike's Newspaper Temptation," *Editor and Publisher Interactive: The Media Info Source,* January 10, 1998.

79. Bill Workman, "In the Corporate Arena," *San Francisco Chronicle,* February 20, 1998; Tim Keown, "Hypocrisy is Nike's Sole Purpose," *San Francisco Chronicle,* November 14, 1997, p. D1.

80. "October 18 Nike Protest Analysis," and "Nike: Two Interesting Items," e-mail messages from Campaign for Labor Rights, October 23 and 25, 1997.

81. William J. Holstein, "Casting Nike as the Bad Guy," *U.S. News & World Report,* September 22, 1997, pp. 49, 50.

82. Bill Carter, "No, It's Just for the Goddess of Victory," *New York Times,* February 22, 1998, p. 6. David Meggyesy, "Superrich Superstars in Sports, Moral Jellyfish in Life," *Los Angeles Times,* October 17, 1997; see also Steve Jacobson, "This Is 'The Right Thing,'" *Newsday,* November 23, 1997.

83. Ira Berkow, "Jordan's Bunker View on Nike's Slave Labor," *New York Times,* July 12, 1996; Harvey Araton, "Standing for More than a Logo," *New York Times,* April 15, 1997, p. B13; George Vecsey, "A Role Model for the Ages Is Honored," *New York Times,* April 16, 1997, p. B11.

84. Tom Cushman, "In Money Quest, Athletes Lose Sight of Bottom Line," *San Diego Union-Tribune,* August 13, 1997, pp. D6, D10.

85. Steve Marantz, "A Model of Understatement," *Sporting News,* December 22, 1997, p. 22; Garry Trudeau, *Doonesbury,* in *San Francisco Chronicle,* January 19, 1998, p. E10; Carol Slezak, "Jordan Has Chance to Help Off Court, Too," *Chicago Sun-Times,* January 25, 1998. Jordan's planned trip to Asia in 1998 did not occur.

86. Harvey Araton, "Student Protests Shame Nike Athletes," *New York Times,* November 22, 1997, p. B17; Keown, "Hypocrisy is Nike's Sole Purpose," p. D1.

87. Hentoff, "The Just War against Nike,"; Robert Lipsyte, "If It's Gotta Be the Shoes, He's Gotta Be the Guy," *New York Times,* July 6, 1997, p. 16.

88. Jeff Manning, "Nike Reports a Gold Medal Year," *Portland Oregonian,* July 10, 1996, p. 1.

89. Jeff Manning, "Questions Arise on Future of Nike Surge," *Portland Oregonian,* April 8, 1997, p. 1; Jeff Manning, "Has the Air Gone Out of Nike?" *St. Louis Post Dispatch,* May 18, 1997, p. 1.

90. Jennifer Steinhauer, "Nike's Shares Tumble after Profit Forecast," *New York Times,* May 30, 1997; Joseph Pereira, "Nike's Rivals Hope Buyers Want Bargains," *Wall Street Journal,* June 2, 1997.

91. Manning, "Nike Cuts Four Factories from Team," p. A1; "Nike Update," e-mail message from Campaign for Labor Rights, July 12, 1998.

92. Sharon King, "Dow Climbs by 52.56 to Reach Its 6th Consecutive High," *New York Times*, February 19, 1998, p. C9. Jeff Manning's "Nike's Asian Machine Goes on Trial," *Portland Oregonian*, November 9, 1997, p. A1, the first of his stellar three-part series on Nike, provided a detailed analysis of Nike's overproduction problems. Ballinger interview.

93. Ballinger interview.

94. Manning, "Nike's Asian Machine Goes on Trial," p. A1.

95. Transcript of CNN coverage of Knight's speech, May 12, 1998, provided to author by Communication Works

96. Press release from Communication Works, "Is Nike a Force of Social Instability in Asia?" May 11, 1998; John H. Cushman Jr., "Nike Pledges to End Child Labor and Apply U.S. Rules Abroad," *New York Times*, May 13, 1998, p. C1; E. J. Dionne Jr., "Nike Proves the Power of Consumers," *San Francisco Chronicle*, May 15, 1998, p. A25. Nike granted a 25 percent wage increase to its Indonesian work force in October 1998.

97. Quan's quotation is from a speech given on October 18, 1997 at San Francisco's Niketown.

Chapter 2: From Challenging American Sweatshops to a Movement for a Global Living Wage

1. See "U.S. Sweatshops Out of Control," *Connection to the Americas* (published by the Resource Center of the Americas), November 1997, p. 2; Sweatshop Watch 1998 calendar; "Who Broke California," *San Jose Mercury News*, April 12, 1998, p. 6C; Common Threads brochure, available at P.O. Box 962, Venice, CA 90294; Robert Ross, Ellen Rosen, and Karen McCormack, "The Global Economy of the New Sweatshops," prepared for the Annual Meeting of the Society for the Study of Special Problems, New York, 1996, p. 15. In noting New York City's relative lack of sweatshops in prior decades, the authors found virtually no stories about sweatshops in the *New York Times* in the 1950s and 1960s, and only four to six stories annually beginning in the early 1980s. The authors' thesis is that the large increase in imports, not immigration, caused sweatshops to reemerge.

2. AIWA news release, October 9, 1992.

3. Media advisory, October 7, 1992.

4. *AIWA News*, November 1993.

5. Jasmin Tuan in *AIWA News*, November 1993.

6. Vanessa Atkins, "Fashion Designer Wins Limits on Pickets," *San Francisco Examiner*, August 26, 1994.

7. *AIWA News*, June 1994, p. 5.

8. Stuart Silverstein and Vicki Torres, "String of Illegal Home-Sewing Sites Found, Regulators Say," *Los Angeles Times*, July 31, 1996, pp. D1, D4.

9. Conversation with Steve Nutter, April 17, 1997; UNITE press release, January 31, 1997.

10. Stuart Silverstein, George White, and Mary Sheridan, "Guess Inc. to Move Much of L.A. Work South of Border," *Los Angeles Times*, January 15, 1997, p. A14.

11. Small's quotation is from Reuters, Associated Press, April 1997, cited in *Nike in Indonesia*, July 1997, p.1.

12. Timothy Egan, "Teamsters and Ex-Rival Go after Apple Industry," *New York Times*, August 19, 1997, p. A10.

13. Sam Dillon, "U.S. Labor Leader Seeks Union Support in Mexico," *New York Times*, January 23, 1998, p. 3. On July 15, 1998, the National Interfaith Committee for Worker Justice released a report, "Cross Border Blues," detailing the deplorable working conditions found in factories producing for Guess in Tehuacan, Mexico. The group can be reached via e-mail at nicwj@igc.org.

14. Ted Tomberg, "Regional Bishops Voice Support for Fired Garment Workers," *Tidings* (Southern California's Catholic weekly), September 29, 1996, p. 1.

15. The author received the flyers from Edna Bonacich, who also provided valuable insights about the campaign. The "Sweatshops and Child Labor" resolutions were adopted at the Union of American Hebrew Congregations's sixty-fourth biennial convention in Dallas, Texas, on October 31, 1997.

16. See Julia Lieblich, "A Union of God and the Worker," *San Francisco Examiner*, July 13, 1997, p. D1.

17. E-mail messages from Joe Goldman to author, January 1998. Duke adopted its precedent-setting code of conduct, which gives the university the right to send independent monitors to garment facilities, on March 6, 1998.

18. Lisa Richardson, "Makers of Guess Jeans Exploit Women Workers, Protesters Say," *Los Angeles Times*, Orange County edition, August 24, 1997; Associated Press, "Rock Star Arrested in Guess Protest," *San Francisco Examiner*, December 14, 1997, p. D12; "New Report on Guess in Mexico," e-mail from Campaign for Labor Rights, July 23, 1998.

19. Stuart Silverman, "Government Berates Guess over Ads on Labor Practices Apparel," *Los Angeles Times*, December 10, 1997; Sweatshop Watch newsletter, summer 1998.

20. See Carl Hartman, "Smithsonian Won't Change Exhibit," *San Francisco Examiner*, September 16, 1997, p. A7.

21. For example, a *New York Times* article on the Guess campaign on July 18, 1997, discussed the apparel industry's failure to adequately monitor

its subcontractors working conditions but ignored AIWA's campaign, the on-going, high-profile anti-Nike campaign, and other campaigns waged around the same issue. The reporter, Steven Greenhouse, has provided strong and favorable coverage of anti-sweatshop campaigns.

22. See Robert Reich, "Trade Accords That Spread the Wealth," *New York Times*, September 2, 1997, p. A15.

23. For a discussion of US/GLEP, see Henry Frundt, "Trade and Cross-Border Labor Strategies in the Americas," *Economic and Industrial Democracy* 17 (1996): 387–417; and e-mail response from Steve Coats to the author, April 22, 1998.

24. John Nichols, "City Bans Sweatshop Products," *The Progressive*, May 1997, p. 14.

25. Interview with Lora Foo, August 10, 1998.

Chapter 3: The New National Environmental Activism

1. Quoted in "Celebrating Hellraisers," *Mother Jones*, January 1996.

2. My discussion of the PIRGs is based on a review of their monthly national newsletters, the *News*, PIRG informational materials, the PIRGs' weekly National Campus Updates, and interviews with national field director Margie Alt on April 21, 1997; national campus organizing director Andre Delattre on June 6, 1997; Andy Macdonald of MASSPIRG on June 11, 1997; Maureen Kirk of OSPIRG (Oregon's PIRG) on June 9, 1977; Seth Levin of WASHPIRG and COPIRG on July 11, 1997; and U.S. PIRG executive director Gene Karpinsky on August 18, 1997. Alt also responded to follow-up questions by e-mail.

3. Canvassing's role as an activist recruitment tool, and especially as a strategy for attracting those who cannot afford to volunteer, is not without controversy. Critics argue that canvassing can be so low-paid as to be exploitative, that the process influences groups to prioritize issues most likely to receive donations from the well-to-do homeowners canvassed, and that it diverts organizational energies from more direct advocacy.

The CALPIRG canvassers I surveyed earned a starting weekly base salary of $200.00, with an incentive package that could bring the amount to $315.00. Canvassers were expected to raise an average of eighty dollars per night. Considering that 75 percent of CALPIRG spending is devoted to programs and only 8 percent to administration, it is difficult to argue that the group is unfairly profiting from the workers' labor. Since the canvassing operation is directly designed to educate and mobilize people about environmental issues, it likely attracts those eager to be paid for work they believe in. Working for the United Farm Workers (UFW) at a weekly wage of five dollars was considered a badge of honor; canvassers who feel exploited have probably lost faith in either their organization or its cause.

I found no evidence that canvassing had a negative affect on agenda-setting by the PIRGs, nor that their canvassing operations subsumed their organizational mission or eclipsed their advocacy and organizing activities. If a better strategy exists for enlisting potential activists who are unable to volunteer, it should be used. Meanwhile, building national campaigns requires the participation of students who often must be compensated for their time, and canvassing has proven an effective vehicle for accomplishing this goal.

4. Conversation with Bob Bingaman, July 22, 1997; *The Planet*, May 1997, p. 3.

5. Ted Williams, "Natural Allies," *Sierra*, September/October 1996, p. 46. I believe a similar dynamic has limited environmentalist support for Ernest Callenbach's visionary proposal to bring back one million bison to the northern plains. Because the plan assumes that some of the buffalo must be slaughtered for sale, many environmentalists want no part of it.

6. David Helvarg, "Sierra Club Slacker," *Terrain, Northern California's Environment Magazine*, May 1997, p. 24; Ree McManus, "Pitchman for the Planet," *Sierra*, September/October 1996, p. 54.

7. E-mail message from Carl Pope to author, September 2, 1997.

8. Marie Dolcini, "Forging Non-Traditional Alliances," *The Planet*, January/February 1997, p. 5.

9. John Byrne Barry, "Clean Air Now," *The Planet*, March 1997, p. 1.

10. John Cushman Jr., "E.P.A. May Extend Debate on Tougher Air Standards," *New York Times*, February 2, 1997.

11. *The Planet*, March 1997.

12. "Dust Mites to Blame, not Pollution, Claims Industry Ad," *The Planet*, March 1997, p. 3.

13. *New York Times*, May 29, 1997, p. A15.

14. Information on the PIRGs' Clean Air campaign is from the group's weekly *Electric Updates* sent to all field coordinators. These internal documents were transmitted to the author on October 14, 1997, by Gene Karpinski.

15. *Electric Update*, June 27, 1997. During the Clean Air Act campaign, the National Environmental Trust was known as the Environmental Information Center.

16. *Electric Update*, May 30, 1997.

17. *Electric Update*, June 20, 1997.

18. *Electric Update*, June 6, 1997.

19. *Electric Update*, May 23, 1997.

20. *Electric Update*, June 20, 1997.

21. Vicki Allen, "Green Groups Pressure Gore to Back Air Rule," Yahoo-Reuters, June 3, 1997 (http://biz.yahoo.com/finance/97/06/03/y0002).

22. Conversation with Kathryn Hohmann, July 23, 1997.

23. Bill Nichols, "White House Quietly Seeks Common Ground," *USA Today*, June 5, 1997, p. 4A.

24. *Electric Update*, June 27, 1997.

25. Conversation with Gene Karpinski, September 29, 1997.

26. Conversation with Bob Bingaman, July 22, 1997.

27. Conversation with Chad Hansen, November 3, 1997.

Chapter 4: The Pentagon:
Reclaiming America by Giving Peace a Chance

1. Quoted in David Corn, "A Frank Talk on the Budget," *The Nation*, March 24, 1997, pp. 23–24.

2. Conversation with Virginia Parks, January 27, 1998.

3. See the *Bulletin of Atomic Scientists*, October 1995; the *Chicago Reader* "City File," July 18, 1997, p. 6, citing the June 25, 1997, online edition of the *Progressive Review*; the Center for Defense Information's *Defense Monitor*, August 1995; *San Francisco Chronicle*, October 18, 1994; Joel Bleifuss, "Warfare or Welfare," *In These Times*, December 9, 1996, pp. 12–14; Doug Ireland, "H.I.V. Negatives," *The Nation*, January 5, 1998, pp. 4–5; Robert Scheer, "What the Poor and Disabled Need Are More B-2 Bombers," *San Francisco Examiner*, August 22, 1997, p. A29; Military Spending Update, June 1998, by Jim Bridgman, distributed to members of California Peace Action, citing the GAO report "Financial Audit: 1997 Consolidated Financial Statements of the United States Government."

4. Conversation with Wayne Jakowitz, July 31, 1997; conversation with John Pike, July 30, 1997; conversation with Elliot Negin, August 5, 1997; conversation with Mary Lord, August 1, 1997; Bleifuss, "Warfare or Welfare," pp. 12–14.

5. Christian Smith, *Resisting Reagan: The U.S. Central American Peace Movement* (Chicago: University of Chicago Press, 1996), p. 165.

6. Conversation with Bob Tiller on August 12, 1997; conversation with Christopher Hellman on August 8, 1997.

7. "From Cold War to Cold Peace?" *Business Week*, February 12, 1949.

8. Robert Reich, *Locked in the Cabinet* (New York: Knopf, 1997), p. 136.

9. J. William Fulbright, *The Price of Empire* (New York: Pantheon, 1989), p. 147.

10. Bill Clinton and Al Gore, *Putting People First: How We Can All Change America* (New York: Times Books, 1992), pp. 75–80.

11. Bill Clinton, *Between Hope and History: Meeting America's Challenges for the Twenty-first Century* (New York: Times Books, 1996), pp. 12,

143, 148. Michael Closson, "Changing Course," *Positive Alternatives*, Winter 1997, p. 1.

12. Among the companies participating in the "move the money" campaign are Tweezerman (the logo will appear on 2.5 million packages of tweezers, combs, and clippers), Gardener's Supply (four million catalogs), and Frontier Natural (three hundred thousand boxes). For a complete list, or to learn how to participate, call Gary Ferdman at BLSP, (212) 964-1109.

13. See Linda Stout, *Bridging the Class Divide* (Boston: Beacon Press, 1996), pp. 122–24.

14. Quoted in Bleifuss, "Warfare or Welfare," p. 13.

15. Quoted in 20/20 Vision 1996 annual report, citing a February 1996 *U.S. News and World Report* cover story.

16. See Bleifuss, "Warfare or Welfare," p. 14.

17. Kelly Lantau, "Students Protest in Chicago," *Daily Vidette*, November 14, 1997, p. 10.

18. See Alison Mitchell, "Leaders of G.O.P. Seek to Overhaul Federal Tax Code," *New York Times*, September 28, 1997, p. 1; and Alison Mitchell, "G.O.P. Tax Debate with One Purpose," *New York Times*, October 19, 1997, p. 14.

19. Conversation with Amy Quinn, May 9, 1997.

20. Joel Bleifuss, "Whose Party Is It," *In These Times*, February 3, 1997, pp. 12–14. A San Francisco Progressive Challenge emerged in 1998 to connect local activists to national struggles. Organizers hope that it will become a forerunner of similar efforts elsewhere.

21. Interview with Fred Ross Jr., September 2, 1997.

22. "Post–Cold War Peace Groups in Search of a Focus," *National Catholic Reporter*, December 9, 1994, p. 16; "Time for a Re-Energized Peace Movement," *National Catholic Reporter*, January 24, 1997, p. 30.

23. The studies are discussed in Peter Steinfels's column, "Beliefs," *New York Times*, August 25, 1997, p. 9.

24. Interview of Kathie Guthrie by David Lubell, August 7, 1997.

25. "The Stealth Boondoggle," *New York Times*, September 19, 1997, p. A15.

26. Ross interview.

Chapter 5: Community-Based Nonprofit Organizations: From Demobilizers to Agents of Change

1. My use of the term *community-based* does not encompass the giant national nonprofits like the Red Cross, the Salvation Army, Catholic Charities, the American Cancer Society, the Jewish Federation, and the Children's Aid Society. Such groups are large bureaucracies that often receive

millions in government funds to perform social services. Although they may have low-income people on their boards, these nonprofits are not rooted in, or accountable to, neighborhood people or low-income constituencies. Such groups do not define themselves, and are not seen as being, community-based. I do not view these groups as likely to provide key resources for national grassroots campaigns, and exclude them accordingly.

2. Conversation with Mary Beth Pudup, December 18, 1997.

3. Conversation with Tim Sampson, October 6, 1997.

4. Sally Covington, *Moving a Public Policy Agenda: The Strategic Philanthropy of Conservative Foundations* (Washington, D.C.: National Committee for Responsive Philanthropy, 1997), pp. 37, 39. The study is available from the National Committee for Responsive Philanthropy, 2001 S Street NW #620, Washington, D.C., 20009. Also see Beth Schulman, "A Wake-Up Call to Liberal Foundations," *In These Times*, October 5, 1997, p. 12. Michael Shuman, "Why Do Progressive Foundations Give Too Little to Too Many?" *The Nation*, January 12/19, 1998, p. 11, reaffirms many of Covington's findings.

5. Rachel Timoner, *Ready or Not? An Assessment of Low-Income Advocacy in California* (Oakland, Calif.: Applied Research Center, 1996).

6. Teresa Funicello, *Tyranny of Kindness: Dismantling the Welfare System to End Poverty in America* (New York: Atlantic Monthly Press, 1993).

7. For the best discussion of CBO lobbying limits, see Bob Smucker, *The Nonprofit Lobbying Guide* (San Francisco: Jossey-Bass, 1991).

Chapter 6: The Media:
Mobilizing through the Echo Effect

1. David E. Rosenbaum, "Why Clinton Is Such an Ink-Stained Wretch," *New York Times*, March 23, 1997, p. 5.

2. David Armstrong, *A Trumpet to Arms: Alternative Media in America* (Boston: Houghton Mifflin, 1981).

3. George Cothran, "The Black Hole of San Francisco," *San Francisco Weekly*, August 27, 1997, p. 14; New Times writer Jill Stewart blamed the poor for their problems in "The Next Eden," *California Lawyer*, November 1996, and in the February 1997 Letters to the Editor.

4. Katha Pollitt, "Their Press and Ours," *The Nation*, November 10, 1997, p. 9.

5. See Jeffrey St. Clair, "Blowing Smoke on Clean Air Rules," *In These Times*, July 28, 1997, p. 9; and "Clean Air Rules: You Really Think Bill Hung Tough?," the nationally syndicated "Nature and Politics" column by St. Clair and Cockburn that appeared in such local publications as *Terrain*, August/September 1997, p. 5.

6. Jeffrey St. Clair, "The Twilight of 'Gang Green,'" *In These Times*, July 28, 1997, pp. 14–16.

7. Jeffrey St. Clair and Bernardo Issel, "A Field Guide to the Environmental Movement," *In These Times*, July 28, 1997, pp. 17–19, quoting journalist Mark Dowie.

8. David Corn, "A Bad Air Day," *The Nation*, March 24, 1997, pp. 16–20.

9. See Joel Bleifuss, "Pacifica's Uncivil War," *In These Times*, December 14, 1997, p. 16.

10. National Public Radio had previously bowed to pressure and refused to run tapes of Abu-Jamal.

11. Felicity Barringer, "Media," *New York Times*, July 27, 1998, p. C9. The study by the Pew Research Center for the People and the Press also found that only 22 percent of men under the age of thirty regularly watch the network news, compared to 42 percent of the general population.

12. See Lisa Bannon, "Commercial Appeal: Jim Carrey Is Coming to a Fruit Bin Near You," *Wall Street Journal*, August 21, 1997, p. B1; Lisa W. Foderaro, "The Vehicle Has Become the Message," *New York Times*, January 16, 1998, p. A19.

Chapter 7: The Internet: Mobilizing in Cyberspace

1. E-mail message from Nick Licata re: Organizing on the Internet, November 20, 1997. Councilmember Licata's e-mail column continues to discuss local issues.

2. IGC NetNews interview, April 4, 1997.

3. Michael L. Dertouzos, *What Will Be: How the New World of Information Will Change Our Lives* (New York: HarperEdge, 1997), pp. 241–43.

4. David Shenk, *Data Smog: Surviving the Information Glut* (San Francisco: HarperEdge, 1997), p. 174.

5. Andrew Zajac, "Where Are the Techno Republicans?" *San Francisco Examiner*, November 9, 1997, p. B1.

6. "Silicon Valley's Poor Get Poorer," *San Francisco Examiner*, January 25, 1998, p. J1, citing a study by Working Partnerships USA that originally appeared in the *Wall Street Journal*; Julia Angwin and Laura Casteneda, "The Digital Divide," *San Francisco Chronicle*, May 4, 1998, p. 1. Blacks and Latinos who are employed in Silicon Valley firms are more likely to work in factory or support jobs than whites and Asians.

7. Tom Tomorrow, "This Modern World," in *Sacramento News & Review*, July 24, 1997.

8. Peter Schwartz and Peter Leyden, "The Long Boom," *Wired*, July 1997.

9. See Christine Miller, "The New Accountability," *New York Times* advertising supplement, October 20, 1997.

10. For a detailed discussion of the group's development, see Patty Wentz, "Bastard Nation," *Flux* (a publication of the University of Oregon School of Journalism and Communication), Spring 1997, p. 13.

11. See Rebecca Eisenberg, "Coping with Virtual Profits," *San Francisco Examiner*, November 30, 1997, p. B1.

12. Rebecca Fairley Raney, "Politicians Woo Voters on the Web," *New York Times*, July 30, 1998, p. D1, citing a telephone survey of 1,021 adults by Bruce Bimber, a political science professor at the University of California at Santa Barbara.

Index

Compositor:	Prestige Typography
Text:	11/13.5 Caledonia
Display:	Officina Sans
Printer and Binder:	Haddon Craftsmen, Inc.